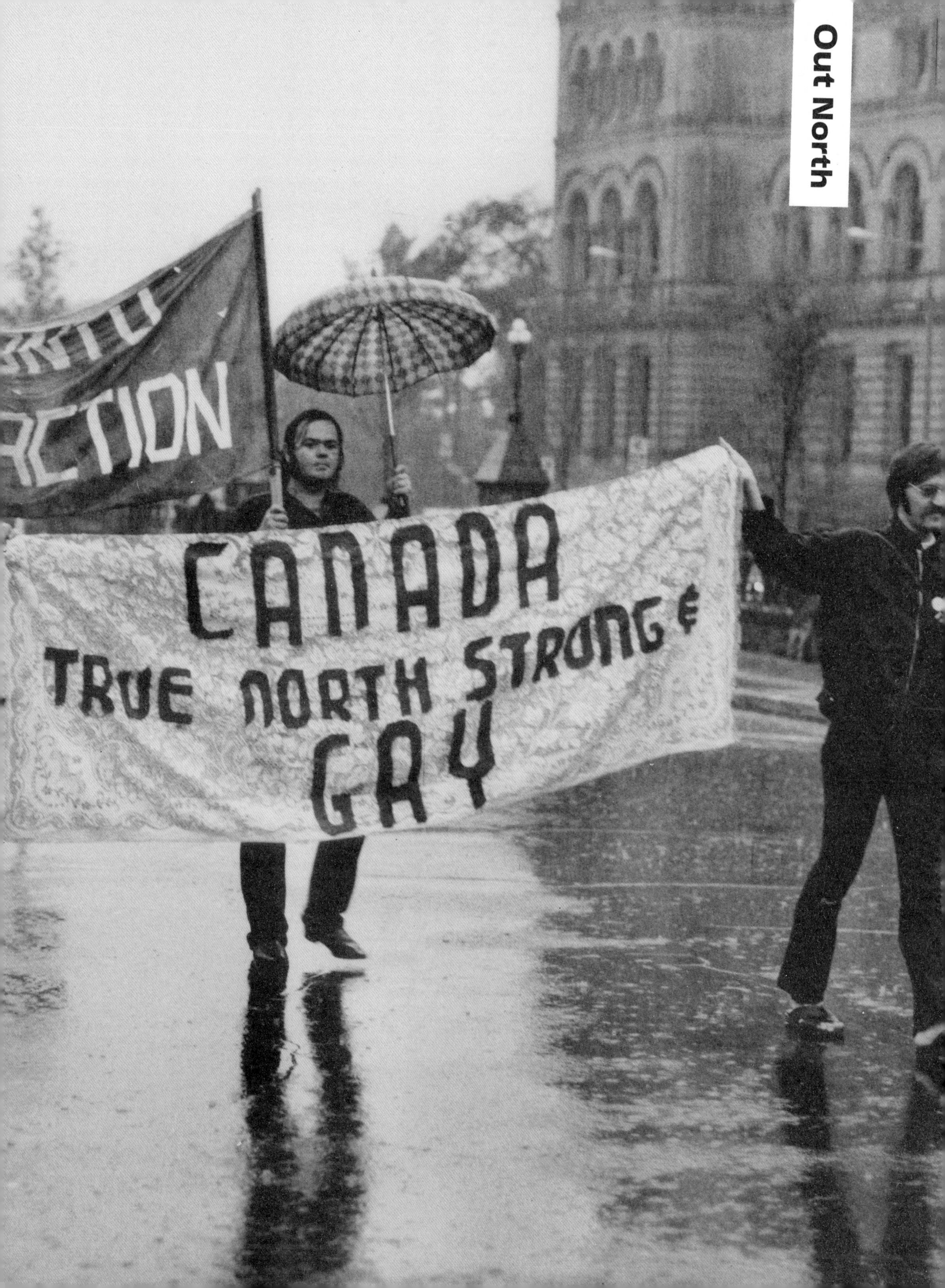

Out North

Craig Jennex and Nisha Eswaran

AN ARCHIVE OF QUEER ACTIVISM
AND KINSHIP IN CANADA

Out
North

Figure.1
Vancouver / Berkeley

THE ARQUIVES
Canada's LGBTQ2+ Archives

1

Dear Richard,   December, 1976

My holiday greetings take a rather different form this year. As you can see from the Varsity article, I've had a rather splashy coming out of the closet. I am more proud of this than anything else I have ever done. It's a great personal success as well: I feel like a whole man for the first time in my life.

The reactions so far range from deafening silence to marvellously positive support on the part of a few students & staff. Since my students are still under my power for now, no one dares say anything negative to me directly—yet. But not all is rosy. I still have to get rehired next year to continue doing my bit to make Gore Vidal's words "homosexuality is what you do, not what you are" come true. At least the department recognizes that they can get rid of me only by way of the annual ritual of the budget problem. Anything else I will fight. However, as the more traumatized staff members see that the sky isn't going to fall, student en-rolement isn't going to drop to zero, funds aren't suddenly going to dry up, and I am not going to start raping every male student in sight, they might come around to the idea that it's no big deal after all. So there is much reason to think I will be back as usual.

With this, I have given myself the best Christmas gift ever. I hope your holidays will be equally happy.

Clarence Barnes

2

Through the experience of researching and writing this book, we developed a meaningful sense of closeness and kinship with individuals we have never met and will never meet—individuals who passed away before we came into our queer politics and before we began working on the collective project of queer liberation. Hundreds of activists' lives have deeply impacted us during this project. We feel a particular closeness with three individuals whose writings have given us access to queer pasts and offered us the opportunity to bask in the queer desires and longings of others:

RICK BÉBOUT (1950–2009)
AIYYANA MARACLE (1950–2016)
ANGE SPALDING (1948–1990)

Their archives—the material traces of their lives—inform and shape this work. This book is dedicated to them and so many others whose lives have made ours possible.

"To write history
is to write
against death."

MICHAEL LYNCH, 1944–1991

CONTENTS

"WE...RESIST THE CALL TO UNCRITI-CALLY CELEBRATE QUEER PROGRESS IN CANADA AND... INSTEAD, TRACE INSTANCES OF COMMUNITY AND KINSHIP THAT CHALLENGE THE LIMITATIONS OF THE STATE."

PREFACE

During the writing of this book, the final report of the National Inquiry into Missing and Murdered Indigenous Women and Girls was released. Entitled *Reclaiming Power and Place,* this report laid bare what many Indigenous individuals and communities have said and struggled against for years: that the settler colonial practices on which Canada rests amount to the genocide of Indigenous women and girls.

This book takes the Canadian nation as its framework for thinking through the queer sexual politics of the twentieth and twenty-first centuries. Like all projects that use this framework, ours risks reifying and celebrating Canada as a benevolent nation—a place that, in securing the sexual rights and freedom of LGBTQ2+ people, guarantees sexual rights and freedom for all. While many queer people are now protected by the Canadian state, the report serves as a reminder that this protection relies on the ongoing oppression of Indigenous communities and the sexual violation of Indigenous women and girls. Amid renewed calls for reconciliation, the protection from which we (the authors) benefit from as non-Indigenous queer people cannot be minimized.

We have thus aimed in this book to resist the call to uncritically celebrate queer progress in Canada and to, instead, trace instances of community and kinship that challenge the limitations of the state. We hope that the narrative here—while framed as part of Canadian history—does not foreclose the possibility of solidarity between Indigenous and non-Indigenous people; rather, we hope this narrative speaks to the connections between queer movements, the fight for Indigenous sovereignty, and the ongoing work of ending sexual violence against women and girls. Written on the traditional territory of the Mississaugas of the Credit First Nation, the Haudenosaunee, the Anishinaabe, and the Huron-Wendat peoples and published on the traditional, unceded territory of the Coast Salish peoples, this book is made possible by the caretakers of these lands, to whom we are grateful.

INTRODUCTION: MEMORY WORK

On December 30, 1977, members of the Metropolitan Toronto Police and the Ontario Provincial Police raided the offices of The Canadian Gay Archives and *The Body Politic,* one of Canada's first and most prominent gay publications. Police seized twelve boxes of the Archives' holdings in order to charge the officers of Pink Triangle Press (the not-for-profit collective formed in 1976 to incorporate *The Body Politic* and the archival project) with the crime of "distribut[ing] immoral, indecent or scurrilous material." The raid is only part of a long history of police raids that targeted gay, lesbian, and trans communities. In "Stashing the Evidence," an essay he wrote in 1979 for *The Body Politic* following the raids, gay liberationist and AIDS activist Rick Bébout recounts the difficulties and the pleasures of archiving queer history under homophobic and hostile political conditions. That essay is the inspiration for the archival work we do in this book. While there have been many social and legal shifts

in Canada since Bébout wrote "Stashing the Evidence," memory work—the act of remembering, holding on to, and cherishing prior experiences, relationships, and possibilities—remains a crucial part of queer life in Canada.

Routinely erased from conventional or state-sanctioned modes of memorialization, queer people have built archives in myriad ways, collecting both tangible and intangible records of queer life: stories, writing, photographs, ephemera, and so much more. Such records are crucial, particularly as queer life is rapidly changing in Canada; as more of us are recognized by the state through the legalization of gay marriage and many of us see ourselves better represented in increasingly "diverse" forms of media, archives of the queer past remain critical. Indeed, many of us retain complex emotional attachments to the forms of friendship, solidarity, sexual freedom, and protest that preceded state and media recognition of certain manifestations of queer life. Both of us (the authors) remember, for instance, how pivotal archival records were to our respective comings of age as queer individuals: materials that evidenced queer people convening, organizing, dancing,

protesting, and building families gave us a sense of history and lineage—an inheritance of a queer past that remains sacrosanct, the impetus for our work here—and a sense of possibility, of a future where queer sexual desires, practices, and communities are alive and flourishing. Our motivation in writing this book is to linger in the emotional attachments we have to such archives and to ask how our connections to the past enable and enliven queer life now.

This book takes as its starting point the vast collection of The ArQuives: Canada's LGBTQ2+ Archives (formerly known as The Canadian Lesbian and Gay Archives). Formed in Toronto in 1973, the organization has grown to be the largest independent LGBTQ2+ archive in the world. We aim to bring the ArQuives' diverse collection of historical photographs, posters, writing, artwork, and ephemera to a broader audience. For us, these materials are exciting and enlivening because of the complicated ways they speak to multiple queer pasts while simultaneously articulating a queer future yet to come. In reproducing and collectively returning to these historical materials, we have considered how the ArQuives' collection

1 Protestors take part in a march during the National Gay Conference, Ottawa, 1975. Photograph by Gerald Hannon.

speaks to both the histories and the future possibilities of queer life in Canada.

Certain narratives of queer Canada are taken as fact—for instance, the idea that we, as a nation, have steadily marched toward progress, tolerance, and acceptance since the so-called decriminalization of homosexuality in 1969. The legalization of gay marriage in 2005, for example, is regarded as evidence of a linear progress through which queer people are recognized and accepted by the state. We recognize the power of this narrative and the comfort that it carries, but part of our interest in this book is to move away from this narrative of progress—a narrative we perceive as too simple, too linear, too easy—and return to earlier moments and the materials created therein that hold unrealized potential for the present.

While we do not deny that queer life changed rapidly in Canada over the latter half of the twentieth century, we aim in this book to consider some of the *unofficial* records of queer life evidenced in the collection at the ArQuives. What does this collection reveal about the hidden histories of queerness in Canada, and how do these stories challenge or add to the official narratives of progress? Which alternative forms of queer resistance and pleasure were at play in the twentieth and early twenty-first centuries, and how do they inflect queer life now? Whose work and life

1

stories are missing from the collection, and, in addressing these absences, can we better understand our collective queer history? The purpose of this book is to consider these many questions through the ArQuives' collection and to build forms of kinship with individuals and movements of the past.

Approaching the Past

In this book, we use the term *queer* when referring to a capacious form of politics, one that includes the struggles of lesbians, gays, bisexuals, trans, and Two-Spirit people. We use *lesbian, gay, trans,* and *Two-Spirit* when referring to a historically specific event or movement primarily organized around a particular conception

of gender or sexuality. In keeping with a commitment to historical specificity, we have organized this book in four temporal sections that follow a chapter on the formation and development of the ArQuives. These sections are organized chronologically, and each focuses on an era of queer collective development in Canada: from burgeoning cross-dressing subcultures, working-class lesbian communities, and homophile movements following the Second World War, gay (and lesbian) liberation, and lesbian separatism to contemporary movements that aim to decentre whiteness (at least partially) from queer organizing that works toward more just futures. Throughout these chapters, we also emphasize the backlash and violence

What is Homosexuality?

Homosexuality is the ability to relate sexually and emotionally to others of the same sex. Homosexuality is a natural form of sexuality found in all mammals and in all cultures.

Our society views homosexuality as either a sin or a sickness. However this view is not typical of the world's cultures. Of the 67 societies surveyed by Ford and Beach in *Patterns of Sexual Behaviour*, 64% considered homosexual behaviour to be "normal and socially acceptable".

Even though forbidden and suppressed, homosexuality is far more common in our society than the myths about it would have you believe. The report of Kinsey, Pomeroy and Martin, the famous team of American sociologists, indicates that while only 4% of the male population is exclusively homosexual, 18% of all men have at least as much homosexual experience as heterosexual experience during some three year period after the age of nineteen, and 34% of all adult males have had at least one homosexual experience resulting in orgasm. One woman in four has a gay experience in her lifetime. Seven percent of all women and 13% of all men are predominantly homosexual throughout their lives. This means, therefore, that the homosexual minority consists of approximately 10% of the population, making it the largest minority group in our society.

Gay is Good!

These studies and others like them point to the same conclusion: that homosexuality is a normal and integral form of sexuality. It is only the arbitrary norms fostered by the Church and traditional psychiatry which say that homosexuality is depraved and unnatural. Society claims that we are evil and sick; but we homosexuals -- gay people -- assert that GAY IS GOOD.

Gays Are Oppressed

Gays are oppressed. On the grounds of our sexuality we are denied many of the basic rights which most members of society take for granted.

We have no legal protection against discrimination in housing, in employment, in immigration, or even in access to services available to the public. It is legal for a businessman to fire an employee whom he suspects to be gay, for a landlord to refuse to rent to a homosexual, or for a bar to refuse to serve homosexuals. This means that we are often forced to live in downtown areas known as "gay ghettos". It means that we must hide our social lives at our work, or accept the constant possibility of dismissal. It means that there are many gay people new to Canada who live in fear of deportation.

The response or government authorities, when confronted with this situation, is often to say that they do not understand how we could be discriminated against unless we "flaunt" our sexuality. Actually there is a grain of truth in this argument. If we cover up our sexual orientation and skillfully manage to pass as straight we are not subject to these overt forms of oppression. But it is easy to see that being forced to play this charade results in an even more vicious type of oppression. The strain of having to play the "normal" role in front of friends, family and business associates is demoralizing and leads to a negative and distorted self-image. And we all remember what it was like to be completely in the closet -- knowing no other gays, having no sex lives, thinking of ourselves as sick or abnormal, in short living an oppressive lie -- yet this is the way most gays still live.

Coming Out

Coming out is the first step toward liberation. By coming out, the gay person begins to live honestly and proudly in spite of the oppressive attitudes of the surrounding society. Coming out does not mean making heart-rending confessions; nor does it mean throwing a party to announce one's homosexuality. Once you decide that your sexuality is good, telling people follows naturally. Coming out means accepting one's sexuality and demonstrating the positiveness of it in our relationships with other people. Coming out is ceasing to play the roles forced on us by a hostile society and beginning to be just ourselves. COME OUT!

2

---

that individuals and communities faced in each of these eras. Anti-queer violence—much of it perpetrated by the Canadian government and its agents—is not unique to one epoch of queer history in this country. Such state-sanctioned violence manifests throughout this history and continues to affect queer individuals today. Although a faithful record of parts of the ArQuives' collection at the moment, this book is not an exhaustive representation of the collection or a complete recounting of LGBTQ2+ movements in Canada. The materials in this book, like the archive from which they come, are Canada-focused but Toronto-dominated, a result of both the ArQuives being based in Toronto and the way that Toronto LGBTQ2+ organizing is often taken as representative of Canadian movements more broadly. This imbalance exemplifies a long-running tension in queer political organizing in Canada. An article in a 1973 newsletter of the Zodiac Friendship Society, a gay liberation organization in Saskatoon, Saskatchewan, for example, laments the "Torontorosis" from which so many of *The Body Politic* writers suffered: "a delusive state in which the patient imagines that Toronto is the seething centre of the universe and anything that happens outside of it (assuming anything ever does) is hardly to be taken seriously."

We (the authors) do our best to navigate this tension. We are, in fact, keenly aware of how Toronto (and Ontario) centrism in queer formation can alienate individuals outside of those geographical spaces. Craig is from the East Coast and Nisha is from the West Coast, but we met in Toronto, to which we both moved because of what we understood to be the city's queer possibilities. This is not, of course, to say that there

1 Individuals pose in front of graffiti during International Lesbian Week, Vancouver, 1987. Photograph by Li Yuen.

2 Pamphlet created by Gay Alliance Toward Equality (GATE), Vancouver, c. 1970s.

are no queer possibilities in Halifax or Vancouver—trust us: there are lots—but to acknowledge the persistent geographical tensions within queer politics in Canada.

Moreover, the ArQuives' collection documents the histories of urban, white, middle-class gay men more thoroughly than it does those of rural queers, people of colour, trans people, and lesbians—absences we do our best to trace back to racist immigration policies and the historically patriarchal nature of public queer community building. In other words, we aim to draw links here between the development of queer communities—of which the ArQuives is a part—and the policies of the Canadian state during the mid- to late twentieth century. The Immigration Act of 1952, for instance, increased the restrictions on Asian and African immigration while also banning "prostitutes, homosexuals, and degenerates." The Immigration Act draws clear links between the so-called moral degeneracy of racialized people and that of homosexuals; yet those Canadian citizens with access to resources and even the most minimal protection of the state were able to organize against institutionalized homophobia in explicit and visible ways. This also means that the voices of gay men were heard louder than those of gay women and that the everyday organizing work of people of colour, lesbians, and trans and rural people—less

visible but no less significant—is not documented as thoroughly in the ArQuives' collection.

This imbalance also stems from the facts that the ArQuives is just one of many LGBTQ2+ archival projects in Canada and that materials evidencing the lives and movements of LGBTQ2+ people in this country are sometimes pulled in multiple directions based on geography and categories of identification. For example, an incredible collection of materials related to lesbian activism, politics, and community is held at the Canadian Women's Movement Archives at the University of Ottawa; so too is a thriving Two-Spirit collection held at the University of Winnipeg Archive. We speak more to this network of queer remembering in Canada in our epilogue (page 268). Indeed, in taking "Canada" as a site through which to chart queer-movement building, this book takes for granted the nation-state that Indigenous movements, queer and not-queer alike, work to denaturalize as a deliberate project of settler colonial violence. Despite these conspicuous absences and issues, we have mined the collections for solidarity and connections across race, gender, sexuality, and urban/rural divides that cannot be evidenced purely through representational politics. In other words, one of our aims here is not to represent the full breadth of queer life in Canada but to find, in the collection we have, the connections

between people that exceed racial, gendered, sexual, and ideological limits.

The images in this book represent a small portion of the ArQuives' holdings, most of which has been donated by individuals and organizations across Canada seeking to preserve their personal records of queer life as part of a broader and collective queer history. We are hopeful that—in bringing the ArQuives' collection to a wider audience—this book engages in the ongoing collaborative project of creating a queerer future. We ask how we might envision another future, one where queer life need not be defined through ideas of linear progress or by recognition from the state. Rather, we ask how we might realize a future where equality is measured not just through the legal right to marry (for instance) but through safety from violence, poverty, racism, and homophobia.

We write this book in a moment of increasing austerity under the Progressive Conservative government in Ontario; cuts to education, social housing, public transportation, public health, and public services such as libraries are all queer issues affecting queer individuals. Under the right-leaning Coalition Avenir Québec, queer and non-queer Muslim women's right to wear the hijab has become the focus of increasing xenophobia and racism under the guise of revived debates in the province on "religious freedom." The 2019 election of Alberta premier Jason Kenney—who oversaw extreme cuts to immigration and refugee funding and the erasure of LGBTQ2+ existence in the nation's citizenship guide as Minister of Citizenship, Immigration and Multiculturalism in the Harper government—threatens to usher in a new era of social and fiscal conservatism on the provincial level. All over Canada, queer and trans youth still experience high rates of homelessness and unemployment and have restricted access to health care; women, queer and straight, continue to have their reproductive and economic rights tested and questioned. And in 2019, Bruce McArthur was charged with the murder of eight men from Toronto's Gay Village. His victims were mostly South Asian and Middle Eastern gay men, suggesting racist and homophobic motivations on McArthur's part and behind the initially lackadaisical approach of the Toronto Police in investigating the disappearance of these men. As Justin Ling notes in the CBC podcast *Uncover*—which seeks to understand these killings in the context of earlier unsolved murders in Toronto's Gay Village—the way these deaths were taken up by police, media,

1 **Winnipeg**

1   Demonstration at the Manitoba Legislature following the ban of *The Joy of Gay Sex* and *The Joy of Lesbian Sex*, Winnipeg, 1980. Photograph by Doug Nicholson.

and in broader public discourse shows that the victims' "sexuality and their skin colour made them easier to forget—easier to write off."

The struggles against homophobia, racism, and poverty persist even in the era of state recognition of gay rights. We hope that the documents we include in this book reveal past methods of queer resistance that remain potentially transformative in the present. In particular, we hope this carefully curated collection of Canadian queer activism

and kinship will direct us to old forms of solidarity and connection that can be taken up anew. By drawing inspiration from the ArQuives' records and in explicitly attending to absences in the collection, we hope this book meaningfully engages with the ongoing work toward better, queerer forms of everyday life. By looking backward and spending time with what came before, we look with optimism toward the future.

Queer Happenings Pre-1939

While this book begins in the mid-twentieth century, there is ample evidence of queer lives and experiences dating to long before 1939. To offer just a few examples:

* "Sodomitical Practices" were reported in the *Halifax Gazette,* the first printed newspaper in the land we now call Canada, in 1752. It's unlikely that 1752 was the first year that soldiers garrisoned in Halifax were participating in such practices—it's just the first year that the paper was printed.

* A leading member of the colonial elite of Upper Canada, George Markland was a little too friendly with young soldiers stationed at the parliament buildings in Toronto in the late 1830s. As Ed Jackson and Jarett Henderson write in "Sex, Scandal, and Punishment in Early Toronto," Markland's career as a respected bureaucrat ended abruptly following an inquiry into his intimate experiences with other men. Margaret Powell, the housekeeper at the parliament buildings, is on record describing Markland's behaviour as "queer doings from the bottom to the top."

* Dr. James Barry, who we would now consider trans (as he was discovered to be "born female" after his death in 1865), saved countless lives in the mid-nineteenth century as the Inspector General of Hospitals in what was then the Province of Canada. He developed sanitation systems in Kingston, Toronto, and Quebec during his time in those settlements. Passing as a man allowed Barry to travel, work, and live with fewer restrictions under the patriarchal logic of the nineteenth century.

* Men met for sex at Moise Tellier's apples and cake shop in Montreal in the nineteenth century so frequently that the shop regularly attracted police attention. The *Montreal Star* reports on police raids of the shop in 1869, noting that "Tellier's business is nominally to keep a small shop for apples, cakes, and similar trifles. But the business is only a cloak for the commission of crimes that rival Sodom and Gomorrah... It has been watched for sometime past by the police, and we regret, for the credit of our city and humanity, to say that several respectable

citizens have been found frequenting it and evidently practising abominations." In his book *National Manhood and the Creation of Modern Quebec,* Jeffery Vacante argues that Tellier's shop, which opened in 1869, "is reputedly Canada's first gay establishment" (43).

4

* John "Ian" Campbell, better known as the Marquess of Lorne, Canada's fourth governor general, was married to Princess Louise (Queen Victoria's fourth daughter) but was not, it seems, entirely exclusive with her. Lucinda Hawksley writes in *The Mystery of Princess Louise: Queen Victoria's Rebellious Daughter* that when the couple was living at Kensington Palace in London, "Louise became so infuriated by her husband sneaking out at night to try to meet sexual partners, usually soldiers, loitering in the park that she ordered the French windows in their apartments to be bricked up" (212). The Marquess of Lorne, a writer and artist, was similarly enamoured with military men during his time in Canada; in his book *Yesterday and Today in Canada,* he writes wistfully of Nova Scotia's "fine seaboard population of excellent sailors" and notes that "those who make up their minds to settle in Nova Scotia will never regret it" (52). Lorne, who served as governor general from 1878 to 1883, founded the National Gallery of Canada and The Royal Society of Canada.

* In May 1895, the front page of the *Medicine Hat Times* reported a "Horrible Crime at Regina: Arrest of Prominent Citizens in Connection with a Most Revolting Offence." The story chronicles the trial of Frank Hoskins, Basil Hume, and William John McPherson, each of whom was charged with "gross indecency of an unnatural character." The same case was widely covered by newspapers in Calgary under the headline "Oscarism at Regina," referencing the well-known case of Oscar Wilde in Britain. According to historian Lyle Dick, "the newspapers' reference to 'Oscarism' would have been clearly understood by most readers. This was the era of two widely publicized same-sex scandals in Britain, the Cleveland Street affair of 1889–1890 and the Oscar Wilde trials of 1895" (108).

* A few years later, in 1898, charges of "Oscarism" surfaced in *Of Toronto the Good: A Social Study: The Queen City of Canada as It Is.* Author Christopher St. George Clark writes, "If saintly Canadians run away with the idea that there are no sinners of Oscar Wilde's type in Canada, my regard for truth impels me to undeceive them. Consult some of the bell boys of the large hotels in Canada's leading cities, as I did, and find out what they can tell from their own experiences" (90).

5

* Court records from Vancouver show that Sikh men were targets of legal attacks on group and public acts of homosexuality during the first two decades of the twentieth century. Gordon Brent Ingram writes that Vancouver police used well-developed entrapment techniques in the early 1900s and that a "program of police interest so intense as to verge on sexual engagement initially targeted one group in particular: South Asian men, nearly all of them members of the Sikh religion recently arrived from… northwestern India" (91). While a relatively small number of South Asians lived in British Columbia during this time, Ingram writes, "Sikh males were defendants in scores of 'oriental cases' and in British Columbia's first legal attacks on group and public homosexuality" (91).

* Arguably Canada's first queer publication, *Les Mouches Fantastique: A Bi-Monthly Publication Devoted to the Arts,* was started by poet and philosopher Elsa Gidlow and poet and journalist Roswell George Mills in Montreal in 1917. In an interview in *The Body Politic* in May 1982, Gidlow recalls: "Instead of accepting society's rejection, we two iconoclasts rejected our rejectors, proud to be the spiritual and passional kin of Sappho… we found reasons for loving ourselves and each other."

* *Hush,* a tabloid newspaper we discuss in more detail in subsequent chapters, was preoccupied with "pansies parading our streets" in the early 1930s. The publication offers sensationalized accounts of these "pansies," including an article in the June 5, 1930, edition about

"Toronto's Love-Sick Pansy Boys" and a front-page story on May 19, 1932, that warns of "Winnipeg's 'Pansy' Traffic." "These boys," the article from 1930 attests, "are prone to lip sticks, rouge, delicate perfumes and extreme cuts of clothes. They are always falling violently in love with one another and their effeminate walk, mannerisms and voice makes the identification of a true Pansy quite easy" (3).

1   Men, including some in drag, 1936.

2   Dr. James Barry, c. 1850s.

3   Postcard showing Moise Tellier's shop next to the Drill Hall on Craig Street, Montreal, c. 1900s.

4   The Marquess of Lorne, Ottawa, 1872.
Image by William Holyoake.

5   Front page of *Hush*, May 19, 1932.

A (Campy) Lexicon

Basher (noun), someone who assaults or seeks to assault LGBTQ2+ individuals. **Related: Dirt** (noun), straight person who seeks to harm LGBTQ2+ individuals, and **Dirt Bitch** (noun), gay male who harms LGBTQ2+ individuals in an attempt to assert his masculinity.

Butch (noun), a masculine lesbian who may date and partner with a **Femme**; a term associated with working-class lesbian bar culture of the 1940s and 1950s. **Related: Long-Haired Butch** (LHB), a long-haired butch.

Chicken (noun), a young, youthful, or boyish male. See, for example, Jackie Shane's live performance of "Any Other Way," in which she explains: "I'm having a good time, me and my chicken." **Related: Chicken Hawk** (noun), pursuer of chickens.

Cruise (verb), to search for sex, often in public places (parks, washrooms, alleys). **Related: Hunt** (verb), to actively search for sexual partners, and **Cottage** (verb), to frequent public washrooms looking for sex (British).

Dyke (noun), a lesbian. **Related: Baby Dyke**, a young lesbian, and **Bulldyke**, a lesbian woman with stereotypical masculine behaviour and style (a.k.a. **Diesel Dyke**).

Faggot (noun), a gay male (often derogatory). **Related: Flamer, Mary, Swish, Pansy**, all synonyms used to refer to particularly effeminate gay men. **Also related: Fag Hag** (noun), a heterosexual woman who cultivates friendships and relationships with gay men (a.k.a. **Fruit Fly**).

Femme (noun), a feminine lesbian who may date and partner with a **Butch**; one half of the femme/butch (or butch/femme) couples who were highly visible in working-class lesbian bar culture of the 1940s and 1950s.

Hasbian (noun), a former lesbian; a lesbian who has turned straight.

Sodomy (noun), historical term used to describe anal sex. **Related: Buggery** (noun).

Switch-hitter (noun), a bisexual person. **Related: Nick-Nack** (noun), term used to denote bisexuals in the mid-twentieth century.

STASHING
THE EVIDENCE

1

2

began in 1973 as an endeavour of *The Body Politic* (*TBP*), a Canadian gay liberation publication. Since its formation, and as a result of decades of dedicated and energetic volunteer labour, the collection has transformed into The ArQuives, the largest independent LGBTQ2+ archive in the world. Over the past few decades, the collection had also gone by the names The Canadian Gay Archives (CGA) and The Canadian Lesbian and Gay Archives (CLGA). Throughout this chapter, we use "the Archives" to refer to the institution in its many manifestations under its many names.

It's difficult to imagine, when sifting through the diverse materials at one of the Archives' three Toronto locations, that the entire collection once fit in a cardboard box stored in a drafty shed on Toronto's Kensington Avenue. In the early 1970s, Jearld Moldenhauer—who co-founded the University of Toronto Homophile Association (UTHA, page 90) and opened Glad Day Bookshop (page 92), which remains the world's oldest surviving LGBTQ bookstore—came up with the idea to establish an archive of the burgeoning gay liberation movement. Members of the *TBP* collective began compiling the materials that would eventually become the foundation of the archival collection. *TBP* collective member and historian Ed Jackson recalls that a primary impetus for the archival project was that *TBP*, as a new gay liberation movement magazine, "became a magnet for newspapers, flyers, buttons, and pamphlets that the new movement was generating." Ron Dayman, who later became a member of *TBP* collective, took the collection started by members of *TBP* and began organizing the materials; it was in Dayman's basement on Boulton Avenue that archival documents were first processed and sorted. Since that beginning in 1973, countless volunteers have built on the collection. The history of the Archives reminds us that processes of remembering, of curating and caring for material evidence of minoritarian lives, is not something that happens naturally or easily—it is a long and arduous process that requires collective effort, communal protection, and, often, the obsessive attention of a few dedicated individuals.

The founding of the Archives was announced at the first national gay conference in Canada, held in Quebec City on October 6–7, 1973. Soon thereafter, an editorial in *TBP* announced the archival project in print, referring to the "painstaking" and vital work of "reconstructing the history of gay people" in this country—a complicated history composed of moments of both oppression and liberation. The editorial identifies "straight historians" and other "guardians of morality" that have participated in the ongoing "obliteration of gay history." In a homophobic reality, the editorial argues, queer individuals must all work to "gather, and make available, resource material relevant to all aspects of gay history."

What began as a depository for the files of *TBP* quickly became an active collecting project with a national scope. In the ten months following the conference in Quebec, gay liberation organizations such as the Toronto and Vancouver chapters of Gay Alliance Toward Equality (GATE, page 108), the University of Western Ontario Homophile Association, the Zodiac Friendship Society of Saskatoon, and the Gay Montreal Association/Association homophile de Montréal all made financial contributions to the Archives. Many more groups and individuals from across Canada donated materials.

TBP collective member, writer, and designer Rick Bébout writes in his 1979 article "Stashing the Evidence" that "there was no shortage of places for such material to come from. *TBP*'s Community Page listed more than 30 organizations in 15 cities across Canada. What might have seemed like isolated protests of a handful of loudmouths three years before had clearly become a well-organized social movement" (21). Some of the first files received and processed came from the University of Toronto Homophile

---

1 Jearld Moldenhauer, 1974.
Photograph by Ian McKenzie.

2 Ron Dayman, c. 1970s.

3 Editorial in *The Body Politic*, No. 10, 1973.

4 Merv Walker (*left*) and Robert Trow (*right*) working in *The Body Politic* offices at 193 Carlton Street, Toronto, c. mid-1970s. Photograph by Gerald Hannon.

gay archives

The task of reconstructing the history of gay people is painstaking work — often yielding little more than speculative sketches of what has been. History can be a tool of both oppression and liberation. It has all too often reflected the world view of the status quo, projecting the historian's own political, moral and psychological biases onto reality, rarely providing an objective and neutral account of the real people and forces involved. These straight historians and other "guardians of morality" have been very conscientious in their near obliteration of gay history. One way to encourage accurate historical research is to gather, and make available, resource material relevant to all aspects of gay history. To this end, The Body Politic has founded the Canadian GLM Archives.

The primary concern of the Archives will be the establishment of a complete Canadian collection, but the scope will be international, and special attention will be given to the U.S., Europe and Australia.

The Body Politic files have provided a fairly complete collection of Canadian material dating from our founding in November 1971. But gay Liberation has been organized here since the autumn of 1969, and previous to this several homosexual organizations existed in Canada during the 50's and 60's.

If our readers have printed matter from these earliest organizational efforts, we would appreciate hearing from you. Or if you can provide information in the form of personal memoirs and correspondence, this would be greatly appreciated as well. Any items you might contribute will be treated with the utmost care. We are at present looking for complete runs of the magazines "Two" and "Exclusive Male" as well as early editions of any books by Edward Carpenter and Magnus Hirschfeld.

Once a significant collection is accumulated and catalogued we will take steps to permanently house the archives within a university or governmental library. From time to time we will print a list requesting specific items needed by the archives. We are dependant upon your generosity for contributions of books, magazines, newspapers, articles, leaflets, photos and letters.

3

4

Association (today known as LGBTOUT, the oldest LGBTQ+ student organization in Canada, page 90) and the Gay Friends of Fredericton. Writer and poet Ian Young's donations in the early years fortified the collection alongside the donations coming from *TBP* writers.

When the collection moved from the basement on Boulton Avenue to the *TBP* offices at 193 Carlton Street, Toronto, in

June 1974, the Archive shared space with *TBP* and the Toronto branch of GATE. The Archive itself didn't take up much space—a year after its founding, the entire collection fit into a two-drawer filing cabinet. The collection was, at the time, known to relatively few—a reality informed both by security concerns and by the fact that many participants in the burgeoning gay liberation movement in Canada were focused on other, more immediate projects. The gay liberation movement in Canada was largely about imagining and working toward a more just and safer future for gays and lesbians. Actions in the present were aimed at constructing a less violent and homophobic world. As Bébout writes, "more often than not, the letters, the flyers, the casual notes that recorded [gay liberation political action] were being tossed away when they were no longer 'needed' " ("Stashing the Evidence," *TBP,* August 1979, 21). Thankfully, in the midst of pressing political actions for a freer, safer, and queerer future, a group of gays and lesbians recognized the profound importance in documenting and archiving the present and the past.

Jackson took over the stewardship of the Archive in 1974. Echoing concerns in the 1974 editorial in *TBP,* in a November 1975 address to the Gay Academic Union in New York City, Jackson emphasized both the political necessity and the world-making potential of archives of gay lives. He argued that "social attitudes toward homosexuality" meant that any gay archival practices and repositories would always "remain a threat to a society organized like ours." To care for histories of minority lives—to remember and hold onto pasts that are so strongly informed and framed by oppression—is to resist and disrupt erasure.

In 1975, the collection was renamed The Canadian Gay

1

2

Archives (CGA), eschewing "liberation movement" from its name to evoke a broader perspective and encourage a more capacious collection. "It wasn't just for gay liberationists," long-time volunteer Alan V. Miller recalls in 2019, "and they wanted to make that clear" (a good reminder that while we may categorize a broad historical era with the label "gay liberation," the politics of the moment are more disparate and complicated than any single term suggests). As Jackson notes, from its beginning the archival effort was about queer history—a genealogy that extended far beyond the liberation movement of the moment. Soon, out of concern that the name unsatisfactorily indicated the expansive way individuals involved in the Archive perceived the term *gay,* a subtitle was added: "For lesbians and gay men." The new name retained the reference to the nation; James A. Fraser and Harold A. Averill write in 1983 that "from the outset, the Archives was determined to develop into a national organization" (2).

In the summer of 1976, members of *TBP* collective incorporated into Pink Triangle Press (PTP), with two projects: *TBP* and the Archives. Momentum for a robust and public collection of materials documenting gay and lesbian experience continued to grow in the mid-1970s. Volunteers at the Archives formed a collective, developed a mandate, and produced a pamphlet that emphasizes the timely political importance of the collective historicizing project. The pamphlet begins with the claim that a "conspiracy of silence has robbed gay people of their history. A sense of continuity, which derives from the knowledge of a heritage, is essential of the building of self-confidence in a community. It is a necessary tool in the struggle for social change." The past, the

3

collective makes clear, is vital for our actions in the present and for the future, and it's important that the work of caring for materials of the past be done by the community. The political perspective captured in this flyer sheds light on a formative decision made by the Archives' collective in 1985 when they turned down an offer from the Archives of Ontario to take some of the materials. While the provincial archives had the funding, infrastructure, and broad support to care for these materials, it was important to the collective that the Archives' holdings (and decision-making power) remain in the hands of a gay and lesbian collective.

In 1976, PTP moved to 24 Duncan Street in Toronto,

where individuals working on the Archives and *TBP* had more space to develop their growing projects. From the new location, the Archives began producing a newsletter—originally named *Gay Archivist* and later published under *Lesbian and Gay Archivist* and *Queer Archivist.* The first newsletter outlines some of the priorities of the Archive, including "locating material in danger of being lost as groups disappear or reorganise" and developing "finding aids for the material on hand" to help researchers. The Archive has always been both a repository for material—a space in which documents are collected and cared for—and a site of learning about and engaging with gay and lesbian pasts.

1 Cover of Canadian Gay Archives booklet, c. 1980s. Designed by David Chang.

2 First page of Canadian Gay Archives booklet, c. 1980s. Designed by David Chang.

3 Chris Bearchell works in the Canadian Gay Archives at 24 Duncan Street, Toronto, c. late 1970s. Photograph by Gerald Hannon.

1

On Friday, December 30, 1977, members of Metropolitan Toronto Police and the Ontario Provincial Police raided 24 Duncan Street and ransacked the Archives. This raid was triggered by an article by long-time collective member Gerald Hannon, entitled "Men Loving Boys Loving Men," published in the December 1977/ January 1978 issue of *TBP*. The issue hit newsstands on November 21, 1977, but outrage over the article didn't foment until Christmas Day 1977, when *Toronto Sun* columnist Claire Hoy wrote an article arguing that, for gay men, "kids, not rights is [*sic*] their craving." (Hoy would remain preoccupied with *TBP* and with gays and lesbians more broadly his entire career.) A few days later, an editorial in the *Toronto Sun* echoed Hoy's concerns under the title "Bawdy Politic."

A week following the raid, Jackson, Hannon, and Ken Popert—the three officers of PTP—were charged with using the "mails for the purpose of transmitting or delivering anything that is obscene, indecent, immoral or scurrilous." Although *TBP* was acquitted on all charges, the case against Jackson, Hannon, and Popert dragged on for years, and materials seized by police were not returned to PTP until 1985. This was not the only time *TBP* members were charged by police; the entire collective was charged in 1982. In both instances, all those charged were ultimately acquitted.

3

2

SEARCH WARRANT

(Form 2)

— ⑨

CANADA
PROVINCE OF ONTARIO
JUDICIAL DISTRICT OF
YORK

To all or any of the constables and other peace officers in the said

Judicial District of York

WHEREAS it appears on the oath of

..... Sergeant M.Jennings .....

of .. Metropolitan Toronto Police Force .....

that there is reason to suspect that *(describe the things to be searched for and offence in respect of which search is made)*

corporate records,invoices and documents pertaining to the business
operations of a publication known as The BODY POLITIC and which
will afford evidence which support a charge of mailing immoral literature
contrary to the provisions of the Criminal Code, Sec. 164.

are contained in

..... business premises .... of Pink Triangle Press .....
(Residence, Building, etc.)

at ..... 24 Duncan Street,5th floor ..... *Toronto* .....
(Address or Location of Place)

THIS IS, THEREFORE, to authorize you to enter between the hours of ....
between 4.00p.m. and 8.00p.m. on December 30th,1977
(as the Justice directs)

into the said premises, and to search for the said things and to bring them before me or some other justice of the
peace.

DATED at the Municipality of Metropolitan Toronto in the Judicial District of York this..... *30 TH* .....day
of.... *DECEMBER* 19 *77*

..... *P. Deacon* .....
A Justice of the Peace in and for the Province of Ontario

4

1 From left to right: Gerald Hannon,
Ken Popert, Mariana Valverde, Ed Jackson, and Clayton Ruby at a press conference following first acquittal related
to publishing "Men Loving Boys Loving
Men," Toronto, 1979.

2 From left to right: Ken Popert, Ed
Jackson, and Gerald Hannon at *The
Body Politic* office at 24 Duncan Street,
Toronto, 1978.

3 *The Body Politic* collective after
acquittal. From left to right: Roger Spalding, Stephen MacDonald, Ken Popert, Ed
Jackson, Gerald Hannon, Chris Bearchell,
John Allec, Rick Bébout, and Tim McCaskell, 1982. Photograph by Bill Loos.

4 Metropolitan Toronto Police Force
warrant for 24 Duncan Street, 1977.

"On December 30, 1977,
the police—leaving the
office of *The Body Politic*
with nearly everything
we needed to stay alive—
likely imagined we'd
quietly fold what was
left of our tent and skulk
off into oblivion. They
were utterly confounded
when we did not."

Rick Bébout, "The Very Long &
Contentious Career of 'Men Loving
Boys Loving Men,'" 2003

The Archives' May 1978
newsletter chronicles the police
action, under the title "Police
Raid Archives" and raises serious
questions about the validity of the
raid: "Can the police, holding a
warrant in regard to a particular
investigation, make any material
in that archives available to themselves? If they can, then what
assurance can archivists give
to donors as regards restricted
access to their records?" The
collective sent a letter to then-
attorney general Roy McMurtry;
it remains unacknowledged.

In spite of the adverse attention from police, the Archives
continued to develop a public
presence in Toronto and in Canada more broadly. Volunteer and,
later, veteran HIV/AIDS activist
Joan Anderson worked to build
awareness of the Archives in the
late 1970s, attending lesbian conferences and forming connections
in broader queer communities. In

Police Raid Archives

On December 31, 1977 five members of the Metropolitan Toronto and Ontario Provinical Police Forces raided the offices of The Body Politic and the Canadian Gay Archives. They came armed with a warrant concerning an investigation of the newspaper. During their search it was pointed out to them that the Archives was separate and independent of the newspaper. This seemed not to matter. In addition to removing certain files related to The Body Politic, they systematically searched the entire Archives, most of whose holdings have no relation to the paper whatever.

This is a very serious matter, and poses certain questions for other archives. Can the police, holding a warrant in regard to a particular investigation, make any material in that archives available to themselves? If they can, then what assurance can archivists give to donors as regards restricted access to their records?

A letter to Attorney-General Roy McMurtry protesting the action of the police and enquiring whether such conduct will be approved in the future has not been acknowledged. The validity of the search warrant was challenged in court and upheld. A further appeal made to the Ontario Court of Appeal on April 14 was lost.

1

fact, a series of national gay and lesbian conferences in the 1970s—starting with the aforementioned Quebec conference in 1973 and subsequent meetings in Winnipeg, Ottawa, Toronto, Halifax, Saskatoon, and Calgary—as well as lesbian conferences in Toronto, Montreal, Ottawa, and Vancouver in the 1970s, enabled members of the Archives collective to develop partnerships with gay and lesbian organizations across the nation.

In 1979, the Archives launched its publication series with Alex Spence's bibliography *Homosexuality in Canada*. Spence's text was the first major bibliography to deal exclusively with gay Canadian material. Soon thereafter, Miller's bibliography *The Genetic*

Imperative: Fact and Fantasy in Sociobiology was published. In his text, Miller compiled as much as possible on this relatively new field of study that, among other goals, attempted to show the evolutionary reasons for homosexual behaviour in society. Miller entered the Archives in 1977 to conduct research on homosexuality and employment, producing three bibliographies that were published by the Ontario Ministry of Labour. Over four decades later, he's still at the Archives, assisting researchers and building the collection six days a week. Other long-time volunteers include Harold Averill, Mario Ciancibello, Colin Dienhardt, Al Duddin, Gerry King, Erica Lee, Gordon

Richardson, and Donald McLeod—the last of whom has published widely on the collected materials.

As TBP faced continued harassment by the Metropolitan Toronto Police, mainstream media in the city, and elected officials into the 1980s, the Archives' collective decided to put some distance between the Archives and the newspaper. When the "cops came in and … took some of our stuff away," Averill recalls, "that made us realize that we had to incorporate to protect our own resources." In 1980, the Archives incorporated with a board of directors. The first six directors were Miller, Anderson, Jackson, Hannon, Fraser, and Chris Bearchell. While most of these people continued to be heavily involved in both TBP and the Archives, the formation of a separate board of directors was meant to allow the Archives to grow on its own and provide some protection from future police actions aimed at TBP.

Nearly a decade into the archival project, the importance of the Archives remained lost on the broader straight community and governing bodies. Gay liberation, growing increasingly aggressive in Toronto in the early 1980s, was still regularly dismissed as a special interest political stance that affected only a relatively small number of citizens. For example, the Archives was denied charitable status because Revenue Canada believed the work of the Archives was not "directed to the benefit of all members of the

1 "Police Raid Archives" in *Gay Archivist*, No. 2, 1978.

2 James Fraser (*left*) and Joan Anderson (*right*), Toronto, 1978.
Photograph by Gerald Hannon.

3 From left to right: Alan V. Miller, Joan Anderson, and Ed Jackson at the Canadian Gay Archives, Toronto, 1979.
Photograph by Gerald Hannon.

4 Ed Jackson working at the Canadian Gay Archives at 24 Duncan Street, Toronto, 1983. Photograph by Gerald Hannon.

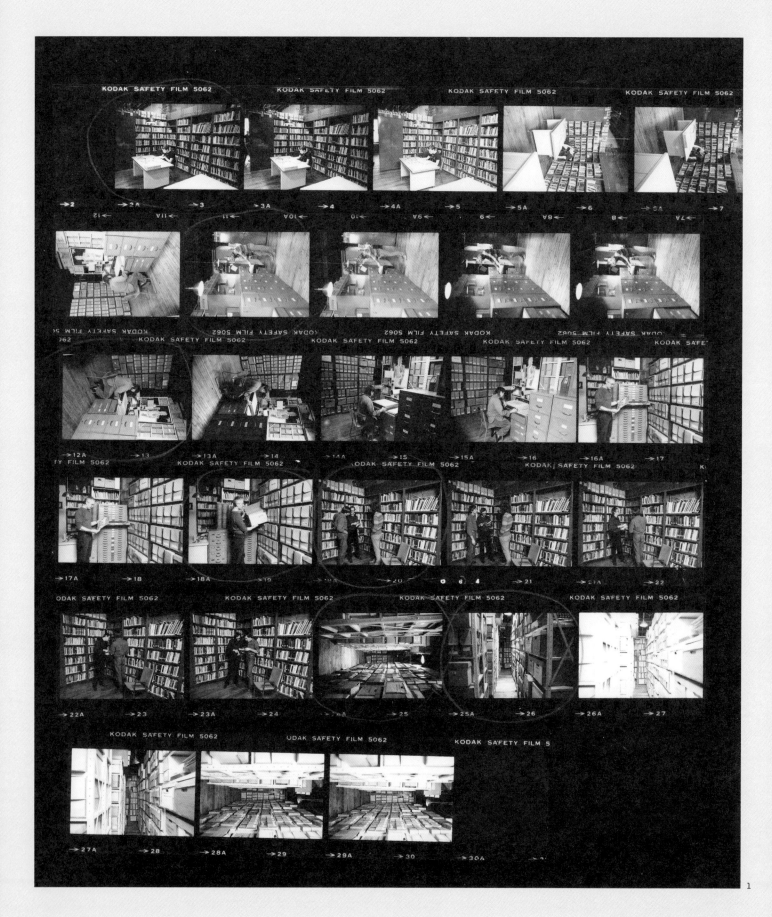

community" but was, instead, "formed by a group of individuals primarily for the promotion, advocacy, or performance of a particular purpose peculiar to them." The Archives eventually won on appeal and received charitable status in November 1981. This is no minor event in the Archives' history: it made financial and material donations tax deductible, giving the Archives a valuable mechanism to help establish financial stability. The June 1986 issue of *Gay Archivist* speaks to this directly, noting that "[u]nlike most archives we have no corporate sponsor and rely heavily on donations. Seventy percent of our revenue in 1984–1985 was from this source."

Regardless of what the Canadian government perceived as the project's peculiarity, the Archives was becoming an important institution in Toronto—a city that was developing a reputation for powerful and productive gay liberation politics—as well as throughout Canada and on the international stage. Alongside *TBP* and other examples of liberation projects, the Archives was participating in a broader shift in the city's reputation, from "Toronto

2

the Good" to "Toronto the Gay." In late June 1982, on the one hundredth anniversary of Oscar Wilde's visit to Canada, the Archives co-hosted Wilde '82— likely the world's first lesbian and gay history conference. A few years later, in July 1985, the Archives co-hosted a second, much larger conference entitled Sex and the State: Their Laws, Our Lives. Both meetings—bringing together scholars, activists, and archivists from the Canada, the United States, the U.K., and farther afield—positioned Toronto as an important site of gay liberation politics.

In 1986, the Archives unveiled The James Fraser Library, a collection of published materials that continues to grow rapidly, specializing primarily in Canadian content and small press

publications. Fraser, an archivist trained at the Provincial Archives of New Brunswick, arrived at the Archives in 1976 with what Rick Bébout, in "Stashing the Evidence," refers to as "a diligence verging on mania." Fraser died from complications from HIV/AIDS in Vancouver in March 1985. In an obituary for Fraser in *Archivaria: The Journal of the Association of Canadian Archivists,* Averill, Victor Russell, and Karen Teeple recall: "Working lunch hours, evenings, and weekends, and often using his own money, James introduced professional archival standards and was particularly adept at attracting volunteers to assist in the archives" (246).

In February 1988, after four years on Wolseley Street (near Queen and Bathurst), the Archives moved to the corner of Yonge and

1   Contact sheet of photographs of the Canadian Gay Archives, Toronto, 1979. Photographs by Gerald Hannon.

2   James Fraser in a Canadian Gay Archives T-shirt at Toronto Pride, 1983. Photograph by Alan V. Miller.

Publications of the Archives

1   *Homosexuality in Canada: A Bibliography,* by Alex Spence (1979).

2   *The Genetic Imperative: Fact and Fantasy in Sociobiology (A Bibliography),* by Alan V. Miller (1979).

3   *Ian Young: A Bibliography (1962–1980)* (1981).

4   *Lesbian Periodical Holdings at The Canadian Gay Archives,* by Alan V. Miller (1981).

5   *Lesbian and Gay Heritage of Toronto,* by James A. Fraser and Alan V. Miller (1982).

6   *Homosexuality in Ancient Greek and Roman Civilization: A Critical Bibliography with Supplement,* by Beert C. Verstraete (1982).

7   *Gays and Acquired Immune Deficiency Syndrome (AIDS): A Bibliography* (1st edition, 1982; 2nd edition, 1983).

8   *Organizing an Archives: The Canadian Gay Archives Experience,* by James A. Fraser and Harold A. Averill (1983).

9   *Homosexuality in Canada: A Bibliography,* by William Crawford (2nd edition, 1984).

10 *Medical, Social, and Political Aspects of the Acquired Immune Deficiency Syndrome (AIDS) Crisis: A Bibliography,* by Donald W. McLeod and Alan V. Miller (1985).

11 *The Writings of Dr. Magnus Hirschfeld: A Bibliography,* by James D. Steakley (1985).

12 *Our Own Voices: Lesbian and Gay Periodicals through Time,* by Alan V. Miller (1991).

13 *Homosexuality, Society, and the State in Mexico,* by Ian Lumsden (1991). Co-published with Colectivo Sol, Mexico City.

14 *Challenging the Conspiracy of Silence: My Life as a Canadian Gay Activist,* by Jim Egan, edited by Don W. McLeod (1998). Co-published with Homewood Books.

1

2

Who Uses the Archives?

Politicians, lesbians, artists, drag queens, students, psychologists, gays, doctors, tourists, musicians, directors, lawyers, playwrights, transvestites, clerics, reporters, historians, librarians, civil libertarians, interior designers, collectors, immigrants, archivists, photographers, architects, dykes, writers, feminists, academics, editors, transsexuals, novelists, sociologists, poets, librarians, leathermen, and actors.

3

4

Grenville. The new location, a space shared with the AIDS Committee of Toronto (ACT) and PTP, was close to other gay and lesbian organizations and businesses in the Church and Wellesley area (a neighbourhood known as the Gay Village) and resulted in a higher profile for the Archives and more regular usage by the public. (A 1990 issue of *Gay Archivist* proclaims, "We Are Being

1   Barb Crisp sorts button in the Canadian Lesbian and Gay Archives, Toronto, c. 1990s.

2   Bruce Jones working in the Canadian Lesbian and Gay Archives, Toronto, c. 1990s.

3   "Who Uses the Archives?" graphic in *Gay Archivist*, No. 9, 1991.

4   Alan V. Miller at the Canadian Gay Archives, Toronto, 1988. Photograph by Marijo Readey.

Used!" alongside a short article about the new, more central location and the higher number of researchers using the Archives.) This increase in usage was comforting: during the move, word spread of gay and lesbian archives around the world shutting down. As noted in the June 1988 issue of *Gay Archivist:*

> A disappointing run of closures of lesbian and gay archives has been reported from around the world. In the past few months the Hall-Carpenter Memorial Archives in London, the International Gay Information Center in New York, and the Lesbian and Gay Rights Resource Centre in Wellington, New Zealand, have all closed their doors. (2)

As gay and lesbian archives around the world were closing, the Archives continued to build a presence in Toronto, across Canada, and on the international stage. In the late 1980s, the Archives collaborated with the Canadian Women's Movement Archives (CWMA)—a collection that has, since 1992, been housed at the University of Ottawa—to produce a set of feminist, lesbian, and gay microfiche of Canadian periodicals. (Microfiche, like all microforms, are reproductions of materials at a much smaller size that are stable to store, cheaper to distribute, and difficult to manipulate.)

In 1992, the Archives began a reorganization, developed a new constitution, severed all legal connections to PTP, and elected a new board of directors: Averill, Miller, Jay Cassel, Robert Champagne,

Canadian
Lesbian
and Gay
Archives

2

"Is the world going to end in 1980 or are we getting a larger office?"

1

Linda Cobon, Michael Lowndes, Michael Rogers, Catherine Shepard, and Andy Visser. In December of the same year, the Archives moved to its first independent location at 56 Temperance Street; one year later, the board voted to change the Archives' name to the Canadian Lesbian and Gay Archives (CLGA).

The Archives launched a National Portrait Collection in 1998, twenty-five years after the institution's founding. The collection of portraits began as an exhibit entitled *25 Lives: Out and Proud,* curated by CLGA president Edward Tompkins, curator Bruce Jones, and vice-president Robin Brownlie. "By setting up

this portrait collection," Tompkins wrote in 1999, "we are actively engaging in the creation of our own historical record. We, as a community, are identifying the people among us whose contributions to the development of out and proud communities makes them worthy of being included in the National Portrait Collection." (See also "The ArQuives Collection: National Portraits," page 266.)

The Archives continued to develop in the early twenty-first century, opening its current home at 34 Isabella Street to the public on September 26, 2009. Toronto city councillor Kyle Rae—the city's first openly gay councillor—facilitated the donation of the building through the City. In addition to housing diverse materials evidencing LGBTQ2+ lives in Canada and around the world, the Archives supports and chronicles exhibitions including *Tape Condition: degraded* by Hazel Meyer and Cait McKinney, which explored the Archives' three thousand (mainly pornographic) VHS tapes and Christina Hernandez's *Marked: Tattoos and Queer Identity.* These exhibits, and many more, bring together the historical nature of archival work with art, photography, and performance in and of the present.

In 2019, the Archives became The ArQuives: Canada's LGBTQ2+ Archives. The Archives' collection grows and develops each year as individuals donate their personal collections of books, buttons, posters, photographs, and periodicals (and so much more), while organizations donate files and other materials. In recent years, the Archives has been privileged to acquire several sizable and important collections from key figures in queer and trans organizing.

Recent accessions include a broad collection of materials from Mirha-Soleil Ross, a Métis trans activist who has organized for years around trans experience and sex work. As one of the founders of the zine *Gendertrash* (page 212), of Meal Trans (a drop-in program for sex-working, street active, and homeless trans people), and of the trans film and performance festival Counting Past 2, Ross's collection is one of the largest trans collections housed at the Archive. The Raj collection—donated by pansexual trans activist, writer, and psychotherapist Rupert Raj—is another

1   Cartoon of James Fraser by Clarence Barnes, 1979.

2   Canadian Lesbian and Gay Archives logo, C. 1990S. Designed by Dennis Benoit.

3   Promotional materials for *Queering Space*, an exhibit curated by James Fowler and Sarah Munro at the Canadian Lesbian and Gay Archives at 34 Isabella Street, Toronto, 2015.

1

sizable trans collection at the Archives that is used regularly by researchers.

Nancy Nicol's donation comprises her award-winning documentary film series From Criminality to Equality and the research materials that informed her films, including original interviews by Nicol with LGBTQ2+ activists from the late twentieth and early twenty-first centuries that evidence a period of profound change in LGBTQ2+ rights in Canada. Edimburgo Cabrera and Anton Wagner's recent donation of 487 DVCAM (digital format video) tapes and DVDs similarly chronicle a wide-ranging history of LGBTQ2+ stories from the late twentieth and early twenty-first centuries; Wagner and Cabrera, who have been donating to the archives since 1999, have produced documentaries on, among other subjects, playwright John

Herbert and Toronto-based female impersonators from the mid-twentieth century on. The Nicol and the Wagner/Cabrera collections are both contextualized by a wide-ranging donation from Inside Out, Canada's LGBTQ2+ film festival. Jearld Moldenhauer, a founding figure in the early gay liberation movement in Toronto, donated an extraordinary collection of books and periodicals that he has been collecting since founding Glad Day Bookshop (page 92) in 1970. In addition to collecting, organizing, and storing these materials, staff and volunteers at the Archives work to digitize holdings so they can be accessible to researchers and community members around the world. As of 2019, the collection is searchable online with an easy-to-use public search interface. As the Archives develops in the digital age, more

and more individuals can access the incredible collection of materials.

Since the Archives' founding in 1973, thousands of volunteers have sustained, developed, and cared for the collection, showing us that the Archives is a collaborative project only made possible through the work of an unknowable and ever-expanding community. In bringing some of its collection to light, this book participates in the aim of the Archives: not only to care for materials of the past, but to make them available in the present as an integral part of the way we live queer life now.

2

1 From left to right: Cecilio Escobar being interviewed by Sajdeep Soomal, Elspeth Brown, and Manuela Accarpio at the Canadian Lesbian and Gay Archives at 34 Isabella Street, Toronto, 2017. Photograph by Celio Barreto. Courtesy of the Family Camera Network.

2 Photograph of The ArQuives: Canada's LGBTQ2+ Archives at 34 Isabella Street, 2019. Photograph by Lauren Kolyn.

Diaries and Journals

The ArQuives collects personal papers of LGBTQ2+ individuals and LGBTQ2+ organizations, with a particular emphasis on Canadian LGBTQ2+ movements. As part of individuals' papers, the ArQuives receives a number of journals and diaries that chronicle individuals' personal narratives and reflections on the queer world and their place therein. For many people, diaries serve as private spaces in which to explore and reflect on their sexuality and desires. As highly personal documents, some journals and diaries are closed—that is, they are unavailable to researchers—until a later date; some, however, are currently open for researchers and provide a window into an individual's life in Canada during the twentieth century.

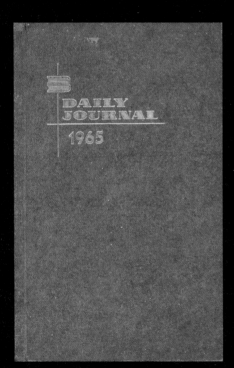

Jeremiah & the Deuteronomic are contemporaries - ... came after Hosea, Amos etc - Joshua, Kings etc are books written after Deut by his followers, with same conceptions of history

Amos, Hosea, Isaiah were spoken - not written - Deuteronomy was first written scripture, comes into existence as purely written book - later books tend more to be written - Ezekiel was author

2 Kings - 22 - 3 on

The time is after David ... Israel had declined ... in relation to other nations and in its service of God - very degenerate religiously

---

December 1960

It all began at church. Jean had met Phil? at a CAS summer camp — and had apparently struck up a friendship. Then Phil was placed at the Boy's Home near Woodgreen Church. It was shortly after Phil's father had died, and he very much needed a friend, that Jean recognized him in church and suggested he pay her a visit some Sunday afternoon.

He was there that afternoon. I was away in Newfoundland, not to return for several weeks. From the beginning Phil was close to Jean.

When I returned, I met Phil and some of the other boys at the Home, and began to take them out for drives, and other places — winter came, and we went out skating.

May 26/55

I am sitting at the table in the men's dorm of the St. Columba House Montreal work camp. Arrived here May 14. Here's the story :

Hitchhiked down from Toronto in 11 hours..an hour less than the bus. My last ride brought me right to the McGill SCM. It was a lot of fun coming down with sleeping bag and brief case overstuffed, and sporting a sign with Montreal on it. Rides varied from businessmen, oil truck, contractor etc. The scenery along the St. Lawrence past Kingston in lovely...lots of islands in the river, red-winged blackbirds, the blues and greens of the river and the shore line on the other side. Saw the new river development, the towns soon to disappear under water... Cornwall, near where I was born,,then into Quebec with a young married couple who had just had very good luck themselves in an accident...My luck all the way was wonderful. I was met after supper at the SCM house by Keith Wright,

---

based on ... humanism,...the strongest I've ever heard(for higher survival value and is thus of greater value (use) ... the supposition that ... the optimistic approach to life is the universe than conflict...this is the source of value truth is utility and survival value. The society which is going to survive and dominate must be technologically advanced, requires democratic education, critical attitude which makes eternal tyranny impossible. No need for the

---

Now I wa... comm... know... and patien... you a great deal for that... only remember with pleasure, I cannot... you werent fatherly but a friend, not too serious...whi... laugh we got when you got around to saying that when man was redeemed he got his freedom back (rather than that man was free after the fall). I guess I managed to show a little of the feeling of frustration and aggression which shows when I taunt you or say somewhat bitterly funny things. You probed me very deeply...wht did I go to the Quakers...was it really something positive or just the negative advantage of a minimum of grating on my sensitivities by the silence . Was I facing reality in rejecting the ideas of communion etc or just giving in to my childhood prejudices. I dont want to

---

that he know good and eveil...morality...otherwise man could never really be free. Not so, Bob said, man lost his freedom and put himself in the condition of life now by knowing what he has not the power to affect. But since God has still given man dominion it is his desire that men strive to do the good and the better even tho they cannot attain the perfection laid upon them by God in the beginning. My idea of man as becoming more and more knowledgeable and powerful was an attempt to replace God by man or at least to put man alongside God...only God possesses real freedom, and man is most free in becoming a creature

1939–1971
BURGEONING SUBCULTURES

1

The Second World War effort moved millions of Canadians (and Newfoundlanders and Labradorians, who did not join the Canadian nation until after the war ended) from the familiar refuges of family homes and small towns and placed them in gender-segregated spaces for sustained periods of time. Mobilization for warfare served as a profound disruption to the authoritative hold of heterosexuality, particularly for young people whose sexual desires and identities were forming during this period. During the Second World War, homosocial—and, for many, homosexual—bonds developed and thrived. As Paul Jackson claims in *One of the Boys: Homosexuality in the Military during World War II*, for many gay men and lesbians in Canada and stationed abroad, "the war was a time of sexual self-discovery, an education into the fact that they were far from alone in their homosexual desires" (17). Although the Royal Canadian Army Medical Corps, in a 1942 document on psychiatric disorders, explicitly identified homosexuality as a threat to military cohesion, changes to societal structures resulting from the war provided exciting opportunities for homosexual experiences at home and abroad.

Postwar Canada was marked by a pervasive desire to return to normalcy in everyday life and to normativity in gender and sexual behaviours. Women who had

answered the nation's call to serve as a powerful wartime labour force were expected to return to the space of the home and serve the nation in a different capacity: as mothers and wives. Cameron Duder explains in *Awfully Devoted Women: Lesbian Lives in Canada, 1900–65* that postwar Canada experienced a "nationwide reinvestment in the traditional nuclear family" and the heterosexual family was "regarded as the building block of the nation and as a bulwark against communism. The nation was the family writ large, and threats to the family were thus threats to Canada as a whole" (95).

In her book *Strangers in Our Midst: Sexual Deviancy in Postwar Ontario,* Elise Chenier shows how notions of sexual and gender deviancy in Canada (and abroad) framed homosexuality as a dangerous abnormality. Accordingly,

while following the Second World War we witness the development of queer subcultural communities and more overt evidence of queerness in Canada, we also see an aggressive response from the state—perhaps most spectacularly in the form of the federal government anti-homosexuality campaigns sparked by the Security Panel on homosexuality (formed in 1946) and subsequent efforts, in the following decades, to purge homosexual military members and civil servants. "Constructed as security risks, blackmailable and suffering from character weaknesses," Patrizia Gentile writes in *We Still Demand: Redefining Resistance in Sex and Gender Struggles,* "gays and lesbians were targets of an extensive national security purge organized by the Security Panel, RCMP Security Services, and local police forces to regulate the lives of 'disloyal'

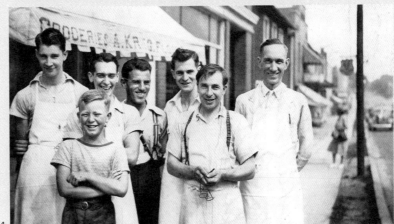

queers" (70). Concerns related to blackmail were informed, in part, by the defection of Igor Gouzenko in September 1945. In what became known as the Gouzenko Affair, the cipher clerk, stationed at the Soviet embassy in Ottawa, defected to Canadian forces and brought with him over one hundred secret documents detailing the USSR's large-scale spying activities in Canada, the United States, and Great Britain—all of which were, at the time, allies of the Soviet Union. Gouzenko's defection in Ottawa, which many historians consider to be the

spark of the Cold War, heightened suspicion of blackmail, difference, and deviance and was used by many to portray leftists and communists as potential dangers to the Western world. Queers, who were living necessarily secret lives, were seen as particularly susceptible to blackmail by foreign agents.

Suburban Lifestyles

Following the Second World War, Canada experienced an economic boom that enabled a different way of living for many of its citizens: a thriving middle class developed, and many Canadians enjoyed a significant increase in leisure time and

disposable income. Suburbs grew—aided by burgeoning automobile culture—and many families moved out of cities' downtown areas to find the ostensible good life. Suburbs were seen as refuges for affluent white families and thus became bastions of racial and class conformity.

As major cities across Canada, but primarily Toronto, became dominated by automobiles and oriented to the ease of car culture, new infrastructure encouraged the development of suburban spaces, which often had a detrimental effect on infrastructure in downtown cores. In the 1960s, many buildings were partially abandoned; some were even demolished to make way for

1 Ann (*left*) with Ted (*right*), c. 1940s.

2 Unknown sailors from HMCS *Stadacona*. Date unknown.

3 Unknown Canadian soldiers, c. 1940s.

4 Unknown individuals. Date unknown.

Maclean's Magazine, April 1, 1948

You don't need a lisp to be a "feminine" man, or bulging muscles to be a "masculine" woman. M-F index proves it

Men Are Men - - or Are They?

1

between these spaces allowed many men to dabble in queer experiences during the workday—cruising on their lunch break or before heading home—and to subsequently retreat into spaces of heterosexual domestic bliss each night. The postwar growth of urban spaces in Canada provided individuals with queer desires more anonymity than suburbs and small towns might have allowed. Development of apartment buildings in Canadian cities allowed for single and shared non-family occupancy. Taken together, shifts in racial demographics and organization of urban space enabled the flourishing of queer community life in urban spaces that were once populated by heterosexual families.

The Increasingly Public Politics of Gender and Sexuality

General awareness of homosexuality increased in Canada mid-century as visible subcultures developed and received significant, sensationalized attention from the tabloid press. Despite an increase in awareness of (and, for many, concern about) homosexuality, the issue was largely absent from respectable mainstream, established media, and as a result the tabloid press became a lurid source of information on the so-called threat of homosexuality. Popular novels that incorporate homosexual desires, experiences, and themes—including

highways that allowed for quicker travel out of the downtown and to suburbia. The deterioration of downtown spaces and communities also resulted in cheaper rents that enabled the development of marginalized spaces—including those that served to bring together gays and lesbians.

Urban centres remained the primary sites of employment, and for many men travelling into the city for work, the distance between the downtown core and surrounding suburbs allowed exciting possibilities for same-sex erotic experiences. The actual and the psychological distances

Gore Vidal's *The City and the Pillar* (1948) and James Baldwin's *Giovanni's Room* (1956)—introduced homosexuality and queer desires to more mainstream literary audiences. Cheap paperbacks exploring homosexual themes and desires were widely available, as were physique magazines that allowed readers to enjoy and marvel at the male body under the guise of health and fitness. (See also "Pulp Fiction," page 94, and "*Face & Physique*," page 70.) In the 1948 book *Sexual Behavior in the Human Male,* Alfred Kinsey, Wardell Pomeroy, and Clyde Martin shocked North American readers and made homosexuality and homosexual desires something of a talking point in the following years. Two of the authors' claims were particularly troubling for heterosexual Canadians mid-century: first, that significantly more men had participated in (or desired) same-sex erotic experiences than one might imagine and, second, that you can't always

identify a homosexual man simply by looking at him. *Sexual Behavior in the Human Female,* by Kinsey, Pomeroy, Martin, and Paul H. Gebhard, was similarly discomforting for ostensibly respectable and proper Canadians; it suggested that a significant portion of women enjoyed sexual experiences outside of marriage and that some desired erotic acts with other women. Kinsey's report coincided with structural conditions that transformed homosexual desires into homosexual identities: the increase in disposable income enabled people (especially men) with queer desires to move away from the heteronormative demands of the family and to live a "gay life."

In a more local context, Sidney Katz's 1964 *Maclean's* article "The Homosexual Next Door" built on what was known as the Kinsey Scale—from the aforementioned studies by Kinsey and his collaborators—and featured Jim Egan (under the pseudonym Verne Baldwin) as a community informant. This article introduced some aspects of homosexual politics in Canada—what Katz refers to as a "drive for 'respectability'"—to mainstream Canadian audiences in the mid-1960s.

Women's liberation had a significant impact on the trajectory of gay life in Canada. Women fought for access to abortion (which began to increase incrementally in 1967), access to contraceptives, the ability to work more freely outside the home, and

1   "Men are Men—or Are They?" in *Maclean's*, April 1, 1948.

2   Promotional card for International Steam Baths in Kingston and Toronto, date unknown.

3   Raymond (*right*) with his boyfriend "Florence" at the Royal Tavern in Saint John, 1966.

4   From left to right: James, Michael, Raymond, (*standing*); Ralph, unknown individual, and Louis (*sitting*) at the Admiral Beatty Hotel in Saint John, 1967.

5   James (*standing*) and Michael at the Royal Tavern in Saint John, 1966.

3

4

5

equal pay for equal work. Indigenous women fought for the right to vote in federal elections, winning it in 1960. Federal divorce reform allowing the legal dissolution of marriage passed in 1968. The Royal Commission on the Status of Women was convened in 1967 to examine the status of women in Canada, and recommendations in its 488-page report included measures to address violence against women, increase representation of women in government, and pay equality. While the role of lesbians within the feminist movement was fraught—factions of the women's movement remained homophobic and committed to a politics of heterosexual respectability—women's increased independence as a result of feminist movements enabled a new phase of lesbian life in Canada.

Gross Indecency

As homosexuality became more widely known and galvanized as an identity rather than a simple act, pushback from the state increased significantly. At the federal level, multiple anti-homosexual campaigns of the 1950s and 1960s targeted suspected homosexuals in the Canadian Armed Forces and the civil service. As Gary Kinsman and Patrizia Gentile argue in *The Canadian War on Queers: National Security as Sexual Regulation,* "thousands of lesbians, gay men, and those suspected

of homosexuality were directly affected by these campaigns… Hundreds (if not thousands) of others were purged, demoted, and forced to inform on friends and acquaintances" (3). The Immigration Act of 1952 was the first version of the Act to explicitly name homosexuals as a class of persons, barring "prostitutes, homosexuals, or persons living off the avails of prostitution or homosexualism" from immigrating to Canada.

At the local level, police in the 1940s, 1950s, and 1960s used disparate laws to harass and arrest men they perceived to be homosexuals, especially if the men in question were wearing women's clothing or otherwise "improperly" performing heterosexual masculinity. In his unpublished memoir, playwright John Herbert notes that "the police of Toronto had several laws on the books by which they could pick up a man dressed in female clothing, one of which was called 'Disguised by Night,' another 'Vagrancy' if the arresting officer could prove to the Judge that the person in drag had no money for food or rent,

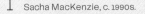

1   Sacha MacKenzie, c. 1990s.

2   Unknown individuals, most likely in Toronto, c. 1950s.

3   Donya Peroff (*left*) with Philip McLeod (*right*) on Hanlan's Point, Toronto, c. mid–1950s.

4   John Herbert, c. 1970s.

5   Title page of John Herbert's unpublished memoir, c. late 1990s.

4   5

INCOMPLETE AND UNEDITED PIECES FOR A MEMOIR to be titled

Writing in the Sand

by

John Herbert

and thirdly, 'Gross Indecency' if the man was caught having sexual intercourse with another male." Herbert's reference to a "Disguised by Night" charge is of note here, as we find very little historical evidence of this charge actually being used. Legal scholar Constance Backhouse notes in *Colour-Coded: A Legal History of Racism in Canada, 1900–1950,* that the charge was "a carryover from an old English statute that was aimed at deterring house burglars" (193–94). The section in which this charge is listed— section 417 of the 1892 Criminal Code of Canada—relates, primarily, to "instruments of house-breaking"; section 417(c) however, reads, "Every one is guilty of an indictable offence and liable to five years' imprisonment who is found… having his face masked or blackened, or being otherwise disguised, by night, without lawful excuse (the proof whereof shall lie on him)." This charge served as a tool for police to harass and

punish men wearing women's clothing. For the state, homosexuality was a social evil that needed to be contained and eradicated through a range of methods at both local and national levels.

This is certainly apparent in the case of Everett George Klippert, a mechanic living in Pine Point, Northwest Territories, in the mid-1960s. Detained by police and asked about a recent arson in the community, Klippert was interrogated for hours and talked openly with police about his homosexual experiences with other men in the community. He was charged with "gross indecency" (an intentionally vague section of the Criminal Code often used to punish consensual sexual acts between men that did not qualify as "buggery") and, in 1967, was declared a dangerous sexual offender likely to commit additional offences of the same kind. During the case, the judge noted that Klippert had never harmed another person

and was unlikely to do so in the future. Ultimately, though, such details didn't matter—Klippert was declared a dangerous sexual offender and sentenced to what the court called "preventative detention." The Supreme Court of Canada dismissed his appeal in 1967, noting that he was likely to commit further offences of the same kind. Klippert's arrest and imprisonment influenced Bill C-150—changes to the Criminal Code in 1969 that altered some laws related to homosexual sex occurring in private spaces between adults. Speaking to the press about the federal government's effort to liberalize regulations and laws related to homosexuality, abortion, and contraceptives, Minister of Justice Pierre Elliott Trudeau uttered his famous quip that "there's no place for the state in the bedrooms of the nation." The rest of Trudeau's

comments in this moment, which are not remembered with the same level of excitement, are useful for understanding the public/private divide that developed in relation to homosexual acts in Canada and, in subsequent years, was used as justification to brutally limit public experiences of homosexuality. "What's done in private between adults doesn't concern the Criminal Code," Trudeau explained; "when it becomes public," he continued, "it's a different matter."

South of the border, the American state's commitment to institutionalized and violent homophobia was challenged by the Stonewall riots in New York City's Greenwich Village in the summer of 1969. Though not the first queer riot to stand up to police violence, the Stonewall riots had an immediate effect on queer collective formation in New

York City: within months, gay liberation newspapers (including *Gay Power* and *Come Out!*) and political blocs (most famously, the Gay Liberation Front [GLF]) developed. The Stonewall riots, held up as the spark of modern gay liberation in North America, had less of an effect on queer organizing in Canada, where attention was wrapped up in changes to federal law through Bill C-150. Informants for Carolyn Anderson's 2001 study on lesbianism in Canada, for example, knew little about the Stonewall riots but were, Anderson writes, "aware of Prime Minister Trudeau's role in the decriminalization of homosexuality and indicated that they had gained a small but significant sense of power by voting for him" (220).

Bill C-150 ostensibly decriminalized homosexual acts between consenting adults in private. In reality, though, the Criminal Code reform exempted certain acts (by certain people, in certain spaces) that were rarely criminalized anyway; both gross indecency and buggery remained on the books for sex in spaces the police defined as "public." As Liz Millward notes in *Making a Scene: Lesbians and Community across Canada, 1964–84,* this "decriminalization applied to men, since only their acts had been criminal offences under existing legislation. For women who desired other women, the act still gave the Crown power to prosecute, under charges of indecency or corruption of a minor" (19). As subsequent sections in this book show in detail, Bill C-150 had relatively little effect on the way local police departments dealt with the so-called problem of homosexuality.

Toronto-based gay activist and politician George Hislop told Marion Foster (the pseudonym of broadcaster and writer Shirley Shea) in the early 1970s that the revisions to the Canadian Criminal Code didn't really change much. In an interview published in Marion Foster and Kent Murray's 1972 book *A Not So Gay World: Homosexuality in Canada,* Hislop explains that while the alterations to the Criminal Code meant little in the legality of most homosexual acts, they did cause a shift in societal attitudes: "There was so much publicity given to it and people think that homosexuality is now legal, when in fact it never *was* illegal to *be* a homosexual. Many gay people, too, now think, 'it's legal, it's OK, I can say it out loud if I want to', but they could always do this. However, there was this new freedom and expansion of discussion on sexuality so the climate was good for the establishment of an organization" (216). Hislop here is referring to collective organizing in Toronto, but the first examples of this activism occurred on the West Coast.

1 Everett George Klippert (*second from right*) seated alongside his family, C. 1940S. Courtesy of Kevin Allen and Klippert Family.

On Our Terms

In April 1964, the Association for Social Knowledge (ASK) in Vancouver, British Columbia, became Canada's first homophile organization (page 84). Like their American counterparts in the Mattachine Society—one of the earliest homophile organizations in the United States—ASK's members downplayed the sexual nature of gay life and focused instead on inclusion within the state and a sense of difference shared with other minority groups. ASK was formed to encourage society to understand and accept individuals who do not live according to the sexual norm. That same month, NDP MP Arnold Peters (Temiskaming) spoke publicly about his efforts to develop a private member's bill to modify the Criminal Code and decriminalize consenting, private homosexual acts. While Peters's bill never reached the floor of the House of Commons, it evidences changing perspectives on homosexual behaviours and the relationship between same-sex acts and the law.

GAY and *TWO*—foundational Canadian gay periodicals—began publishing out of Toronto in 1964. (See more about *GAY* on page 85, and *TWO* on page 86.) Homophile movements eventually gave way to the more overtly political and aggressive goals of gay liberation, but the University of Toronto Homophile Association (UTHA, page 90), the first contemporary gay liberation organization in

Canada, retained the "homophile" moniker into the 1970s.

In the years 1939–71, we thus see pivotal developments in Canadian queer formation: the development of subcultural communities marked by non-normative sexual and gender behaviours; the production of artwork, periodicals, and magazines that speak to queer individuals as an identifiable and burgeoning audience; the beginnings of self-representations of gays and lesbians in Canada; and, ultimately, the collective formation of activists bound together by their interest in homophile and, eventually, gay and lesbian liberation politics. In *Never Going Back: A History of Queer Activism in Canada,* Tom Warner writes, "Activism and organizing since the late 1960s have left a profound legacy, and built a strong foundation. Because of the profound change wrought by small bands of defiant and courageous individuals in communities across Canada, queers can now more confidently proclaim that they are always moving forward—not in pursuit of monochromal assimilation—but towards their liberation" (358). Throughout this period, queer citizens faced sustained, coordinated, and often violent repression of their desires and identities by fellow citizens, established media, and the state. The materials in the following section evidence the complicated ways queer citizens attempted to live their lives during this period in Canadian history.

SECOND
WORLD WAR

The Second World War marked a major shift in the way gender organized the social and political world. As men left to fight on the front lines, women took up work outside the home and life was organized around the homosocial—rather than the heterosexual—unit.

While homosexual experiences were readily available and regularly enjoyed during wartime, Canadian military personnel worked to ensure these experiences were as covert as possible. Identifying, policing, and censoring evidence of homosexual behaviour was complicated by a number of factors. The Second World War resulted in profound shifts in gender behaviours and expectations, challenging simplistic notions of what "men" and "women" did and were. Close relationships developed among soldiers on the front lines; articulating the difference between a caring and loving friendship and a romantic relationship could be difficult. Even cross-dressing was regularly incorporated into morale-boosting projects in the military, and cross-gender performance didn't read as "gay" as it might in contemporary culture. In short, identifying a homosexual was much more difficult in practice than it was in theory—the lines of "proper" gender and sexual behaviour, unclear to begin with, were shifting rapidly.

Much of the material evidence of same-sex experiences and desires during wartime may have been lost forever. Careful and complex censorship practices were in place from the beginning of the war effort, and the vast majority of letters written by soldiers were screened for inappropriate messaging by commanding officers, personnel of the Women's

Royal Canadian Naval Service (WRCNS), or both. In his book *One of the Boys: Homosexuality in the Military during World War II,* Paul Jackson recalls an WRCNS member's surprise in discovering love letters between men. The woman explains:

> The first thing was one of the girls coming to me and she said "[Margaret], here's a man writing to another man!" And she said, "It's a love letter!" And she was totally surprised and I said, "Well, I think you'd better discuss it with the officer in charge." Which is how the whole subject came to our attention… And the officer said, "If you find any letters of that sort, please bring them to our attention as a matter of security." (39)

There is little evidence of homosexual desires in the written materials that survive from this era—a result of both the careful nature of the writers and the aggressive work by the censors.

1 Elgin Blair (*left*), 1945. Handwritten text on the back of the photograph notes he is "with Tom (from Hamilton) and Johnny (from Calgary)."

RAA1104 17 GLT COML XCI OPT

WEATHARTLEPOOL 29   1943 APR 29 PM 10 28

LIEUT WILLIAM ATKINSON   1519

CARE CPR TORONTO

GREATLY APPRECIATE TEMPTING PROPOSAL BUT FEAR FIANGE MAY

DISAPPROVE

RENE WILSON

2   Mary (*left*) and Rita (*right*) during the Second World War, c. 1940s.

3   Telegram sent from Rene Wilson to William Atkinson, 1943.

4   HMCS *Fraser* sailor blowing a whistle, c. 1940s. Photograph by James Skitt Matthews. Courtesy of the City of Vancouver Archives.

5   Unknown woman, c. 1940s.

DEAR MOTHER, DAD & J.B.:- this in the late evening..they have just
been reading the news from london..the peace begins tomorrow..the
150 watt bulb in the ceiling here is burning and the blinds are up..
there is no more war..the lamps outside the mess hall building are
on and all the lights inside are shining thru the windows..there are
lights on in every building...and the blinds are up..oh god its incredible..i hear that in london they have gone wild..the same in new
york, in paris, in brussels evenin rome..i don't believe it but i
hear it rumoured the holy father himself is stinkin from drinkin!..
i'm wrong..i do believe..i'll believe anything tonight..come one come
all..i'm ready for conversion and immersion..oh joy..its over...
when i'm done here i'm going to walk out in the defeated german night
and look at the lights falling thru the windows..let your light so
shine before men that they will see your good works and glorify your
prime minister which is at no. 10 downing street..i wish i were in
picadilly tonight, milling with the crowds there..its a hideous spot
picadilly..all sign boards and theatre marquees and streets loaded
with traffic of buses and taxis and prostitutes loitering against
the building and people circulating and mingling along the sidewalks
..and yet i love it..it would be good to stand under the high solit-
ude of nelson staring nobly out over the tremendous city to or to
walk in the heavy darkness of hyde park and be concious of the lovers
on the grass under the trees..or to stroll pompously down the mall
toward the palace and look at the great ugly building those two pre-
posterous mortal live in..i could even settle for an amble thru the
close quartered rue neuve in brussels and the back streets with their
sordid little cafes where ugly women with nothing but bodies try to
seduce you from other tables with crude gestures and obvious postures
..best of al would be home and montreal..what has it got?..i don't
know..my heart is there..or most of it anyway..i can't claim to love
the mountain, except perhaps on a winter night withno one up there
and the weird music of the wind blowing in the frozen naked trees
and the great black trunks creaking to bring you nearer to the myster
of things than any experience i know..i often remember the view of
the great hump from our parlour window in autumn..the trees (someone
hear shakily blowing the last post on a trumpet) all red and the
houses perched on the slopes beginning to emerge,with the autumn dying and the leaves drifting,from the deep rish obscurity of summer..
it was a clean view from our kitchen window of the flat irregular
ribbon of the river flowing round the island, i used to like after
coming home from work for supper..i hope i will go back to it many
times and be surrounded by the same familiar voices..instead for
tonight i'll have to find consolation in the lights here..they're the
best thing..at the moment they're driving a moth or some fluttery
th ing mad..absolutely mad..he has been beating himself against the
window here for the last ten minutes in one frenzied attempt after
another to reach the luminus it bulb in our ceiling..i think i'll
let him in and just as he reaches it, switch the current off..

                    LOVE, EVER
                              Phil.

may 7 th (i think) /45 (i'm positive)
germany (i'm damned positive..too damned positive!)

1

2

1 Letter written by Philip McLeod to his parents indicating that he just learned the Second World War was ending, 1945.

2 Members of the Canadian Women's Army Corps, 1945.
Photograph by James Skitt Matthews.
Courtesy of the City of Vancouver Archives.

MID-CENTURY CROSS-DRESSING

Part of the postwar changes in social formation was the development of gay and lesbian subcultures that were increasingly visible and, thus, identified by those interested in the possibilities of gay and lesbian life. In particular, cross-dressing became a hallmark of queer life after the war. In Toronto, for instance, the Letros Tavern's Nile Room (campily referred to as "The Vile Room") quickly became known as an overtly gay cocktail lounge, particularly during its high-profile Halloween drag balls. Similarly, the Continental, located in Toronto's Chinatown and frequented by lesbians, was marked visible by its butch/femme clientele.

Because cross-dressers, drag queens, and female impersonators faced so much scrutiny from the police in public spaces, private networks of drag performance developed in urban areas, including a Toronto garden party circuit in which performer George Bailey thrived.

Unsurprisingly, cross-dressing and the homosexual subcultures in which it occurred were of interest to academics and sociologists seeking to understand the roots of homosexuality as a behavioural phenomenon. Maurice Leznoff's 1954 McGill University MA thesis, "The Homosexual in Urban Society," analyzes the lifestyles and experiences of homosexual men in "a large cosmopolitan Canadian city which we shall refer to as 'Easton' " (16). The city was clearly Montreal, and Leznoff's is one of the first sociological studies on male homosexuality in Canada. The Addiction Research Foundation procured a study on the Letros Tavern called *Working Papers on the Tavern: Notes on the Gay Bar,* which sought to understand the relationship between sexuality, cross-dressing, and alcohol addiction. Similarly, *Men in Women's Clothing,* edited by Dr. Crichton Allison, took a medical approach to cross-dressing and identified the link between dress, gender, and sexual behaviour.

1

Fags In 'Drag'

Toronto's fagdom is breathlessly looking forward to that annual spectacular, the selection of Miss Letros 1962. As usual, the "Tournament of Pansies" will be held at Letros Tavern, King St. E. Above, couple of unidentified local contestants stage a preview of their "drag" finery.

2

1   The Letros Tavern, Toronto, C. 1950S. Courtesy of the Archives of Ontario.

2   "Fags in 'Drag,'" in *TAB*, 1962.

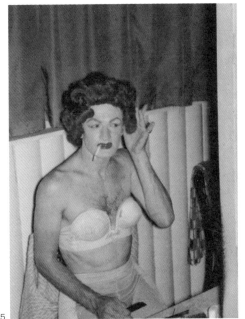

3   George Bailey, Toronto,
c. 1950s.

4   Riki Tik performing onstage,
Toronto, c. 1960s.

5   Madam Melba prepares for a
performance, Toronto, c. 1960s.

STRIPPING, SEX,
AND INCARCERATION

John Herbert (who would use his stage name Carol Desmond when in drag) and Allan Maloney (better known by his stage name Brandee/Brandy/Brandi) were staples of Toronto's burgeoning cross-dressing community. In his unpublished memoir, Herbert writes about working convention shows in downtown Toronto, remembering that "[t]he law did not allow women to strip at convention shows at this time of Toronto's entertainment scene, so drag-queens who could dance were expected to be strippers. Carol was described as an 'exotic' dancer, stripping to music such as [Maurice] Ravel's 'Bolero' and [Leroy] Anderson's 'The Blue Tango.' "

> "We hit Halifax in what's called 'Navy Week' there. If they'd known that Allan and I were men they would've carried that tent down the midway." **John Herbert, in** *John Herbert: Fortune and Men's Eyes,* **dir. Anton Wagner, 2003**

Homophobic laws targeted visible manifestations of queerness, and cross-dressers were frequently harassed and assaulted by police. Such harassment also resulted in the incarceration of many gay individuals in the 1940s and beyond. Both Herbert and Maloney were incarcerated in Guelph Reformatory in the late 1940s for, respectively, gross indecency and hustling. After his release, Herbert went on to write the play *Fortune and Men's Eyes,* based on his experience in the reformatory. It was first staged in Stratford, Ontario, in 1965 before opening off-Broadway at the Actor's Playhouse in February 1967. A film version of the play premiered in Toronto in June 1971.

Following his release from the Guelph Reformatory, Maloney hosted strip shows at the Warwick Hotel in Toronto and travelled as an emcee and stripper across Ontario. An advertisement for one of Brandee's shows in Kirkland Lake, Ontario, speaks to her popularity: "When we say fabulous we mean exactly that. BRANDEE has packed night clubs, wherever 'She' has appeared. You may not believe your eyes but your ears will tell you BRANDEE is the greatest. All the old favourites and a lot more we don't dare tell you." Maloney hosted the Warwick's *All Star Nude Strip Revue* for decades, until the bar—known for being the "sleaziest bar in Toronto"—closed in 1980.

1

2

1   John Herbert/Carol Desmond, 1953. That year, Herbert and his friend Allan Maloney/Brandee travelled through Ontario, Quebec, New Brunswick, and Nova Scotia.

as performers in a show titled *Paris after Midnight*. Brandee stripped, sang, and emceed; Carol was billed as "The Tallest Showgirl in America."

2   Guelph Reformatory, 1948.
Courtesy of the *Toronto Star* Archives.

John Herbert's Memories of Carol Desmond (1953)
in Paris After Midnight, Model Shows tour.

Carol at start of the
Show's tour (Hamilton),
hair too short to swing
in burlesque style. SHIRT
AND SLACKS—STREET CLOTHES.

Carol, several months
later, feeling like
Gypsy Rose Lee, an
artist she admired.

Carol, wearing silk snood
and holding her 'chinchilla'
(Canadian rabbit) jacket.
• STAGE COSTUME •

Carol, as casual Dietrich,
in black beret, black and
white slacks and silk scarf.
• STREET CLOTHES •

1

---

1 Page from John Herbert's unpublished memoir, c. late 1990s. In this text, Herbert remembers his performance as Carol Desmond in 1953 while on tour as part of the *Paris after Midnight* revue: "Carol made her first appearance in the Toronto drag community at Toronto's first gay night-club, Letros's Nile Room, on King St. E., across from the King Edward Hotel, wearing a black slipper-satin evening gown, a copy of the one worn by Rita Hayworth in the movie 'Gilda', Carol's gown made by designer Mary Grey in her salon on Bloor Street, between Bay St. and Avenue Rd., designing the costume from a sketch made by Carol. Carol was a hit that night but lost the prize of a crown of rhinestones and a dozen red roses to a short and hairy-legged Swan Queen in white tulle ballet costume."

2 Allan Maloney/Brandee, c. 1960s. Brandee would, for decades, perform in bars and taverns in southern Ontario. She was particularly well known for hosting shows at the Warwick Hotel and performing "A Hard Man Is Good to Find," her campy rendition of the classic blues standard "A Good Man Is Hard to Find."

RONALD MCRAE

Ronald McRae was a Canadian artist, designer, and illustrator. In the 1920s he worked for *Vogue* in New York City, where he developed a close relationship with Carl Van Vechten (novelist, photographer, cultural critic, and important figure in the Harlem Renaissance, a transformative artistic and intellectual movement centred on Black politics and culture in Harlem, New York, in the early 1920s) and provided the illustration for the cover of Van Vechten's 1928 book *Spider Boy*. An openly gay man, McRae participated in New York City's drag balls and queer subcultures. Upon his return to Canada, McRae developed his illustration collection Fashionable Women—an exoticizing depiction of women from around the world.

1   Ronald McRae, c. 1930s.
Photograph by Ashley and Crippen.

2/5   Artwork from Ronald McRae's Fashionable Women series, c. 1940s.

2

3

4

5

TABLOID REPRESENTATIONS
OF QUEERS

In the 1950s, disparaging media representations of homosexual men and women were widespread. A primary source for such representations was the thriving tabloid industry. Toronto-based tabloids like *True News Times, Justice Weekly,* and *Hush* published sensationalized articles on "sex deviants," "pansies," and "perverts" who were "infecting" the city and the nation more broadly.

In many instances, these tabloid articles' homophobia was bound with racism. One spectacular example is a 1954 article in *Flash* entitled "Sodomy City!" Its unnamed author recounts a racy story about a "huge… 80-year-old Negro… prostitute" who serviced as many as "400 men and boys" in the town of Collingwood, Ontario—a town with a population of just over 7,000 according to the 1951 census. Of course, little (if any) of the information that appears in articles such as these is true.

To a lesser extent, tabloids also targeted lesbians as a "threat" to the proper functioning of Canadian society. As much as these tabloids reflected broader racist panics about immigrants and people of colour, they also spoke to a widespread fear of the changing nature of women's roles and the development of feminist politics: lesbians were seen as a danger that threatened to "take over" cities, convert straight women, and destroy the institution of marriage.

While the tabloids used sensationalized headlines about homosexuals to sell papers to curious heterosexuals, many also featured gay gossip columns that, while dubious at best, are useful archives of gay life during this period. *True News Times,* for example, featured columns called A Study in Lavender and Toronto's Gay Nights, and *TAB*'s columns Fairy-Go-Round and The Gay Set similarly told tales about homosexual happenings. The June 2, 1956, issue of *TAB,* for example, informed readers about the "alarming" number of same-sex weddings happening in the city:

"Toronto's queer set are having mock weddings like CRAZY! Now that spring is here, gay romances are thriving just too-too much. We know of at least three recent weddings that have been modelled on Grace Kelly's recent smash hit. The trouble is—both of the partners want to be the Grace Kelly, and very few of the fairies want to be the Prince Charming" (4).

It wasn't just sensationalized headlines that referenced homosexuality and non-normative gender and sexual behaviours. Some of these publications provided in-depth reports on queer behaviours.

Though she would be the last to admit it, the confirmed Lesbian is a tragic figure. In following her way of life she rejects all the special privileges of being a woman: home, the right to be cared for, and above all, motherhood. Hers is a complex problem and we should try to understand it.

1   "Understanding the Lesbian," in *TAB*, 1961.

A MIDNIGHT SURVEY ON...
Homosexuality In Canada!

Observers who have occasion to be aware of such things saw a fantastic upsurge of homosexuality in Canada in the years from 1943 to 1946. Now in 1958 the same pattern is being repeated. The "homo" populaton of Canada has increased tremendously, and of major significance is the fact that not even the most observant expert can pick them out "just by looking".

Worse yet, homosexuality is getting more young people involved. Ignorance of the subject should not continue. Now is the time for investigation, information and action.

Hiding its head in shame, closing its eyes and wishing it would go away, and snarling at any publica- 'tion daring to speak about the subject, present day society has erected a wall of apathy, opposition and ignorance against the developing moral menace of today.

Just as veneral diseases were public secrets until discussed and over-powered, so is the subject of homosexuality.

For this our hypocritical society should be thoroughly ashamed. It is not.

Canada has at least 300,000 active or potentially active homosexuals. Can you say this is not correct? A recent check in the U.S. set the figure at over 7,000,000.

Because they are law-abiding citizens they rarely get into public trouble. Social workers, scientists, professors hate to discuss the subject. Police and prison guards regard the topic with loathing.

There is little factual knowledge, but every report or survey sees increases.

FANTASTIC FACT

Before he died Dr. Alfred C. Kinsey was planning to do research specially on the subject and stated: "We were totally unprepared to find such data as the research revealed. Something like 37% of the population has had at least some homosexual experience between adolescence and old age".

There are many viewpoints towards the homosexual.

The common one today seems to be that he is an unfortunate sick creature who only harms himself.

Until a few years ago gutter humour and imitations of a hip-swinging, limp - wristed, falsetto-voiced fairy was the only attitude of most male to homos. It was a standard vaudeville gag.

"This attitude is wrong. The homosexual is all too often a seducer of the young, and he presents a problem because he is not willing to be a degenerate alone, but must make others degenerate, and so seeks his victims among the youth of the country," a special investigation told MIDNIGHT. "This is something that the parents of all young boys should recognize and be aware of."

Each year at least 15,000 young Canadians are introduced to the weird practise of the homosexual. The settings for such affairs can be anywhere. Sometimes it is a car, other times at school, in offices, buildings.

A young Montrealer died in the West Indies a few years back in the same little shack as his giant Negro male friend of many years. He came from one of the weathiest of Westmount families and was a victim of a perverted teacher in an English school he attended. He never returned to normal.

Mark is a Montrealer who decided to take 1948 off in New York before he went into business with his father. The result was that he fell in with a homosexual con man in that city. The crook managed to get Mark to shake down the father for some $40,000 before the latter discovered his son's sex deviation. He cut off all ties with the lad. Ten years have passed and Mark is today a pathetic Harlem derelict despised by the Negro residents, and seeking only the companionship of males.

Juvenile Courts often face serious problems as to their handling of homosexuality. They usually have no answer. One man was caught in a Dorchester Street rooming with a 16-year-old youth. He merely lost his job and paid a small fine. Authorities could do little

DO IT FOR MONEY

Police have often found young men who give their occupations as "male prostitutes". For a period of time Montreal's Peel and St. Catherine was swarming with these youths. About fifty descended on the city 3 years ago and only after some heavy-handed treatment by the police were they driven away to Toronto and Vancouver.

Once a man assumes the role of a homosexual and resorts to relationships with youth he seems to throw off all moral restraint and reasoning. They often goad youths on to sadism, drug addiction, torture, and all types of crime.

Some of the brutal beatings administered to innocent citizens stem from perverts who want to show off their "manhood".

There is no question that many of them are physically powerful and appear to be very "male". Some are in and out of jail on other charges, but their report never indicates for police information that they are homosexuals.

"We almost take it for granted that about 75% of the men in the pen will get involved in homosexual antics," a penitentiary warden told MIDNIGHT. "So why put it on their file cards?"

IT IS A SICKNESS

What can be done about the growth of homosexuality among our youth?

Cancer was once a naughty word. Syphilis was never murmured outside of medical books, This was prudery. But since the clean breath of information has been turned on them and this attitude banished, the cure has progressed.

Homosexuality is a sickness, 'a moral menace and a serious problem — ask the parents of any son who has been contaminated!

The psychiatrist recognizes that homosexuality is a form or arrested emotional development. Sometimes it is a craving to be different, for self expression, or to be a producer of bizarre relationships.

But eventually it becomes a way of life. The dedicated try to increase their membership by adding those who are on the edge—one way or the other. They offer a refuge from humdrum society. The newcomer needs no money and he finds himself in a circle of handsome, talented, influential, well dressed and prosperous persons. These people are not poor or unemployed. They are personalities in the arts, entertainment, decoration and many other important phases of endeavour. They stick for mutual protection, help each other, and although they live in constant terror of losing the object of their affections, they still have a very strongly developed "herd instinct".

HOW IT STARTS

Scientific research has proven that the following are main causes for homosexuality:

(a) Cultivation of dependence and infantilism in the son by the mother.

(b) Distortion of values, principles and relationships through life in the field of art and creativeness.

(c) Inability of some youth to cope with the problems of economic life and inability to get proper guidance and relationship from other sources.

(d) Glandular imbalance from earliest childhood.

These patterns can best be studied in cities like Montreal, Toronto, Vancouver rather than in smaller centres. The mannerisms of the homosexual are too apparent in the small town. They leave at an early age. Violence is often turned against them in the smaller cities and they know this.

The sensitive introverted male arrives in a metropolis like Montréal. By some sure instinct he can find the centre of a group of males of his type. Contact with these groups generally means some form of emotional security and financial protection.

It is estimated that Montreal now has over 30,000 homosexuals.

MEANS OF PROTECTION

The way to protect your child is simple:

(a) Make sure that you have a happy home with love freely exchanged between members of the family. No baby talk, greeting the children as if they are not responsible, or that they are precious.

(b) Educate the kids about sex from the start. Let them know the facts of life. They generally know but you make sure that there is little or no hypocricy about normal sex practices.

(c) Encourage the children to privately discuss any sex problems they have with you.

(d) Keep a sharp eye out for homosexuals among your children's friends and be suspicious of any relationship with your boy and a man several years older.

(e) Make sure that your children do not take off with strangers, indulge in excessive drinking or any other form of addiction.

(f) Bring up the subject of homosexuals and carefully listen to the attitude of your children on the subject. If sympathetic they will reveal it. Then check more closely.

(g) Investigate your boy's school, camp, social clubs or organizations where he might have time and occasion to practise such things. Bring to the attention of the heads of the organization any information you are sure of on this point. They will act.

HYPOCRISY DANGEROUS

Discussion of homosexuality is not obscene.

Perhaps in the front parlour with a group of young girls and boys it might be indelicate, but it is information they all should have and it is the responsibility of parents to be aware of this.

The challenge is up to the mothers and fathers of Canada. Can they face it?

Truth is the best protection. Hypocricy is the worst danger.

"A page sixteen special" Hollywood's Susan Hayward.

---

1 "A *Midnight* Survey on... Homosexuality in Canada!" in *Midnight*, May 9, 1958.

64

Working Papers on the Tavern:

Notes on the Gay Bar (excerpt)*

A unique aspect of social interaction in the Gay bar, which strikes the uninitiated almost at once, is the distinctive language of its patrons: "she" is consistently used for "he" and "her" for "him." There are also many special terms and usages. Some of those heard, and for which a definition was obtained after the visit, are as follows:

Bitch—n. a particularly effeminate person;

Bitching—v.i. a game of insult;

Butch—n. a person with hypermasculine mannerisms (syn. stomper);

Camping—v.i. act of seeking to gain attention;

Cruising—v.i. act of looking for a homosexual partner;

Drag-queen—n. a queen (see below) dressed in female clothing;

Gutter-gay—n. unattractive, old or indigent homosexual (syn. for old homosexuals—auntie);

Queen—n. a homosexual with haughty or regal mannerisms, usually a focal point of a Gay group;

Trade—n. male prostitution;

Turn-a-trick—v.i. to have intercourse with a male prostitute

Notes on the Gay Bar, part of Robert E. Popham's 1976 publication *Working Papers on the Tavern*, is based on ethnographic fieldwork conducted at the Letros Tavern in Toronto in 1955–56.

JIM EGAN'S
LETTERS

Within this broader context of tabloid sensationalism, Jim Egan—arguably Canada's first public gay liberation activist—began a letter-writing campaign. In *Challenging the Conspiracy of Silence: My Life as a Canadian Gay Activist,* Egan wrote that, in the 1950s, "even though homosexuality was coming under the spotlight, it was almost always viewed as an abnormality or sickness. There were never any articles published from a gay point of view, which in my mind equalled a conspiracy of silence on the true nature of homosexuality" (43).

On May 16, 1950, one of Egan's letters to the editor was published in the *Globe and Mail.* The same month, another of his letters was published in *Flash.* Both were published under the pseudonym "Leo Engle"—the name of Egan's grandfather. Later, Egan published letters and articles under "J.L.E.," including a twelve-part series in *Justice Weekly* entitled "Homosexual Concepts" that ran from December 5, 1953, to February 27, 1954. A second series of his writings was published in *Justice Weekly* from March 6, 1954, to June 12, 1954.

Egan's published writings were met with derision in both tabloids and the mainstream press. In a 1963 issue of *TAB,* for example, Joe Tensee wrote that Egan's defense of homosexuality in the *Toronto Daily Star* "was enough to make the paper's founder, 'Holy Joe' Atkinson, spin crazily in his grave."

"Disease or otherwise," Tensee continues, "there can be no rationalization of homosexuality… [W]hether fag or lesbian, he has set himself up against the human race, against its propagation and preservation, fundamental laws of nature."

"Every time I saw one of these ridiculous articles, or a negative comment on homosexuality, I sat down at my old Underwood typewriter and did up a letter of complaint to the editor." **Jim Egan,** *Challenging the Conspiracy of Silence,* 1998 (44)

1

1   Jim Egan (*right*) with partner Jack Nesbit (*left*), 1954.

2   Announcement of Jim Egan's series on homosexuality in *Justice Weekly,* November 28, 1953.

Series Of Articles On Homosexuality And Homosexuals Begins Next Week

Purpose To Bring About A Better Understanding Between Hetero And Homo

In next week's issue of "Justice Weekly" there will appear the first of what is hoped will become a regular series of articles dealing with homosexuality. Their continuance will depend largely on reader-reaction and response. Need for some enlightenment on homosexuality and homosexuals is very evident, particularly in view of the widespread ignorance and intolerance reflected in newspaper reports of homosexual affairs. Until now, however biased thinking and violent prejudice have prevented any other publication from carrying a contribution that attempts to present the homosexual as well as the heterosexual viewpoint,

To do just this, and thus bring about a better understanding between the heterosexual world and that of the homosexual will be the prime purpose of this column, which will be titled "Homosexual Concepts," by J.L.E.

It will present the homosexual viewpoint on various aspects of law, public opinion, and current events dealing with homosexuality in Canada, the U.S. and England. Court cases, both past and present which involve homosexuals, will be discussed and the findings analysed.

While admittedly sympathetic to the homosexual and his fight for equal civil rights, the writer will attempt to present the facts with as little bias as possible, certainly with far less than is used by some tabloids in their vituperative reports of homosexual court cases. Rather than appeal to the reader's sympathy and emotion, the facts, pro and con, will be reviewed and from these the reader himself will be able to form his own opinion as to the merits of the case. No stereotyped condemnation based on editorial policy will be offered the readers of this column at any time. This deplorable situation, all too commonly observed to-day, will be dealt with more fully at a future date.

However, it should be clearly understood that notwithstanding the sympathetic approach to and the defence of homosexuality, nothing that appears in this series is intended to incite anyone to the commission of any illegal act. It will not, in any way, be suggested that a state of homosexuality is superior to, or more desirable than a state of heterosexuality, (except, of course, insofar as genuine homosexuals themselves are concerned). Neither will it demand moral license or a special dispensation from the law for sexual deviates. Its readers will be asked to do nothing more than THINK!

In the belief that all acts of intolerance, prejudice and injustice to which the average homosexual is subject are solely caused by ignorance and misunderstanding — as are all forms of discrimination against any minority group— it is hoped that this series will be able to supply such facts and information that will, perhaps, be of some help in correcting the present unfortunate situation.

This column, aware that the onus is upon the homosexual to prove to Society that he is capable of assuming the rights and privileges that he demands, and is prepared to accept his place as a responsible citizen, will in no way condone or defend the actions of those few inverts who become involved with minors, or who make such spectacles of themselves as to constitute an outrage of public decency. The attitude of society that created the environment of which these men are the victims, and the unjust and outmoded law under which they are prosecuted are both deplored, but the right and the duty of Society in punishing such behaviour are indisputable.

Comments, criticisms or suggestions will be welcomed from any reader, and questions that are sent in will be answered from time to time. All opinions and comments are solely those of the writer and do not necessarily reflect the agreement or editorial policy of this paper or its editor and publisher.

In next week's column the writer, "J.L.E." discusses the current investigations into homosexuality in England, and will attempt to evaluate the validity of the claim that sexual inversion is rapidly increasing there every year.

JE SUIS GUILDA!

Born Jean Guida de Mortellaro in Paris, France, in the mid-1920s, Guilda (who, inspired by the 1946 film *Gilda,* added an "L" to his last name and used it as his performance moniker) established himself as a female impersonator in Montreal, where he relocated in the 1950s and lived until his death in 2012. A cabaret performer with an unparalleled talent for embodying the gestures, vocal inflections, and mannerisms of female celebrities—including Marlene Dietrich, Edith Piaf, Rita Hayworth, and Marilyn Monroe—Guilda performed regularly in Montreal and attracted huge, mixed audiences of hetero- and homosexual men and women in the 1950s and beyond. Guilda, who would often sing live as part of his elaborate, over-the-top performances, also released multiple LPs. Gilles Latulippe recalls that Guilda

did a minimum of 100 shows a year. He never missed a season. He was a perfectionist. He left nothing to chance. He was not the first female impersonator in Quebec, but he was the most celebrated, the first to be accepted without moral judgement by audiences who recognized his talent. A large part of his following were women, who admired his makeup artistry. Often, in a room filled with women, he was the most beautiful. (Quoted in Hustak, 2012)

1

1   Program for Guilda's cabaret at Casa Loma, Montreal, c. 1960s.

2   Inside the program for Guilda's cabaret at Casa Loma, Montreal, c. 1960s.

2

FACE &
PHYSIQUE

In the mid-twentieth century, physique magazines delivered homosexual men sexualized images of young, athletic men directly to their mailbox. Like most physique magazines of the time, Quebec-based *Face & Physique* was ostensibly created for two groups: people interested in physical fitness and artists who wanted male models for their work. In practice, the magazines were enthusiastically taken up by homosexual men as erotic texts. Artists and photographers would often publish under only their first name and their geographical location (often the city or country in which they worked). Some became famous—Tom of Finland is one; lesser-known ones include Keith of Quebec and Stephen of Canada. Alan B. Stone was perhaps the most prolific physique photographer in Canada; the Archives gaies du Québec in Montreal holds his collection of over thirty thousand negatives as well as thousands of slides and printed photographs.

A Canadian bodybuilder worth knowing is Arthur Nelson whose magnificent physique was built with intelligent weight training, hard physical work and the hard natural environment of the Canadian North which has produced so many husky physiques.

1

1 "Husky" Canadian featured in *Face & Physique*, Vol. 4, December 1962. Because physique magazines would share their photography among an international network, models would often be described in relation to their nationality. *Face & Physique*, for example, would regularly credit hard living in the Canadian North for models' impressive "husky physiques."

2 Cover of *Face & Physique*, Vol. 3, October 1962.

3 Cover of *Face & Physique*, Vol. 4, December 1962.

4 Cover of *Face & Physique*, Vol. 5, March 1963.

5 Feature spread in special issue of *Face & Physique*, 1963.

LESBIANS IN
THE STUDIO

Gays and lesbians played a pivotal role in mid-twentieth-century Canadian arts and culture. After years of service in the Air Force, Shirley Shea became one of Canada's best-known female broadcasters, living and working in Sudbury, Calgary, Victoria, Guelph, and Toronto. In addition to her popular radio shows on shopping, Shea wrote lesbian mystery novels under the pseudonym Marion Foster. She also used this pseudonym for her book, co-written with Kent Murray (also a pseudonym), *A Not So Gay World: Homosexuality in Canada*—the first published, monograph-length study of homosexuality in Canada. Shea, a well-known part of Toronto's gay community and the lesbian bar scene, met her partner, Betty Burrows, in 1966.

"It seemed normal to me to like women and to like them better than men because I never thought men amounted to much." **Shirley Shea, oral history interview with Amy Gottlieb of Lesbians Making History, 1987**

Alma Duncan and Audrey "Babs" McLaren—partners in every sense of the word—formed the film company Dunclaren Productions in 1951, specializing in stop-motion animated short films. Some garnered international attention, including *Kumak, the Sleepy Hunter* (1953), *Hearts and Soles* (1956), and *Friendly Interchange* (1959). A 1951 Canadian Press article published in the *Globe and Mail* describes the filmmakers as "brimming over with ideas." "The two women," the article continues, "both in their early 30s, have a busy time ahead. Starting from scratch, they will rent and equip their own studios, make their own sets—and their own film stars... wooden puppets... carved and dressed with meticulous care." While Dunclaren Productions ceased productions in the early 1960s, Duncan and McLaren continued to live together for decades and encouraged each other's individual creative projects.

1

1 *The World and Its Women with Shirley Shea* logo, c. 1950s.

2   CJVI 900 billboard promoting Shirley Shea's radio show, Victoria, 1953. In an oral history that Lesbians Making History conducted with Shirley Shea and Betty Burrows in 1987, Shea recalls her excitement when recognizing groups of lesbians in Victoria. "The first time I went into a tea room on the main street in Victoria and saw all the women coming in for lunch," she tells Amy Gottlieb, "I couldn't believe it, and I was with the girl I had been with from Sudbury. We just looked at each other open-mouthed because they were gorgeous women, and you could tell they were gay." Photograph by Jim Ryan.

3   Alma Duncan (*left*) with Audrey "Babs" McLaren (*right*), c. 1950s.

4   Shirley Shea, 1947.

RIKI TIK AT VICTORY BURLESQUE

Ricky Sheldon—better known as Riki Tik or Riki Tick—worked as a burlesque dancer in Toronto and regularly passed as a woman for heterosexual male clientele. She was also a central figure in cross-dressing performances in the 1960s, starring in the popular Toronto shows *Facad* and *She-Rade*. A 1969 press release for *She-Rade* indicates that Riki Tik performed a number called "Goldfinger" covered head to toe in gold paint, until she was advised by a doctor that the paint was poisonous and making her ill.

In a 1969 *Sunday Sun* article, Ivan Prokopchuk wrote about Riki Tik's performance at the Victory Burlesque, noting that "Ricky… twice appeared at the Victory Theatre as a stripper, unknown to anybody that he was a man. He said he had done this because the girls at the Victory were paid well and he saw no reason why he shouldn't make good money by posing as a girl!" When Riki Tik is onstage, Prokopchuk wrote, he "highlights his features to the point where no one could tell he's a man."

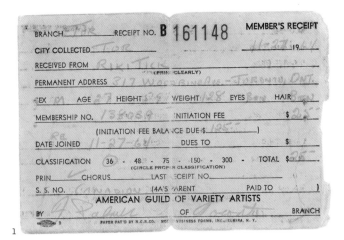

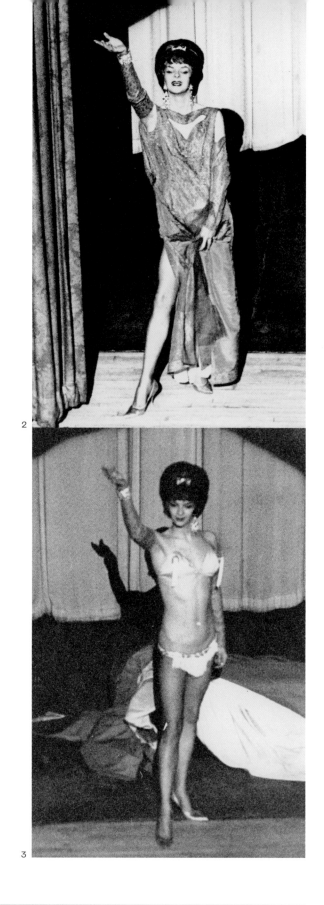

1 Riki Tik's receipt for membership to the American Guild of Variety Artists, 1964. Riki Tik sometimes went by "Riki Tick," as this receipt shows.

2 Ricky Sheldon/Riki Tik performs at the Victory Burlesque, Toronto, 1962.

3 Ricky Sheldon/Riki Tik performs at the Victory Burlesque, Toronto, 1962.

JACKIE SHANE

Nashville-born R&B singer Jackie Shane made
Toronto home in the 1960s, regularly performing
at the Sapphire Tavern and captivating crowds
with tales of her experiences as her band vamped
behind her. Shane first arrived in Canada in the
late 1950s as a carnival performer in Montreal and
Cornwall, Ontario. In *Any Other Way: How Toronto
Got Queer*—the title of which comes from one of
Shane's most popular recordings—Steven Maynard
writes that Shane's gender was the subject of
public speculation, discussed both in mainstream
publications like the *Toronto Star* and in popular
tabloids. In 1962, Shane recorded a hit version of
"Any Other Way" that became popular not only in
Toronto but across Canada and the United States.
The song featured the hook "tell her that I'm happy,
tell her that I'm gay / tell her I wouldn't have it any
other way."

   At the time, Jackie would have probably
been considered by many to be gay or perhaps
"transsexual," since *transgender* hadn't yet entered
the lexicon. Later in life, she identified as a woman,
and emphatically eschewed labels. In interviews
conducted in the last two years of her life, Jackie
regularly commented: "I'm just Jackie."

1

2

1   Jackie Shane, 1967. Courtesy of
Numero Group.

2   Cover of *Jackie Shane Live*,
1967.

THE MUSIC ROOM

Located at 575 Yonge Street, just north of Wellesley, the Music Room was a private gay club managed by Sara Ellen Dunlop, who co-owned the club with Richard Kerr. With music, drag shows, and dancing, the venue drew crowds of drag queens, gay men, butch and femme lesbians, as well as the ire of Toronto police. The Music Room was open only from 1962 to 1966, but, as John Forbes writes in "Sara Ellen Dunlop and the Music Room: A Memory," the club's influence on the creation of a spaces in Toronto—as well as the role Dunlop played in keeping gays and lesbians safe—should not be overlooked. In their November 15, 1963, *Ryersonian* article "A Visit to the Gay World," Mike Graham and Paul Sufrin chronicled the night they "crashed the society of the homosexual in Toronto" and met Dunlop at the Music Room. They wrote about the night in vivid detail:

> Dressed in what we hoped was appropriate clothing that this group affects, we climbed the long staircase and were confronted at the top landing by a solidly-built, soft-spoken woman. "Do you know where you are?" she asked. She looked at us suspiciously as we assured her we certainly did know where we were and that we hoped to join the club… "Just call me Sara," smiled the hostess sweetly.

1

very much out... and about.

MUSIC ROOM
PRIVATE MEMBERS CLUB

by PETER ALANN

The steep, barren staircase is an unlikely entrance to a place so warm and vital. Once the red and gold door is passed, the world of Yonge Street swiftly fades from memory. Rich wine drapes with the flocked wallpaper, plush red wall-seats and the textured white ceiling all combine to relax the visitor into an easy mood of gaiety.

The M-R, as it was fondly known until the Melody Room introduced an element of c o n f u s i o n into the initials, seems to have the easiest "take-off" of any gay club in town. Three or four couples can "launch it into orbit" for a lively evening. So intimate and unintimidating is its rich decor, that even a lone couple on the dance floor need feel no embarrassment. Yet the floor is large enough for two lively lines of the "chicken-scratch".

S o c i a b l e mixing is easy at the Music Room; it is small and bright enough for a friendly smile to be visible across the room. The wall-seats make it possible to sit strategically near someone, while working up the courage to propose a dance, without actually walking up to the table. Those who choose to devote themselves to each other without unwelcome interruption, may do so in the alcove corner just off the stage.

1 Advertisement for Music Room and Melody Room in *TWO*, Vol. 2, 1964.

2 "Very Much Out ... and About" by Peter Alann (pseudonym of John Alan Lee), in *TWO*, 1964.

3 Performers at the Music Room, Toronto, c. 1960s.

4 Performer at the Music Room, Toronto, c. 1960s.

Matchbooks

Matchbooks were among the most popular forms of advertising mid-twentieth century. They were, at the time, affordable to purchase in large quantities and adorned with a logo and/or information. The production of these small, practical objects peaked in the 1940s and 1950s and steadily declined once disposable lighters (and, in part, anti-smoking campaigns) became commonplace. The ArQuives collection of matchbooks—which continues to grow—chronicles bars, institutions, and organizations that might not otherwise be remembered.

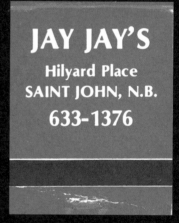

HULL, Québec

LE DOMINO
A man's cruising bar

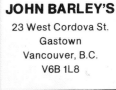

LEATHER
& UNIFORM BAR

JOHN BARLEY'S
23 West Cordova St.
Gastown
Vancouver, B.C.
V6B 1L8

CLOSE COVER, FERMEZ S.V.P.
EDDY MATCH CO. LTD. PEMBROKE, ONT.

**GAY COMMUNITY
CENTRE OF
SASKATOON**

P.O. Box 1662
SASKATOON

**INFORMATION AND
CRISIS LINE**

652-0972

CELEBRATING TEN YEARS OF SERVICE

1974
HALO
1984

TO THE LESBIAN AND GAY COMMUNITY

Close Cover Before Striking

HALO

**649 COLBORNE ST.
LONDON, ONTAIRO
N6A 3Z2**

LES CAVALIERS   977-4702
CLUB IVORY   977-4702

**THE BARN
TORONTO**

Close Cover Before Striking

Les Cavaliers

TORONTO, CANADA

Le Jardin

**1258 STANLEY
MONTRÉAL - QUÉ.**

**DISCO
&
CRUISING BAR**

POUR HOMMES SEULEMENT
❊
FOR MEN ONLY

Fully Licensed Disco~Draught Beer

Gandydancer

684-7321

*Gandy
~dancer* FOR MEN

1222 HAMILTON ST.,
VANCOUVER, B.C.

AIRCONDITIONED

OPEN 24 HOURS

the
CLUB

Close Cover Before Striking

the
CLUB

231 MUTUAL STREET
AT
CARLTON STREET

TORONTO

Hollywood

**1252 STANLEY
MONTRÉAL - QUÉ.**

**DISCO
&
PIANO BAR**

FEMMES SEULEMENT
*
WOMEN ONLY

AIDS

Close Cover Before Striking

COMMITTEE OF LONDON
256 Oxford St. E., Suite 4,
London, Ontario
N6A 1T7

DRAG BALLS AND BASHING AT THE ST. CHARLES TAVERN

The Halloween Drag Ball at St. Charles Tavern in Toronto was an annual event in the 1970s, an offshoot and continuation of the Letros Tavern Halloween balls of the 1950s and 1960s. Every year, the event drew crowds of competing drag queens, but, as Christine Sismondo writes in "Halloween Balls: From Letros to the St. Charles," the St. Charles ball became the site for extraordinary manifestations of hatred. Mobs of angry onlookers threw eggs while chanting "Kill the Queers" as drag contestants entered and attempted to leave the tavern. In 1979, nearly two thousand people gathered at the St. Charles Tavern, pelting participants with eggs. Volunteer gay street patrol programs, including Operation Jack O'Lantern, which launched in 1977, saw groups escorting gays and lesbians through the area on Halloween night. The mob violence at the St. Charles Tavern persisted until 1980, when police intervened after a decade of mobilization by lesbians and gays in Toronto.

"The crowd was like thousands out on the street and a lot of them were out there to see the queers and yell and scream at them and all that. I got ink thrown at me and so…all I did was go home, change my dress and my wig and came back out again. I mean, you couldn't stop me from doing what I wanted to do—ever." **Michelle DuBarry, recalling 1970s drag balls at the St. Charles Tavern on CBC's** *Uncover: The Village*, **2019**

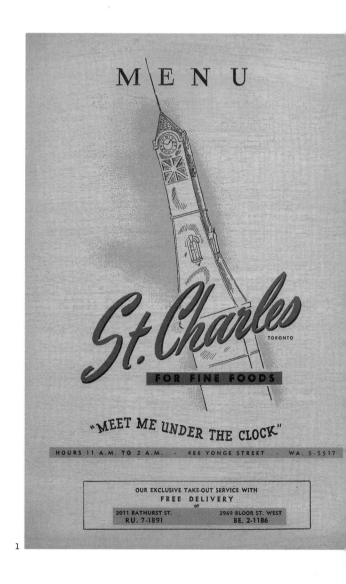

1

1   St. Charles Tavern menu, c. 1960s.

2   Unidentified drag queen in front of St. Charles Tavern, Toronto, October 31, 1979. Photograph by Gerald Hannon.

3   Police escort unidentified drag queen into St. Charles Tavern, Toronto, October 31, 1979. Photograph by Gerald Hannon.

4   Crowd of onlookers/assailants in front of St. Charles Tavern, Toronto, October 31, 1979. Photograph by Gerald Hannon.

HUNTING
HOMOSEXUALS

In the 1950s and 1960s, the federal government attempted to rid the civil service and military of the "threat" of homosexuals, similar to the U.S. purge under Joseph McCarthy. Hundreds of civil servants lost their jobs, pensions, and communities. The hunt for homosexuals in the civil service and military was part of a broader campaign that included attacks on other left-leaning communities and political movements—including immigrants, women's liberation organizers, and anti-racist and civil rights movements—as well as unions and organized forms of workers' collective power. Harold Averill recalls the impact:

> Thousands of dedicated men and women in the federal civil service and the military had their careers destroyed and their lives dramatically altered in the 1950s and the 1960s in the name of "national security," solely because of their sexual orientation. In many cases, those affected suffered in silence, piecing together their lives as best they could. Others resisted in a variety of ways. But everyone would bear the scars. (*Lesbian and Gay Archivist*, no. 15, 1999)

William Atkinson, who served as a lieutenant-commander in the Royal Canadian Navy during the Second World War, was forced to resign his post in 1959 because of his homosexuality. Interrogated for hours by individuals only identified as members of Security Agency B (RCMP), Atkinson was encouraged to divulge the names of all suspected homosexuals he had knowledge of. In a detailed account he submitted to the ArQuives, Atkinson recalled agents telling him, "If you resign, nobody will hear anything of the events of the last few months."

During the purge, the federal government invested in a series of tests and devices meant to detect homosexuality. In his 1962 *Report on Special Project*, Dr. Frank Robert Wake of Carleton University identified a number of disparate tests—the polygraph, the Hess-Polt pupillary response method, palmar sweat tests, projective word association tests, and a series of examinations he named "masculinity-femininity tests"—that could be utilized to test for homosexual desires. In *The Regulation of Desire: Homo and Hetero Sexualities,* Gary Kinsman writes that this series of tests was given the name " 'fruit machine'... by members of the RCMP who did not want to be recruited to be the 'normals' who were to be tested on it" (178). Ultimately, Kinsman argues, "the 'fruit machine' never worked and it was abandoned in 1967" (181). As we show in subsequent chapters, the broader purge of homosexuals persisted into the 1980s.

1

1 Portrait of William Atkinson, c. 1940s.

Report on Special Project
by Dr. F.R. Wake (excerpt)*

<u>SECRET</u>: THIS DOCUMENT IS THE PROPERTY
OF THE GOVERNMENT OF CANADA

Apparatus:

73. The Hess-Polt pupillary test with suitable visual stimuli; a measure of skin perspiration (McCleary Palmar Sweat test or an apparatus recently developed by the National Research Council); the plethysmograph with a modification to measure pulse rate.

Subjects:

74. Fifteen normal males; fifteen normal females; fifteen homosexual males; fifteen homosexual females. As the experiment progresses, additional normal and homosexual subjects in unspecified numbers. All subjects to be supplied by the R.C.M.P.

Procedure:

75. The subject is seated in front of the pupillary apparatus, and the modified plethysmograph and sweat apparatuses are attached to the subject's hand. He is told that he will see pictures in the pupillary apparatus, that he should concentrate on them for, after the test, he will be examined on general information and memory. Pictures then will be run in sets—experimental stimuli—neutral pictures—experimental stimuli, and so on. The experimental stimuli will be pictures designed to elicit the subject's interest in males and females.

76. When the pictures have been shown, the subject will be asked to name the magazines from which the pictures were selected (general type of reading) and to recall the pictures he remembers best (memory test). His statements may reveal direction of sex interest, although presumably he does not know this.

77. His responses to the various physiological measures thus will be recorded photographically and electronically, and may give valuable data.

78. The first sixty subjects will be processed to determine the reaction patterns of normals and homosexuals. Then, using these patterns as criteria, the experimenter will attempt to distinguish homosexuals presented by the R.C.M.P., where nothing of the subject is known to the research team. Those methods proving successful will be retained for continuing research.

*Wake submitted his report to the Security Panel on homosexuality in December 1962. In the early 1990s, as a result of successful Access to Information Requests from LGBTQ2+ activists and historians, the Canadian Security Intelligence Service declassified and released the document.

THE ASSOCIATION
FOR SOCIAL KNOWLEDGE

The Association for Social Knowledge (ASK) was formed in April 1964 as Canada's first homophile association. Early literature distributed by the group indicates that the primary goal of ASK was to "help society to understand and accept variations from the sexual norm." The association began publishing the *ASK Newsletter* in 1964, hosted dances, and ran a gay community centre (the first in Canada) and a resource library on Kingsway in East Vancouver. In April 1964, ASK hosted its first public lecture—entitled The Church and Homosexuality—during which Reverend J.M. Taylor of the East Burnaby United Church called for volunteer treatment centres where medical professionals could help homosexuals return to heterosexuality.

"All that is desired by the sexual variant is an equal right to understanding and acceptance as a fellow human being, to work and play, to suffer and rejoice as an integral part of society." *ASK Newsletter,* **vol. 1, no. 1, 1964**

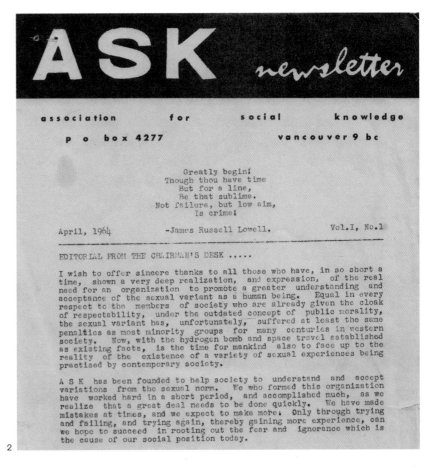

1 ASK logo, c. 1960s.

2 *ASK Newsletter*, Vol. 1, No. 1, 1964.

GAY

GAY began publishing in Toronto in March 1964. The tabloid featured an odd mix of content; the first issue, for example, comprised a letter from the editor, clip art, stories on a range of topics (high-heel stimulation and the experiences of a call boy, among others), photographs, an excerpt of Pietro Aretino's 1536 work *Ragionamenti* translated by Bernhardt J. Hurwood, and a recipe for veal cutlets. One particularly notable feature of the paper includes GAY-brial's Column—personal advertisements (under the heading "New Men") from men in Canada and the United States. The first issue carried with it advertisements for men in Ontario, Manitoba, New York State, Missouri, and Pennsylvania. "The first issue of *GAY*," Donald McLeod writes in *A Brief History of* GAY: *Canada's First Gay Tabloid, 1964–1966,* "was printed in a modest edition of 500 copies, [and] sold out almost immediately" (18). The publication was renamed *Gay International* in January 1965 and ceased publishing a few months later.

1

2

1   *GAY*, Vol. 1, No. 1, 1964.   2   *GAY*, Vol. 1, No. 2, 1964.

TWO: THE HOMOSEXUAL VIEWPOINT IN CANADA

TWO: The Homosexual Viewpoint in Canada began in July 1964 as a magazine, publishing art, essays, reviews, news, and physique photographs. Published by Gayboy Publishing (later renamed Kamp Publishing), *TWO* was initiated by Richard Kerr, co-owner of the Music Room (page 76), and listed the Music Room as its editorial offices. According to the editorial in the first issue, *TWO* was meant to "promote knowledge and understanding of the homosexual viewpoint among the general public and to educate homosexuals as to their responsibilities as variants from the current moral and social standards." The publication's name was very likely inspired by *One*, an early American homophile magazine published in Los Angeles beginning in the 1950s that featured a supplement entitled *Truth Will Out* (*TWO*).

1 2 3

⚓ SAILORS...A Sex Symbol ?

It has often been contended that sailors are a sex symbol for male homosexuals. Wherever there is a large naval depot, there also seems to be a large homosexual population, whether by accident or design is open to conjecture.

The many cases involving sailors and homosexuality would also lead one to believe that sailors are, to say the least, 'open minded' about their camp followers. However it is in the field of physique publications that the formation of the sailor as a sex symbol has reached its ultimate.

The physique publications are now the male equivalent to the girly magazines and while they occassionally develop a "star" they more often feature unknowns. Where as the girls in the girly magazines, are invariably wearing flimsy negligees, you are sure to find at least one sailor suit(or part of it anyway)in any Physique magazine, you may pick up.

It would appear that the addition of a sailor hat and pants gives an other wise non descript model, some added attraction.

This would seem to be an endorsement of the theory that sailors are indeed a sex symbol for homosexuals. On the opposite page is a collection of clippings from various physique publications around the world, and on the following pages some "nautical terms" from CAN-ART STUDIOS.

If there is one thing that may rival the naval uniform as a sex symbol, it could be a cowboy outfit or perhaps a leather jacket.

The only common denominator · of all these is that thay are all overt indications of male virility, which may explain their acceptance as sex symbols by the homosexuals.

Whatever the reasoning, the sailor suit does seem to have some fascination for the homosexual. Then of course there is also the theory that sailors often find homosexuals just as fascinating!

One last comment. We do consider it strange that no matter what the country of origin of the prints or the publication, it is invariably an American sailor suit that turns up.

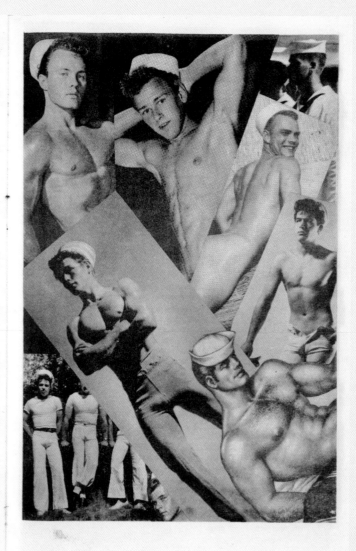

4

SELF-REPRESENTATIONS
IN THE 1960S

In the 1960s, various individuals published fictional work that dealt overtly with homosexual themes. These self-representations functioned as counter-narratives to the homophobic and sensationalist mainstream media representations of homosexuality. They also gave a literary voice to the politics occurring on the ground: lesbian fiction, for instance, spoke to a generation of women who were fighting for their bodily autonomy, for the right to work freely outside the home, and for sexual freedom and independence from the institution of marriage.

In these texts, we can trace a history of more contemporary forms of self-representations that characterize life in twenty-first-century Canada, as queer and trans people document their lives through photo series, plays, film, art exhibits, pride parades, and social media. The desire for us to represent ourselves remains a driving force of contemporary queer cultures.

1

1   Edward A. Lacey's *The Forms of Loss*, 1965.

2   Jane Rule's *The Desert of the Heart*, 1964.

3   Scott Symons's *Place d'Armes*, 1967.

4   John Herbert's *Fortune and Men's Eyes*, 1967.

5   Ian Young's *Year of the Quiet Sun*, 1969.

2

3

4

5

THE UNIVERSITY OF TORONTO HOMOPHILE ASSOCIATION

The University of Toronto Homophile Association (UTHA)—the city's first gay liberation organization and the first gay student organization in all of Canada—was sparked by a chance meeting in one of the university's most popular cruising spots. In a washroom at University College, Jearld Moldenhauer (who had recently moved to Toronto from the United States) met Charlie Hill (at the time, a graduate student in Art History). The two discussed an advertisement Moldenhauer had recently placed in *The Varsity,* the University of Toronto's student newspaper, in October 1969. Elspeth Brown suggests in "Canada's First Gay Student Activist Group,"

> If one ever wanted to make an argument as to the centrality of sex to queer organizing, the founding of the University of Toronto Homophile Association (UTHA) would be exhibit A—because it was through having sex in the basement washroom in U of T's University College that Moldenhauer met University of Toronto art history MA student Charlie Hill, who went on to become a key student organizer for UTHA.

The UTHA hosted dances and discussions, bringing the ideas of homophile politics to the community at the University of Toronto and the city more broadly. After the university's Student Advisory Council (SAC) ratified the UTHA, the *Globe and Mail* published a letter to the editor in which the author argued that it was a mistake for the SAC to have given the UTHA status as a student group. Moldenhauer responded with his own letter to the editor in which he identified himself as the founder of the UTHA and a homophile. Soon thereafter, he was dismissed from his position in the University of Toronto Department of Physiology. Nevertheless, the UTHA grew in popularity and conducted important work throughout the city.

The University of Toronto's LGBTOUT traces its genealogy to the UTHA and claims to be the longest-running LGBTQ student organization in Canada.

1

1 Poster for a gay dance organized by the University of Toronto Homophile Association (UTHA) and Toronto Gay Action (TGA), 1971.

ANYONE INTERESTED IN DISCUSSING THE

ORGANIZATION OF A

STUDENT HOMOPHILE LEAGUE

PLEASE CONTACT: J MOLDENHAUER

922-2050 between 5-7pm

2

University of Toronto
TORONTO 5, CANADA

DEPARTMENT OF PHYSIOLOGY   MEDICAL SCIENCES BUILDING

3rd February

Mr Moldenhauer.

You are dismissed from your position as laboratory technician
as from 3rd March 1970.

R.M. Preshaw

3

2 Advertisement for the
University of Toronto Homophile
Association (UTHA), 1969.

3 Jearld Moldenhauer's dismissal
letter, sent from R.M. Preshaw,
February 1970.

GLAD DAY
BOOKSHOP

Jearld Moldenhauer started Glad Day Bookshop in 1970 as a response to the censorship of gay material in Canada, both overt and implicit, and to the widespread disinterest (and disdain) that straight booksellers had for books about gays and lesbians. As he writes in "A Literary Breakthrough: Glad Day's Origins,"

> After Stonewall, publishers started to issue books about gay and lesbian life, written by a generation of newly "liberated" homosexuals. This literary breakthrough began to combat the traditional negative images of homosexuality… While Toronto served as the centre of Canada's publishing industry and had an abundance of bookshops, I could never find copies of these new releases, even though most were being reviewed by *The New York Times* and *The Village Voice*. (158)

Glad Day began in Moldenhauer's backpack, which he filled with books to sell at meetings, rallies, and parties. Soon thereafter, Glad Day operated out of his apartment in the Annex before moving to the top floor of a house in Kensington Market. While Glad Day was—and remains—a bastion for queer literature and people, it has also been affected by the forms of censorship that motivated Moldenhauer to create a queer bookstore in the first place: Canada Customs would frequently withhold materials deemed "obscene," and Glad Day employees became targets of the so-called Morality Department of the Metropolitan Toronto Police. In 1974, the *Toronto Star* refused to print an advertisement for the bookstore, claiming that it attempted to "proselytize for the homosexual movement," though, as Donald McLeod writes in *Lesbian and Gay Liberation in Canada: A Selected Annotated Chronology, 1964–1975,* the *Star* later suggested it would print the advertisement if the word "gay" was changed to the more palatable "homosexual"; Glad Day refused. In October 1974, the Ontario Press Council ruled that the *Star*'s refusal to print the advertisement was discriminatory.

Glad Day Bookshop
Statement on Censorship

We deplore censorship. State censorship is simply incompatible with Canadian democratic principles. Democratic decision making and social evolution need the kinds of literary and artistic (and even scientific) investigations, expressions and communications that censorship seeks to control. Censorship is a tactic for maintaining power and privilege by intimidating and prosecuting selected groups and individuals. It is fundamentally anti-democratic.

As gay people we know how important literature is in informing our own evolving identity and furthering our social empowerment. Because our "difference" as gay and lesbian people is largely defined by our sexuality, it is especially important for us to be able to communicate and share experiences about this subject.

As booksellers to the gay and lesbian communities it is our moral responsibility to provide public access to the literature of our community. This is especially true for those books and periodicals which address complicated, problematic or un-examined areas of sexuality—areas where discussion and enlightenment are most needed: women's sexuality, youth sexuality, S/M sexuality, man-boy love and paedophilia, and sexual experiences in other cultures. Censorship means darkness in these areas when illumination is called for.

Liberation from oppressive social arrangements where sexuality and politics overlap will come about through free and thoughtful discussions about our sexualities, and from the political transformations that result from these discussions. Social policy in areas related to human sexuality should arise from rigorous and conscientious study of the nature of human sexuality and its cultural manifestations, not from the kind of fear, ignorance and prejudice that censorship creates.

1

2

1   Glad Day Bookshop's commercial space at corner of Yonge and Collier streets in Toronto, Ontario, C. 1970S. Photograph by Norman Taylor.

2   Glad Day Bookshop staff at 598a Yonge Street location, 1985. From left to right: Paul Jenkins, Jearld Moldenhauer, Robert Banks

(*front, leaning forward*), Alan Li, James McPhee, and Russell Armstrong.

Pulp Fiction

Small enough to fit in a purse or a pocket and cheap enough to purchase and discard after reading, paperback novels that dealt with taboo subjects—adultery, prostitution, lesbianism, male homosexuality, interracial relationships—dominated the literary market in the mid-twentieth century. These formulaic texts regularly featured covers with suggestive, lurid artwork and descriptions of the racy story to be found between them. Publishers, most of which were based in the United States, also acknowledged the controversial nature of the "shocking," "exciting," or "explosive" subject matter.

Both lesbian and gay male pulp fiction were formative for readers and lay important groundwork for the gay and lesbian subcultures that were developing after the Second World War. For many readers, these cheap, suggestive pulp fiction novels were the only available representations of non-normative sexual and gender behaviours other than sensationalized tabloid journalism. The forms of representations available to gays and lesbians through pulp fiction novels were not necessarily positive: lesbian texts, for example, allowed moments of lesbian eroticism, sex, and desire, but they almost always end with tragedy, closing off any sort of possibility that may have existed in the narrative.

In their 1992 film *Forbidden Love: The Unashamed Stories of Lesbian Lives,* Lynne Fernie and Aerlyn Weissman explore the ways in which lesbian pulp fiction sparked desires for finding community and kinship in Canada in the mid-century. The wonderfully campy film features Ann Bannon, an American author considered the "Queen of Lesbian Pulp Fiction," as well as interviews with nine women from across Canada—Keely, Stephanie, Reva, Lois, Nairobi, Jeanne, Amanda, Carol, and Ruth—who discuss their individual identity formation and their experiences of finding lesbian community.

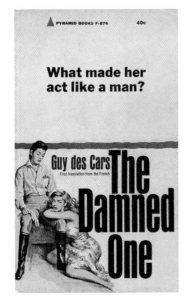

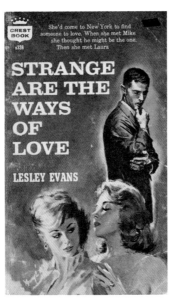

1971–1981

COLLECTIVE FORMATION

The decade following the Criminal Law Amendment Act of 1969 was turbulent in both national and provincial contexts. Decriminalization of certain (homo)sexual acts, in private, between consenting adults over twenty-one, was considered indicative of a larger "liberalizing" of Canadian society under Pierre Elliott Trudeau's government; indeed, the Act decriminalized the selling and possession of contraceptives and legalized abortion under particular conditions, including that the procedure was deemed necessary by a committee of doctors. Such changes were part of Trudeau's mission to build what he deemed a "just society" that preserved the rights of minorities and distributed the nation's wealth more equitably among its citizens.

The reality of Canadian life in the 1970s and 1980s was, not surprisingly, more fraught and complex than the ideological push toward a "just" society would suggest. During the 1970 October Crisis in Quebec, for example—when members of the Front de libération du Québec (FLQ) kidnapped British diplomat James Cross and kidnapped and killed Minister of Labour Pierre Laporte—Trudeau invoked the War Measures Act, allowing government officials to search people without warrants and detain people without charge

1

and leading to the arrest of more than four hundred people in Quebec. For many people, Trudeau's action called into question his commitment to individual rights and liberty. The tension between an increasingly multicultural and socially liberal Canada and the restrictive demands of the Canadian state was palpable.

The social liberalism of the Canadian nation was similarly called into question later in the decade when, in 1977, Barbara Thornborrow went public with her experience with the Canadian Forces' Special Investigations Unit (SIU) and became the first individual pushed out of the armed forces for her sexuality to publicly challenge the action. SIU officers who suspected Thornborrow of being a lesbian searched her room and, after finding love letters from her girlfriend,

Colleen, alongside pamphlets for gay and lesbian organizations, gave her two options: sign a document confirming her lesbianism and be discharged from the armed forces, or agree to psychiatric counselling. Her treatment, which was widely publicized by Gays of Ottawa and garnered a great deal of public attention and sympathy, served as a necessary precursor to legal protections for gay men and lesbians in the 1970s and beyond. In June 1977, Thornborrow was given official notice of her discharge from the Canadian Forces for being a "sexual deviate" who was thus "not advantageously employable."

Taking Action
We document in this section the flurry of collective queer formation that occurred in the decade after the passage of the

2

Criminal Law Amendment Act. New forms of political organizing occurred during the early years of the 1970s. The idea of collective formation in the name of gay and lesbian liberation organizing took hold, and a politicized and identifiable community manifested through action. Most of this work was done under the watchful eye of the nation state as the RCMP conducted extensive surveillance of these gay and lesbian liberation groups on the grounds of "national security." The Community Homophile Association of Toronto (CHAT, page 106), for instance, began in December 1970/January 1971 and, under the direction of George Hislop, became a central site of queer political and social organizing in Toronto, along with branches of the Gay Alliance Toward Equality (GATE) in Vancouver and Edmonton (both formed in 1971), Gays of Ottawa (GO) in Ottawa (1971), Le front de libération des homosexuels (FLH) in Montreal (1971), Gays for Equality (GFE) in Winnipeg (1972; earlier known as the Campus Gay Club),

1 Gay Alliance Toward Equality (GATE) demonstration, Vancouver, 1977.

2 Demonstration against police repression organized by Comité homosexuel anti-répression (CHAR), Montreal, 1976. Photograph by Michel Cambert.

and the Zodiac Friendship Society (1972; grew out of the Gay Students Alliance and later known as the Gay Community Centre of Saskatoon). In 1971, Toronto Gay Action (TGA) spearheaded the pivotal We Demand rally on Parliament Hill in Ottawa. Decrying the myth of "the homosexual problem," the protestors vocalized a list of demands for freedom from discrimination in housing, employment, health care, and legal status and directly critiqued the changes to the Canadian Criminal Code made two years prior. The protestors made clear: the superficial changes made to the Criminal Code were neither sufficient nor just. Ed Jackson tells us that these demands, written by Herb Spiers with assistance from David Newcome, quickly became a strategic blueprint for the Canadian movement more broadly.

These demands preceded changes to Canadian legislation, including, six years later, changes to refugee and immigration legislation that removed the ban on homosexual men as immigrants to Canada. Before 1977, "homosexuals" were listed as categories of persons to be prohibited from immigrating to Canada, along with "prostitutes," "pimps," and "persons coming to Canada for these or any other immoral purposes." While the reference to homosexuality was removed in 1977, the law continued to discriminate against gay and lesbian immigrants by prohibiting them

1

from sponsoring their spouses as family-class immigrants until an amendment passed in the early twenty-first century.

Social Politics

While much of the decade's organizing took the form of groups advocating for specific legal changes that would enable the flourishing of queer life, resistance to the violence of homophobia took a variety of creative, intellectual, and social forms as well. The Gay Community Appeal, for example, a Toronto-based organization, was founded in 1979 to raise funds for queer community organizations and projects. Later called the Lesbian and Gay Community Appeal and, in recent years, Community One Foundation, the Appeal brought together seemingly disparate aspects of the movement to sustain and inform one another,

showing how social, political, and fundraising projects are all integral to a sense of collectivity and collaboration. Collective dance experiences were vital to queer movements in the 1970s (and subsequent decades), as such events engender a sense of belonging and agency, often while also raising funds for specific legal challenges facing gays and lesbians. Posters and ephemera at the ArQuives document various dances held in the 1970s, such as those in support of John Damien, who was fired from the Ontario Racing Commission in February 1975 because he was gay, and Douglas Wilson, a graduate student at the University of Saskatchewan who, in September 1975, was suspended from supervising student teachers because of his involvement in the gay liberation movement. Wilson had placed an advertisement in the university's student newspaper that read, "Anyone interested

2

in participating in a campus gay organization, contact Doug Wilson." Dance events were also held in solidarity with the Brunswick Four (page 131), a group of lesbians who were beaten by police after their performance of "I Enjoy Being a Dyke" (a variation on the show tune "I Enjoy Being a Girl") at the Brunswick Tavern in Toronto in January 1974.

Dances and similar social events were crucial to building relationships between gays and lesbians active in political

1   *The Body Politic* collective, from left to right, back row: Roger Spalding, Gerald Hannon, Stephen MacDonald (*bent over, face not clear*), Ken Popert, Ed Jackson, Kevin Orr (not member of *TBP* collective, manager of Glad Day Bookshop), Tim McCaskell; in front: John Allec, Chris Bearchell, 1982. Photograph by Bill Loos.

2   Members of the Cabbagetown Softball League, Toronto, 1977. Photograph by Gerald Hannon.

struggles. The Gay Alliance for Equality (GAE) in Halifax, for example, organized popular dance parties for gays and lesbians at the Turret, a downtown building at 1588 Barrington Street; the dances fostered a sense of collective agency and community across differences between gays and lesbians while simultaneously raising funds for the activist efforts of the gay liberation movement (see also "GAE's Turret," page 138). We focus on the GAE's dance space, paying particular attention to how the events at the venue transformed gay and lesbian political formation in Halifax, but opportunities for social dance were fundamental to gay and lesbian formation in the 1970s across Canada. As Valerie Korinek argues in *Prairie Fairies: A History of Queer Communities and People in Western Canada, 1930–1985,* "[g]ay and lesbian socializing at community dances was a formative development in

the early 1970s" (171). In an attempt to emphasize the role of music and collective dance in gay and lesbian formation in the 1970s, we think through historical documentation of dance playlists at Gemini Club dances in Saskatoon (see "Zodiac Friendship Society," page 116). Across Canada, such community-building efforts worked to sustain the gay and lesbian movement and the forms of kinship developing therein, not only throughout the 1970s but also in subsequent decades. The 2019 documentary film *Our Dance of Revolution,* for example, beautifully chronicles the important role of collective dance and performance in the broader political history Toronto's Black queer community.

Similar bonds developed between attendees at the National Gay Conferences held in Quebec City, Winnipeg, Ottawa, Saskatoon, Toronto, and Halifax.

1

These conferences were attended by lesbians and gay men and occurred alongside smaller, regional conferences. Starting in Toronto in 1973, lesbian activists in Canada began hosting lesbian conferences, which allowed for different conversations than those held at the mixed gay and lesbian conferences. As Liz Millward notes, lesbian conferences of the 1970s "were often intensely sexual and erotic spaces, where women encountered other lesbians as part of a culture of woman-centred possibility. These experiences were distinct from those at the mixed national lesbian and gay conferences, which could be hostile, hierarchical spaces filled with conflict over decision-making power and the purpose of lesbian and gay community" (171).

The Body Politic (*TBP*), which began publishing in 1971, played a pivotal role in the formation of gay and lesbian community throughout Canada. (Its collection also formed the basis of the ArQuives.) The images we reproduce here from *TBP* demonstrate how crucial this publication was to the development of queer political life. As the long list of periodicals that emerged in 1970s shows, *TBP* did not do this work alone—the diversity of writing across Canada became a crucial part of ongoing political conversations within the burgeoning queer community.

Collectivity and Coalition

The marked shifts in queer politics resulted not only from organizing explicitly focused on gay and lesbian issues, but also, and crucially, from the increasing diversification of urban areas by immigration, which enabled new and generative forms of queer collectivity. According to the Canadian census, the demographics of the nation changed drastically beginning in the 1970s. Before 1971, the majority of immigration to Canada was from European countries, with some immigration from countries in Asia (primarily China and Japan) and comparatively little from other parts of the world. After Canada's immigration regulations underwent major amendments in the 1960s, the number of immigrants from non-European countries started to grow dramatically. Immigrants of colour (referred to in the census as "visible minorities") made up only 12.4 percent of immigrants who arrived before 1971, whereas during the 1970s this proportion more than quadrupled to over half of all newcomers (53 percent), further increasing to 67.4 percent of

newcomers in the 1980s. Many of the immigrants of the 1970s were from the Caribbean and Central and South America. Importantly, the late 1970s saw the arrival of sixty thousand refugees from Vietnam, Cambodia, and Laos. As immigration to Canada continued to increase over these decades, the cultural makeup of populations in urban centres, including Vancouver, Toronto, and Montreal, was transformed. For example, while almost 96 percent of the

1 Map of Gay Toronto from the Gaydays Souvenir Programme, 1978.

2 Ange Spalding, c. 1970s. Photograph by Lamar Van Dyke.

3 Sherona Hall of the Committee against the Deportation of Immigrant Women speaking at the International Women's Day rally in Convocation Hall, University of Toronto, 1978. Photograph by Gerald Hannon.

population of greater Toronto was of European ancestry in 1971, this proportion declined to 60.2 percent in 2001.

In this section, we aim to draw connections between the gay liberation movement of the 1970s and the anti-racist and feminist work that also shaped this decade in order to demonstrate the connections, conversations, and coalitions that exist between different forms of political movement building. In 1969, the Trudeau government proposed eliminating Indian status for Indigenous people in Canada, spurring the growth of Red Power in the form of Indigenous organizing, demonstrations, and anti-government protests across the country, which effectively pressured the government to rescind its proposal. Lesbian and feminist organizing brought the broader demands of

women into conversation with the often male-dominated gay movement: Wages Due Lesbians and Lesbian Mothers' Defense Fund emerged in the 1970s from the feminist struggles for wages for housework, access to child care and abortion, and legal rights for mothers. In 1970, the feminist protest movement Abortion Caravan travelled from Vancouver to Ottawa to gather support against continued legal restrictions to abortion. And the dreams of lesbian separatism remained strong and increasingly relevant to many women's lives—Ange Spalding's diary chronicles the journey of the Van Dykes in their travels from Toronto across the U.S. and Mexico in search of a lesbian utopia away from men and the restrictions of heteronormativity, monogamy, and marriage (see also "The Van Dykes," page 140).

1

2

Lesbian and gay organizing against police violence brought the struggles of queer people into conversation with people of colour and racial minorities in Toronto at a time when both Red Power and Black political consciousness were growing. Albert Johnson, a thirty-five-year-old Black man of Jamaican descent, was killed in his own home by two white Toronto police officers in 1979. The coroner's report—verified by an account from Johnson's nine-year-old daughter—indicates that Johnson was forced to kneel and was shot "execution style" by the officers. Both officers were charged with manslaughter but were eventually acquitted. As Tanisha Taitt writes in the National Arts Centre study guide for Dionne Brand's play *thirsty,* Johnson's murder was, a "watershed moment for the black community in Toronto" that sparked coalitional political formation against police violence in the 1970s and 1980s. Lemona Johnson—Albert Johnson's widow—spoke at a February 20, 1981, rally organized by the Right to Privacy Committee (RTPC) and claimed that "the raids and arrest of the Toronto gay community is a further indication that the police force of this city is lacking in discipline and proper supervision. The police force in this city is being used as a political tool by politicians ... who achieve their personal and political gain at the [price] of the people of Ontario."

In reaching back to the coalition politics of the 1970s and early 1980s, this section documents the

3

violent backlash faced by gays and lesbians as they became more outspoken about their lives and rights. John Alan Lee received death threats and hate mail as a high-profile, openly gay professor

and writer; Montreal "cleaned up" areas in the city frequented by gays and lesbians in preparation for the 1976 Olympics; and bathhouse raids occurred throughout the nation: Club Baths in Ottawa was raided on May 22, 1976, Montreal's Sauna Aquarius was raided on February 4, 1975, and on February 5, 1981, police raided four bathhouses in Toronto as part of Operation Soap.

These are only a few of the many police raids of spaces in which gays and lesbians could amass during this period. Historian Tom Hooper's chart of bathhouse raids in Canada between 1968 and 2004 shows the sheer number of raids and arrests following the 1969 amendments to the Criminal Code, reminding us that the often-celebrated changes did little to dissuade local police departments from harassing gays

and lesbians (Hooper, 2018). As such, we end this section with what seems like the crucial message of queer organizing of the 1970s: while the legal limits on queer life changed under the Criminal Law Amendment Act, freedom from persecution, violence, poverty, and homophobia remained the impetus for a decade of significant and diverse movement building for queers in Canada.

1   Cora Women's Liberation Bookmobile, 1974. Photograph by Lynnie
Johnston. Volunteers would drive the
bookmobile, named after E. Cora Hind,
a pioneering suffragist and writer, to rural
towns in Ontario to spread information
about the Women's Liberation Movement
and to learn about and participate in
local organizing.

2   Women on the back porch of The
Farm, Cavan, Ontario, 1977. Front: Lamar
Van Dyke; second row, from left: Pam
Godfrey, Artemis Pallas, Guy (holding
dog), Alison Fraser, Vicki Treirse; third row,
from left: Jeannie, Nia (mostly hidden);
back row, from left: Jen, Ange Spalding,
BJ Danylchuk, Judith Zutz, Chris Fox, Elby.
Photograph by Shey Smith. Courtesy of Chris Fox.

3   Police raid Back Door Gym and
Sauna on Elm Street, Toronto, 1983.
Photograph by Gerald Hannon.

COMMUNITY HOMOPHILE
ASSOCIATION OF TORONTO

The Community Homophile Association of Toronto (CHAT) grew out of the University of Toronto Homophile Association (UTHA, page 90) in late 1970/early 1971 and opened a community centre at 58 Cecil Street (near College and Spadina) in Toronto in 1972. The space housed all of the group's operations, including its counselling phone line and its popular drop-in sessions. Early CHAT dances provided gays and lesbians (and their friends) with a space to come together on the dance floor and get a sense of their collective power. Peter Zorzi explained, before CHAT opened the community centre, that

> Areas where we are permanently and openly accepted are limited and money has taken advantage of this. With their bars and clubs and baths... entrepreneurs have fed on our need for some ground where we can associate, where society's restrictions are relaxed. They are the only places that tolerate us for any length of time and they know it. They tolerate us as long as we keep paying. It is this totally commercial exploitation of our isolation which makes gay life the way it is. Many people cannot or won't take it and instead have been driven away into further isolation... gay organizations have been formed by people coming together to open their lives to some alternative. The CHAT Community Centre is at 58 Cecil Street and opens at the beginning of February. There will be a coffee house, a dance hall, a library, a book shop, as well as the usual counselling, 24-hour crisis phone, court assistance, etc. that's been going on for the past year. Cecil is one block south of College on the east side of Spadina. (*Guerilla*, January 1972)

The CHAT Community Centre was, for activists at the time, a promising development in queer organizing in Toronto—a space in which gays and lesbians could foster community that was not driven by commercial exploitation. The second issue of *The Body Politic* (TBP) featured the community centre on its cover and presented the space as an alternative

to the (minor) commercial gay scene in Toronto at the time. CHAT would later move into a building at 201 Church Street.

Within CHAT, tensions resulting from sexism within the organization challenged the cohesion of the group. In late 1971, a group of lesbian members of CHAT, self-identified as the Cunts, delivered a statement to the broader membership of the organization demanding that gay male members of CHAT confront their sexism and that each male individual put in the work to raise his consciousness. The document, signed "THE CUNTS," does not equivocate:

> As lesbians we are oppressed both as cunts and as dykes. Until the gays of CHAT see the necessity of struggling against sexism, until the structure of CHAT is revolutionized, then CHAT will reflect the status quo through legalization and acceptance. This is shuffling. Our energies will not be wasted on raising the consciousness of the members of CHAT who should be raising their own...
>
> The amendment: Dykes and faggots in CHAT shall share equally in decision making. This means equalization at all official decision making levels.

Chris Fox, a member of the Cunts, recalls the inflammatory nature of the statement and the proposed amendment; while the use of "cunts," "faggots," and "dykes" was a form of reclaiming language, she suspects the terminology was "why many who might have would not vote for it. Clearly," she continues, with a smile, "we were angry young women. We felt we were excluded on the basis of sex, so we wanted our language to emphasize that, and we wanted to have the organization right that injustice."

Alongside political tensions within the association, economic challenges made it difficult to sustain CHAT. The organization, like many gay liberation groups in the 1970s, had trouble convincing well-off and closeted queers to support the movement and had no real chance of accessing funding from the city, province, or federal government.

In 1972, CHAT hosted a panel entitled "Homosexuality: Myth & Reality" at the St. Lawrence Centre Town Hall. Moderated by journalist Barbara Frum, the panel featured lawyer A.K. Gigeroff, journalist Sidney Katz, and CHAT members Kathleen Brindley, George Hislop, Pat Murphy, and Herb Spiers. The event was disrupted when two members of the right-wing Western Guard sprayed the 450 attendees with tear gas. The next night, a Molotov cocktail was thrown through a window of CHAT's community centre. (Earlier, a Molotov cocktail meant for CHAT's building was thrown through the window of a neighbouring house.)

In 1979, George Hislop—one of the founding members of CHAT and a hugely influential gay activist in Toronto—served as the first openly gay candidate for public office in Canada. Until his death in 2005, he was affectionately known by many as the (unofficial) mayor of gay Toronto.

1 Poster for CHAT dance party at 72 Carlton Street, Toronto, c. 1970s.

2 Exterior of CHAT office at 201 Church Street, Toronto, c. 1970s.

3 CHAT members, with signs, at Hanlan's Point, Toronto, c. 1970s.

4 CHAT panel, "Homosexuality: Myth & Reality" held at St. Lawrence Centre Town Hall, Toronto, 1972.

GAY ALLIANCE
TOWARD EQUALITY

The Gay Alliance Toward Equality (GATE) formed
in 1971 in Vancouver with an emphasis on militant
and aggressive strategies to attain gay and lesbian
civil rights. GATE's public protests and marches, as
well as their newspaper, *Gay Tide,* brought the group's
vociferous politics to a wider audience. Though dominated by men, GATE incorporated feminist analysis
of patriarchy into its political projects; the group was
also heavily informed by Marxism and Marxist analysis. Maurice Flood played a leadership role in the
organization and brought to the fore detailed anal-
yses of gay liberation politics. Significantly, in 1973,
GATE filed a human rights complaint against the *Vancouver Sun* after the newspaper refused to publish an
advertisement for subscriptions to *Gay Tide.* The ad,
which read simply, "Subs. TO GAY TIDE. gay lib. paper.
$1.00 for 6 issues," was deemed offensive. After the
B.C. courts ruled in favour of the *Sun* on the grounds
that "homosexuality was offensive to most people,"
GATE appealed to the Supreme Court of Canada in
1979, where the court again ruled in favour of the *Sun,*
citing freedom of the press. Although unsuccessful,
GATE's human rights complaint against the *Sun* was
the first time in Canada that sexual-orientation discrimination was investigated by a human rights board
and heard by the Supreme Court of Canada. *Gay Tide*
was published from August 1973 to June 1980.

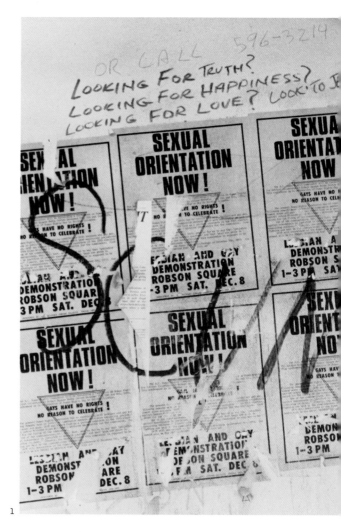

1

2

YOU CAN OVERCOME YOUR HETEROSEXUALITY

3

GAY IS GOOD

4

5

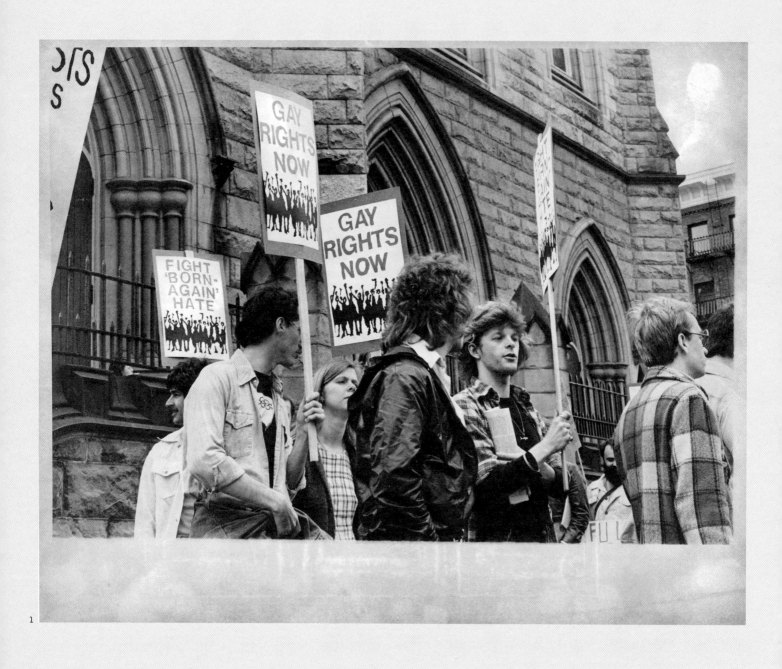

| 1 | GATE protest, c. 1970s. | 2 | GATE poster, "Fight 'Born-Again' Hate," c. 1970s. |

FIGHT 'BORN-AGAIN' HATE

2

LE FRONT DE LIBÉRATION
DES HOMOSEXUELS

Le front de libération des homosexuels (FLH) formed in Montreal in 1971. Comprising both francophones and anglophones, it was the first gay liberation political organization in Quebec. It grew quickly, boasting over two hundred members a few months after its founding. But the organization faced vicious harassment by police in Montreal, which, not long after its founding, led to its demise. When the FLH moved to their new location on Sainte-Catherine Street in June 1972, Montreal police raided the open-house event and dance and arrested over three dozen attendees. "The blame for the FLH's demise," Patrizia Gentile argues in " 'À bas la répression contre les homosexuels!': Resistance and Surveillance of Queers in Montreal, 1971–76," "rests squarely on the shoulders of police harassment and repression. After the June 17–18 raids, the FLH executive resigned" (73). Their announcement was powerful:

We are homosexuals. We are PROUD. We refuse to hide. We do not accept that we must live in a society that oppresses us because we are homosexuals and Quebeckers. We want a free Quebec because we want our liberation on all levels, sexual as well as political, economic, and cultural. We fight because we want every Quebecker to be able to express their sexuality without restraint and wherever they choose. For us, the oppressors are those who hold on to a system that forces too many of us to hide our real identity in order to earn a living; these are psychologists and sociologists that observe us like curious animals; these are priests that treat us as perverts; these are finally ordinary guys that call us "tapettes." (Quoted in Gentile's " 'À bas la répression contre les homosexuels!' " 71)

HOMOSEXUELS POUR UN QUEBEC LIBRE

On est des homosexuels. On en est FIER. On refuse de se cacher.

1   "Homosexuels pour un Québec libre," document produced by the FLH, c. 1970s.

VIVE LE QUÉBEC LIBRE; VIVE LA LUTTE DE LIBÉRATION DES HOMOSEXUELS

LONG LIVE A FREE QUEBEC; LONG LIVE THE FIGHT FOR GAY LIBERATION

GAYS OF OTTAWA

Gays of Ottawa (GO) was founded in September 1971. The organization was education-focused, running discussion groups, creating publications, and giving presentations on homosexuality. Founding members were also committed to lobbying federal and provincial governments on behalf of lesbians and gays.

GO hosted events, ran a counselling and drop-in centre, and provided a crisis phone line for gays and lesbians. They worked with both anglophone and francophone communities and organized on local and national levels.

1 Gays of Ottawa protest, 1977.
Photograph by Claude Jutras.

2 Poster for dance hosted by Gays of Ottawa, c. 1970s.

GAYS FOR EQUALITY

What began as the Campus Gay Club at the University of Manitoba became, in 1972–73, Gays for Equality (GFE)—an organization committed to radical and public gay liberation political action. GFE offered a phone line, peer counselling, information on gay-liberation politics and gay community organizing in the city, a research collection and library, social activities, support groups for a variety of gay issues, as well as a popular "rap session"—a structured discussion group to think through the politics of coming out. The aggressive liberation politics espoused by Gays for Equality caused tension in Winnipeg gay organizing, particularly in relation to the work of The Mutual Friendship Society, Inc., and their community space, Happenings Social Club. While the two groups featured some overlapping membership, GFE was committed to a more overt gay presence in the city. While publications and promotion materials coming out of Happenings in its early years usually featured pseudonyms and coded language, GFE was more public about their membership and goals. According to Valerie Korinek in *Prairie Fairies: A History of Queer Communities and People in Western Canada, 1930–1985,* "Gays for Equality became a driving force in Winnipeg's gay and lesbian community because it acted as the incubator for many other gay organizations in Winnipeg" (128). The group had staffed an office on the University of Manitoba campus since its inception; in 1983 it moved to the Winnipeg Gay Community Centre. This progression was a natural outgrowth of geography, Korinek shows:

> Geographically, the city of Winnipeg, as the province's largest urban centre, continued to pull gays and lesbians into the city from the outlying rural

Love and Let Love

Gays For Equality
Winnipeg, Man.
474-8216

1

areas and the smaller cities. In particular, the movement of students into the city to attend the Universities of Manitoba and Winnipeg was a key factor that attracted younger gays and lesbians to the city. (116)

Korinek also articulates a tension in Winnipeg during the 1970s and 1980s that surfaced in other Canadian cities as well as lesbians were pulled between gay liberation politics and feminist (and, at times, lesbian-feminist) political organizing. In 1974, for example, the Winnipeg Lesbian Society developed out of A Woman's Place (an exclusively lesbian organization in Winnipeg founded in 1972) to push back against the patriarchal reality of gay and lesbian groups in the city. While Gays for Equality and The Mutual Friendship Society, Inc., were mixed—welcoming both gay men and women—they were, in reality, male-dominated in both membership, leadership, and political priorities.

1   Pamphlet produced by Gays for Equality, Winnipeg, c. 1970s.

ZODIAC
FRIENDSHIP SOCIETY

The Zodiac Friendship Society was formed in 1972. "Similar to other prairie cities," Valerie Korinek writes, "they purposefully chose a slightly playful, coded name that would not trigger concerns or cause cautious members to avoid the group for fear of exposure" (169). The Society curated a small library of books on lesbian and gay life and politics and, in subsequent years, developed a phone line for individuals interested in gay liberation politics and opportunities for gay and lesbian social life. The Society soon developed a social wing—which they named the Gemini Club—and began hosting dances at the Unitarian Centre on Main Street. Gemini Club dances, which began in February 1972, were hugely popular; profits from the events enabled the organization to rent space and enabled more public political action. For example, in November 1972, the Gemini Club hosted the first Western Canadian Gay Clubs Conference, gathering together representatives from five private clubs: their own plus Club 70 in Edmonton, Club Carousel in Calgary, Happenings Social Club in Winnipeg, and Odyssey Club in Regina.

1

2

In March 1973, the Gemini Club opened the first public gay and lesbian centre in the Prairies in a space rented on 2nd Avenue North in Saskatoon, across the hall from the Saskatoon Women's Centre. The physical location of the Gemini Club, Korinek argues, was vital to the development of gay liberation and women's liberation politics in the city: "a small core of feminist lesbians began to participate in local gay activism, changing the group's focus and analysis" (171). In January 1975, the Zodiac Friendship Society and Saskatoon Gay Action officially merged and transformed into the Gay Community Centre of Saskatoon.

A Soundtrack of the Zodiac Friendship Society

An undated document in the Neil Richards Collection at the University of Saskatchewan Archives chronicles some of the LPs played on high rotation at Zodiac Friendship Society dance parties. The playlist is composed of disco and soul—the primary dance music of the era—as well as rock and show tunes, making for an eclectic soundtrack.

B.T. Express, *Do It ('Til You're Satisfied)* (1974)

Bette Midler, *The Divine Miss M* (1972)

Deep Purple, *Deep Purple in Rock* (1970)

Gloria Gaynor, *Never Can Say Goodbye* (1975)

Kool & the Gang, *Light of Worlds* (1974)

Liza Minnelli, *Liza with a "Z"* (1972)

The Pointer Sisters, *The Pointer Sisters* (1973)

The Three Degrees, *The Three Degrees* (1973)

Van McCoy, *Love Is the Answer* (1974)

Van McCoy, *Disco Baby* (1975)

Yvonne Fair, *The Bitch Is Black* (1975)

3

1 Elizabeth Noton at the Gay Community Centre of Saskatoon, 1977.

2 Two people playing pool at the Gay Community Centre of Saskatoon, 1977.

3 Doug Hellquist (*on ladder*) and two other members of the Zodiac Friendship Society prepare for the opening of the Gemini Club, Saskatoon, 1973.

Music Recordings

Musical recordings have the capacity to articulate queer politics, connect listeners with others, and encourage listeners to imagine a more just world. With this in mind, the ArQuives collects a wide array of music—including vinyl LPS, 33s, and 45s, audiocassettes, compact discs, and digital files—from all genres of music that are significant to LGBTQ2+ movements in Canada and beyond. In the collection process, preference is given to musical recordings by LGBTQ2+ musicians and musicians whose work is significant to LGBTQ2+ communities in Canada.

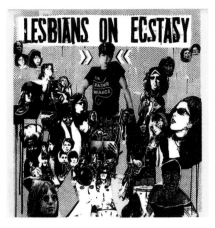

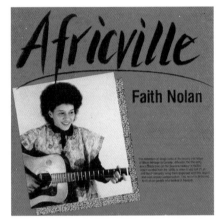

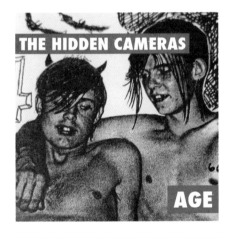

WE DEMAND
RALLY

On August 28, 1971, gay groups amassed on Parliament Hill in Ottawa to demand recognition and equal rights for gays and lesbians in Canada in what was the first large-scale public demonstration for gay rights in Canada. Toronto Gay Action (TGA) coordinated the action and compiled a list of demands—written by Herb Spiers and David Newcome—that dealt specifically with federal legislation. George Hislop and Pat Murphy, on behalf of CHAT (page 106), and Pierre Masson, representing Le front de libération des homosexuels (page 112), spoke at the rally. Charlie Hill welcomed the approximately one hundred demonstrators, noting that "we are here to demand equal rights." Hill made it clear that so-called "decriminalization" of homosexuality had, in reality, done little to create equitable conditions for sexual minorities.

A corresponding demonstration, organized by the Gay Alliance Toward Equality, was held at the Vancouver courthouse on the same day.

Patrizia Gentile, Gary Kinsman, and L. Pauline Rankin write in *We Still Demand: Redefining Resistance in Sex and Gender Struggles* that the 1971 action "critiqued the limited decriminalization and the public/private strategy of sexual policing followed by the Trudeau government and focused on the actual, daily discrimination that queer people continued to face" (4).

1

2

1 We Demand rally on Parliament Hill in Ottawa, 1971. Photograph by Jearld Moldenhauer.

2 Charlie Hill speaking during We Demand rally on Parliament Hill in Ottawa, 1971. Photograph by Jearld Moldenhauer.

Charlie Hill's Speech on Parliament Hill: "Today marks a turning point in our history"

There's no homosexual problem in Canada. There's a heterosexual problem. It is they who have made the laws to protect themselves from us.

Two years ago the Criminal Code Amendments came into effect. After months of debate, during which ignorant Members of Parliament amused themselves making anti-homosexual jokes and vaunting their religious and sexist bigotry, sexual acts between persons over 21 were made not illegal in private. This did nothing to ameliorate the situation of Canadian homosexuals. This merely brought the law into line with police practice.

In October of the same year, the Canadian homophile movement was revived with the formation of the University of Toronto Homophile Association. Beginning with eight people in one association, we're now thousands of men and women in many groups right across Canada and we're here today to assert our rights and make our demands. We're no longer willing to quietly give thanks for a few crumbs begrudgingly given [to] us by our own government. We're here to demand full equality.

For thousands of years homosexuals have been the scapegoats of anti-homosexual societies. Throughout Canada's history our sisters and brothers have been thrown in jail, hounded into hospitals, forced to hide and pass for straight, conforming to other people's prejudices. Even today Canadian homosexuals are having their careers ruined, being kicked out of their churches, having their children taken away from them and being assaulted in the streets of their own cities. What have we done to deserve all this violence and hate? LOVE. All we want to do is love persons of the same sex and live our lives as we decide for ourselves and for this we're taught in our schools to hate ourselves.

We're labelled sinful, criminal and sick, and fired from our jobs. No longer!

Today marks a turning point in our history. No longer are we going to petition others to give us our rights as gifts. We're here to demand them as equal citizens on our own terms. Homosexual men and women in Canada are fed up with being the butt of other people's jokes. We're fed up with the lack of basic respect due to all human beings. We're fed up with having to hide to preserve our jobs. We're fed up with having to hide to preserve our own freedom. We're fed up with the genocide of gays fostered by psychiatrists using medieval tortutres [*sic*] to destroy us. We're fed up with being discriminated against in employment, housing and the courts. We're fed up with being arrested and harassed by police forces paid for by our own taxes. In fact we're fed up with paying the price of other people's hangups.

No longer are we going to accept the lie foisted on us that there is a homosexual problem. There's no homosexual problem in Canada. There's a heterosexual problem. It is they who have made the laws to protect themselves from us. They're the ones who employ the R.C.M.P. to identify us, isolate us and evict us from our jobs. They're the ones who control the schools that teach hatred of homosexuals. They're the ones who control the churches that label us sinners. They're the ones who control the courts that label us criminals. No longer!

We've come here today to assert our pride in ourselves. To say we're homosexual and proud of it. We're coming together and uniting to manifest our own power as Gays. Two million homosexual men and women in Canada are watching us. We're going to show them it can be done, that we can go anywhere we choose as homosexuals and as Canadian citizens with full civil rights. Gay is proud and Gay is good. Let's say it wherever we go.

And here's how things look to Dick Smyth this morning

August 30 1971

The prospect of a group of homosexuals prancing about Parliament Hill in a demonstration for equality not only repels and repulses me, it makes me wonder if perhaps it's all an insane nightmare from which I shortly will return to reality.

The prospect is about as savory as a demonstration for equality and acceptance by militant alcoholics, militant lepers or militant lunatics.

All are people who need help and understanding.

To stamp such afflictions with the acceptance of normal behaviour is senseless.

The entire Gay Liberation movement is based on the false assumption that homosexuality has some redeeming or positive aspect to it. It is negative and unproductive. It is a mental and a sexual abberation.

The position of these various gay action groups is roughly akin to a situation in which Alcoholics Anonimous was advocating acceptance of drunkeness rather than trying to help those afflicted with a drinking problem.

Like alcoholics, homosexuals are sick people who indeed do need help..not the help of lawyers and politicians but that of doctors and psychiatrists.

Two, four, six eight, gay is just as good as straight. Really!

As a normal and healthy male who thrills to a shapely thigh or a full breast, I know otherwise.

The lie inherent in that rallying cry, as much as anything, tells me how sick the guys really are.

THIS IS A REPRODUCTION OF THE ORIGINAL TRANSCRIPT FURNISHED BY CHUM-1050.

DICK SMYTH – NEWS DIRECTOR

1050 chum ALL THE NEWS

1331 Yonge Street, Toronto 290, Ontario · 923-1133

1

1 Dick Smyth's editorial on CHUM Radio in response to the We Demand rally in Ottawa, August 30, 1971.

2 We Demand rally on Parliament Hill in Ottawa, 1971. Photograph by Jearld Moldenhauer.

THE BODY
POLITIC

The Body Politic (*TBP*) began in 1971 as Canada's national gay liberation newspaper. *TBP* played a pivotal role in galvanizing the gay and lesbian community, as mainstream newspapers often refused to publish material related to homosexuality. In 1973, for example, the *Toronto Star* refused to print an advertisement for *TBP* on the grounds that it was obscene and sexually explicit material; eventually it revoked *TBP*'s printing contact with the *Star*'s subsidiary printing company.

In early January 1978—after the late December 1977 raid on the Archives—Ed Jackson, Gerald Hannon, and Ken Popert were charged with using the mail for the purpose of delivering obscene materials. One year later, the three men were found not guilty, but Ontario attorney general Roy McMurtry appealed the ruling. In response, the *TBP*'s Free the Press Fund—established in 1978 to raise financial support for Jackson, Hannon, and Popert's legal defence—placed an advertisement with over eight hundred signatories in the *Globe and Mail* urging McMurtry to end the appeals. In 1982, the entire collective of *TBP* was charged for publishing obscene materials (related to an article entitled "Lust with a Very Proper Stranger"), of which they were subsequently acquitted.

The last issue of *TBP* was published in February 1987. Pink Triangle Press (PTP) continued with *Xtra* as its flagship publication. *Xtra*, designed to be less radical and less serious that *TBP*, was aimed at a broader audience. In 1993, PTP began publishing *Xtra West* (Vancouver) and *Capital Xtra* (Ottawa).

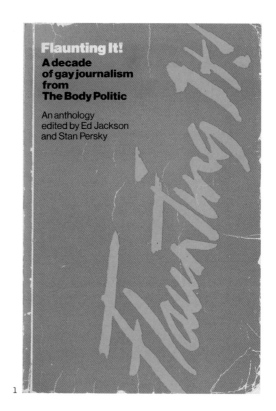

1

1 *Flaunting It! A Decade of Gay Journalism from* The Body Politic, edited by Ed Jackson and Stan Persky, 1982.

2 *The Body Politic*, No. 1, 1971.

3 *The Body Politic*, No. 4, 1972.

4 *The Body Politic*, No. 11, 1974.

5 *The Body Politic*, No. 16, 1974.

6 *The Body Politic*, No. 19, 1975.

7 *The Body Politic*, No. 25, 1976.

8 *The Body Politic*, No. 76, 1981.

9 *The Body Politic*, No. 80, 1982.

10 *The Body Politic*, No. 98, 1983.

the **body politic**
gay liberation newspaper
25¢

GAY RALLY OTTAWA
CHARTER

no. 1 november–december 1971   toronto

2

the **body politic**
gay liberation newspaper
25¢ 35¢ OUTSIDE TORONTO

NO. 4   MAY – JUNE   TORONTO   1972

FASCISTS GAS GAYS P.4
CREATIVE PSYCHE AND HOMOSEXUALITY P.6
THE MYTH OF THE NEW HOMOSEXUAL P.3

3

the **body politic**
no. 11 1974
u.s. 50¢ 35¢ u.k. 15p
gay liberation journal

4

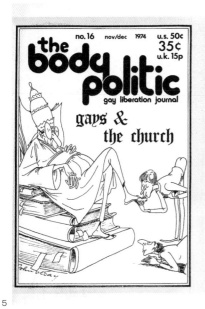

no. 16   nov/dec 1974   u.s. 50¢ 35¢ u.k. 15p
the **body politic**
gay liberation journal

gays &
the church

5

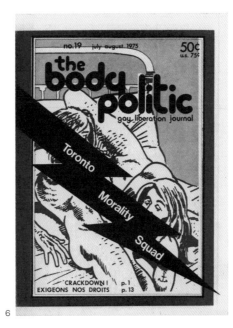

no.19   july·august 1975   50¢ u.s. 75¢
the **body politic**
gay liberation journal

Toronto
Morality
Squad

CRACKDOWN !   p.1
EXIGEONS NOS DROITS   p.13

6

THE **Body Politic**   50¢
Gay Liberation Journal   No. 25 August

POLICE:

Entrapment
Olympic crackdown

United States 75c.   Other countries as marked.

7

Out in the City
THE CITY'S OWN GUIDE TO GOINGS ON IN TORONTO   GAY PRIDE ACROSS CANADA: TWO PAGES OF PHOTOS
Body Politic

DIRTY MOVIES
OPENING THE DOOR ON VITO RUSSO'S CELLULOID CLOSET
Special
Edition

WORLD
SERIES '81
PLAYING BALL WITH THE SERIES' HOSTS, TORONTO'S CABBAGETOWN GROUP SOFTBALL LEAGUE

8

JANE RULE • MICHEL TREMBLAY • DAVID SEREDA • GARY OSTROM • AND THE WHOLE TBP GANG
BodyPolitic
A MAGAZINE FOR GAY LIBERATION

CELEBRATING A DECADE!
Tenth Anniversary Issue
The biggest Body Politic ever—50 pages!

9

BodyPolitic
A MAGAZINE FOR GAY LIBERATION
OUT OF COURT AT LAST!

THE DANCEABLE REVOLUTION

DRUGS
Chocolate to Morphine: John Alfee looks at changing perceptions on changing perceptions

10

1970S
PERIODICALS

Periodicals and other small publications were pivotal to the development of lesbian and gay politics during the 1970s and came to house the early writings of important lesbian and gay activists. They also were able to intervene in the isolation felt by many lesbians and gays—especially those living in rural areas without access to the resources concentrated in Toronto, Montreal, Halifax, and Vancouver—while creating a shared sense of political values based on feminism, gay liberation, and working-class union organizing. *After Stonewall,* for instance, a gay liberation journal written and published in Winnipeg (and, in later years, Saskatoon), galvanized gays and lesbians in western Canada. As the first issue of *After Stonewall* made clear, "[g]ay liberation is alive in western Canada. Every day we hear new reports in media of this or that event which reaffirms that gay people will not accept their lot in silence…*After Stonewall* aims at being a publication to serve gay liberation in the prairies of Canada and adjacent American states."

The Other Woman, a feminist newspaper published in Toronto, focused on the struggles of women around the world, with special attention to reproductive rights, labour politics and working-class resistance, lesbian sexuality, and women in music.

Published in Montreal from 1973 to 1976, *Long Time Coming* was the first regularly produced publication for lesbians in Canada. It focused on arts, poetry, politics, and lesbian sexuality.

1

2

1   *Long Time Coming*, Vol. 2, No. 6, 1975.

2   *The Other Woman*, Vol. 4, No. 3, 1976.

2nd Anniversary

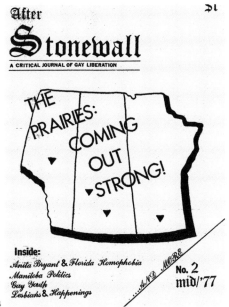

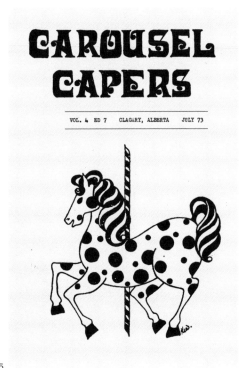

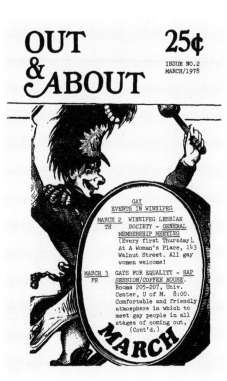

3   *Aboutface* (St. John's), Vol. 2, No. 4, 1976.

4   *After Stonewall* (Winnipeg), Vol. 1, No. 2, 1977.

5   *Carousel Capers* (Calgary), Vol. 4, No. 7, 1973.

6   *Out & About* (Winnipeg), Vol. 1, No. 2, 1978.

THE METROPOLITAN COMMUNITY CHURCH

The gay and lesbian Metropolitan Community Church (MCC) established a Toronto congregation in 1973. The following year, the *Toronto Star* refused an advertisement for the MCC because it was "distasteful to our readership." Led by Brent Hawkes from 1977 to 2017, the MCC provided (and continues to provide) services that have extended beyond spiritual support over the years, including, since the 1980s, hospice care and support groups for people living with HIV/AIDS. MCC supported the establishment of Parents and Friends of Lesbians and Gays (PFLAG) and provided office space for the Toronto Counselling Centre for Lesbians and Gays, Lesbian and Gay Youth Toronto, and the Coalition for Lesbian and Gay Rights in Ontario. It also provided critical support for gay and lesbian rights in Canada, backing provincial and federal bills that recognized sexuality and equal rights for gays and lesbians over the years. In the early 1970s, branches of the MCC served gay and lesbian Christians in Edmonton, Hamilton, Ottawa, and Vancouver.

Significantly, the MCC married two same-sex couples in 2001 and challenged the Registrar General of Ontario for refusing to register the marriage documents. MCC took the provincial government to court, and in 2002 the Ontario Superior Court of Justice ruled in favour of the MCC, declaring that marriage rights must be extended to same-sex couples. The federal government appealed this judgment. In 2003, the Ontario Court of Appeal again ruled that marriage rights must be extended to same-sex couples as their exclusion violated the Canadian Charter of Rights and Freedoms. This was not the first time the MCC performed same-sex marriages; as documents reproduced here indicate, the MCC celebrated holy unions between same-sex couples since the mid-1970s.

1 Reverend Brent Hawkes, Toronto, 2015. Photograph by Nigel Dickson.

2 Program for MCC Service, 1976.

1

CELEBRATION OF HOLY UNION

LAWRENCE C. GAUER AND ROBERT S. WOLFE

September 24, 1976

The Reverend Troy D. Perry, Officiating
The Reverend David Gunton, Assisting
The Reverend Philip Speranza, Assisting

PSALM 100   Reverend Speranza

An ancient song of praise and
thanksgiving.

PRAYER OF INVOCATION   Reverend Speranza

SPECIAL MUSIC   Ian, MCC-Ottawa

ASSURANCE OF ABSOLUTION   Reverend Gunton

Bob and Larry are asked to confess
their pasts, that the past may be
set behind them and they may enter
a new life.

AVOWAL OF INTENT   Reverend Perry

Larry, do you now before God and this
company proclaim your love for Bob?

Do you seek to live with him in a
union that is holy, and is based on
mutual love, trust, and understanding?

Bob, do you now before God and this
company proclaim your love for Larry?

Do you seek to live with him in a
union that is holy, and is based on
mutual love, trust, and understanding?

READING OF SCRIPTURE   Reverend Perry

from the letter of Paul, to our
brothers and sisters at Corinth,
Chapter 13.

WORDS OF ADMONITION AND SPIRITUAL ADVICE
                             Reverend Perry

SPECIAL MUSIC   Joanne and Do, MCC-Toronto

OFFERING OF THE RINGS AND THE BREAD AND WINE

PRAYERS OF CONSECRATION

WORDS OF COMMITMENT* AND EXCHANGE OF RINGS

ADMINISTRATION OF COMMUNION

PRAYERS OF BLESSING

+++++++++++++++++

*
Words of commitment;

WITH THIS RING I ACCEPT YOU AS MY LIFE-MATE
AND PLEDGE MY LIFE TO A UNION WITH YOU THAT
IS HOLY AND IS BASED ON MUTUAL LOVE, TRUST
AND UNDERSTANDING, FOR AS LONG AS GOD SHALL
BLESS OUR LOVE.

Guests are invited to celebrate with Bob and
Larry, with refreshments, at the back of the
church.

Special thanks to Reverend Perry, Reverend
Gunton, Reverend Speranza, Wayne Hagen,
John Paul Napier, Ian, Joanne, Doreen, Lyn,
Linda, Norm, Lloyd, Maddy and John Bodis.

2

ANDROGYNY BOOKSTORE/
LIBRAIRIE L'ANDROGYNE

Community bookstore Androgyny Bookstore/
Librairie l'androgyne opened in Montreal in 1973
and specialized in gay and lesbian and feminist
literature in both French and English. In " 'À bas
la répression contre les homosexuels!': Resistance
and Surveillance of Queers in Montreal, 1971–76,"
Patrizia Gentile argues that the bookstore "played a
critical role in bridging these linguistic divides and
providing a much-needed space" for gay, lesbian,
and trans activists in the city (73).

THE BRUNSWICK
FOUR

On January 5, 1974, Adrienne Potts, Pat Murphy, Sue Wells, and Heather Byers took to the stage of the Brunswick Tavern in downtown Toronto to perform "I Enjoy Being a Dyke" (a rendition of the classic show tune "I Enjoy Being a Girl").

> I've always been an uppity woman
> I don't run I stand and fight
> 'Cause I'm gay and I'm proud and I'm angry
> I enjoy being a dyke!
>
> When I see a man who's sexist
> And he does something I don't like
> I can tell him that he can fuck off
> I enjoy being a dyke!
>
> I don't dress up cute and frilly
> And in clothing that I don't like
> I just go in my jeans and stompers
> I enjoy being a dyke!

It was amateur night at the Brunswick and, as Becki Ross writes in *The House That Jill Built: A Lesbian Nation in Formation,* the women received a "surprisingly warm response from the largely straight male clientele" (47). The manager of the venue, however, felt differently—he cut the power halfway through the performance and demanded that the women leave the bar. When Potts, Murphy, Byers, and Wells refused, the manager called the police to report "a lesbian riot." At least eight police officers arrived on the scene, forcefully removed the four women from the bar, threw them in a paddy wagon, and took them to 14 Division, where the women were held for several hours. When they were finally released, the women returned to the Brunswick Tavern to locate witnesses to the verbal and physical abuse they had experienced from police.

At this point, Murphy, Byers, and Potts were arrested for creating a public disturbance (Wells was not arrested) and thus received the moniker "Brunswick Four (minus one)" that is used on much of the literature describing the event and its aftermath. Following their arrest, the Brunswick Four (minus one) publicized their case and the physical abuse they received from police, including, Ross writes, "torn ligaments, bruising, punches to the back of the head, twisted arms," and "verbal taunts such as 'You fucking hosebag, I bet you drive a tugboat' and 'Did you ever put your finger in a dike?' " (48).

1   From left to right: Adrienne Potts, Pat Murphy, Sue Wells, and Heather Byers, 1974.

NATIONAL
ORGANIZING

The 1970s saw the development of sustained national gay and lesbian organizing in Canada. The politics of gay liberation, barely on the radar in Canada just a few years prior, had taken hold in cities across the country. In an effort to sustain and build on movements across Canada, liberationists met in various cities to debate broader questions of the movement, socialize with other politicized gays and lesbians, and work together toward the ideals of gay liberation politics. The attendance at these conferences varied: the 1973 conference in Quebec City hosted by Le Centre humanitaire d'aide et de libération (CHAL) and the 1974 conference in Winnipeg hosted at the University of Manitoba by Gays for Equality each attracted about eighty participants; the conference in Ottawa in 1975 had more than two hundred delegates. In *Lesbian and Gay Liberation in Canada: A Selected Annotated Chronology, 1964–1975,* Donald McLeod calls the 1975 Ottawa conference, organized by Gays of Ottawa, "the largest and most geographically representative meeting of lesbians and gays in Canada to that time" (225).

At the 1974 meeting in Winnipeg, Ron Dayman proposed the formation of a national gay rights organization that could continue to build on the national energy at these conferences and sustain political organization at the national level; the National Gay Rights Coalition/Coalition nationale pour les droits des homosexuels (NGRC/CNDH) was officially formed at the conference in Ottawa the following year. Two issues regularly surfaced at these national conferences: the Toronto-centric nature of what was meant to be a national movement and its male-dominated nature, including the lack of autonomy of lesbians within this movement. The issues affecting lesbians were indeed, in certain ways, different and unaccounted for by a male-dominant gay movement. As Liz Millward argues, the 1969 Criminal Law Amendment Act decriminalized consensual acts between men but did not address women who slept with other women; as such, the Act "still gave the Crown power to prosecute under charges of indecency or

1 **Winnipeg, 1974**

corruption of a minor" (19). Lesbians were also affected by broader "women's issues" that were sometimes seen as distinct from gay organizing; access to abortion, the rights of lesbian mothers to keep their children, and freedom from sexual and domestic violence linked lesbian struggles to the larger feminist movement. Accordingly, this decade saw the development of smaller, regional conference networks as well as a series of hugely influential lesbian conferences more directly informed by the feminist politics of the moment. For example, the Gay Women's Festival of June 30, 1973, held at a YWCA on McGill Street in Toronto, featured discussion groups on legal rights for women and lesbian mothers as well as on lesbian feminism—a political movement that encouraged women to challenge the patriarchy and pursue the creation of a feminist society by forming social, sexual, and political bonds with other women. According to Millward, this conference "set the blueprint for most subsequent conferences" (176).

1   Poster for Second National Gay Conference, Winnipeg, 1974.

2 Quebec City, 1973

3 Ottawa, 1975

4 Toronto, 1976

5 Saskatoon, 1977

6 Halifax, 1978

7 Ottawa, 1979

2 Participants at the First National Gay Conference, Quebec City, 1973.

3 Protest march during the Third National Gay Conference, Ottawa, 1975.

4 Gathering at the Fourth National Gay Conference, Toronto, 1976.

5 March during the Fifth National Gay Conference, Saskatoon, 1977. Photograph by Gerald Hannon.

6 Audience at the Turret during the Sixth National Gay Conference, Halifax, 1978.

7 March during the Seventh National Gay Conference, Ottawa, 1979.

T-shirts

The ArQuives artifact collection includes a variety of fabrics in forms that include T-shirts, protest banners, dresses, drag clothing, and leather gear. The collection of T-shirts demonstrates the important role that clothing, as a mode of identification and political expression, has been for individuals and the varied ways in which LGBTQ2+ people have used clothing to articulate political messages to broader publics. Articulating a public queer presence throughout the city as individuals model these garments in everyday life, T-shirts make possible the widespread promotion of queer ideas, initiatives, media, and institutions.

SEPERATING THE MEN FROM THE BOYS

ROCK & ROLL
FAG BAR

IOI JARVIS · FRIDAYS · TORONTO · CANADA

2003

LESBIAN ORGANIZING

In addition to national lesbian conferences (see "Social Politics" section, page 100), more regional examples of lesbian and feminist organizing thrived in the 1970s. Groups like Wages for Housework, Wages Due Lesbians, Women Against Violence Against Women, Lesbian Mothers' Defense Fund, and the Lesbian Organization of Toronto were all instrumental in expanding political critiques of heteronormative patriarchy and the violence done in its name.

The Lesbian Organization of Toronto (LOOT) emerged out of feminist organizing and the women's movement of the early 1970s. Lesbian consciousness-raising groups were held by the Women's Liberation Movement in Toronto beginning in 1971, and many lesbian members of LOOT came out through their involvement in the Women's Place, a women's centre for feminist organizing that held a Friday-night lesbian drop-in. Nevertheless, relations between straight and lesbian women within the feminist movement were fraught. In 1976, lesbians voiced their concerns about sexism within the gay liberation movement at the National Gay Rights Coalition conference (see also "National Organizing," page 132) in Toronto. Subsequently, Toronto lesbians, frustrated with both the women's movement and gay liberation efforts, identified the need for lesbians to gather, organize, and build community as lesbians. LOOT secured a house at 342 Jarvis Street, which they occupied along with *The Other Woman* lesbian newspaper (page 126) and the Three of Cups lesbian coffee house. In 1977, LOOT celebrated the establishment of Canada's first lesbian-feminist centre.

In the first LOOT newsletter in March 1977, the group positioned itself as "an umbrella organization for lesbians" that "serves social, recreational, personal, cultural, political, and educational purposes for the women involved," enabling "a lesbian to meet and get together with other lesbians who share her interests." In the late 1970s, LOOT offered a variety of services to Toronto-area lesbians, including telephone counselling and peer support; organized events for lesbians in the city, such as dances, concerts, other performances, and potlucks; and facilitated lesbian political organizing. Rock band Mama Quilla II regularly performed at LOOT events, including a New Year's celebration concert on December 30, 1978. Mama Quilla II—and, later, Parachute Club, which featured some of the same members—provided a soundtrack for the broader gay and lesbian liberation movement in Toronto and more broadly throughout the 1970s and 1980s, performing many concerts that helped raise funds for lesbian and gay liberation organizing.

Similar organizations thrived all over Canada and helped created a nationwide network of resistance: the Lesbian Action Group in Victoria, the Winnipeg Lesbian Society, the *Saskatoon Women's Liberation* newsletter, and a lesbian drop-in organized by the Edmonton chapter of GATE, among others, galvanized women all over the country.

1   Poster for "Toward a Strategy for the Lesbian Movement" event hosted by Wages Due Lesbians, Toronto, 1976.

2   Winnipeg Lesbian Society protest, c. 1970s.

3   Lesbian Organization of Toronto (LOOT) marching for International Women's Day, Toronto, 1980. Photograph by Gerald Hannon.

4   Wages Due Lesbians protest, Toronto, 1977.

Wages Due Lesbians (Toronto) Invites **All Women** To A Conference On Lesbians And The Wages For Housework Campaign

TOWARD A STRATEGY FOR THE LESBIAN MOVEMENT

INTERNATIONAL SPEAKERS: WILMETTE BROWN - FROM SAFIRE: BLACK WOMEN'S GROUP (NEW YORK)
RUTH HALL - FROM WAGES DUE LESBIANS (LONDON, ENGLAND)
TORONTO JULY 23-25

IT WILL BE AN OPPORTUNITY TO CONFRONT THE MOST CRITICAL QUESTIONS NOW FACING US AND OUR MOVEMENT:

WHY WE WANT AUTONOMY

An international panel of lesbian women from Canada, England and the United States, on why we need autonomy from men - including gay men, and from straight women, so we don't subordinate our own interests to those who have more power than us. Our own organizations are necessary in order to guarantee that we won't have to hide our lesbianism, and that more and more women will have the power to choose whether to be lesbian or not. Lesbian autonomy is in the interest of everyone fighting for sexual choices and full human liberation.

SEXUALITY

Our fight as lesbian women for control over our sexuality, within the context of all women's fight for sexual choices.

What does it do to our sex lives to always be thinking about having to go to work in the kitchen, the typing pool, or on the assembly line the next morning?

Is it our fault if our sex lives aren't what we think they should be?

How the state organizes our sexuality through abortion laws, population control, and wagelessness, and how our fight against it explodes the separation between "personal" and "political".

OUR LIVES AS LESBIANS

Informal rap sessions on areas like:
Closets: Problems of coming out and staying out -- What's at stake?
Lesbians in smaller towns
Younger lesbians, older lesbians
Relationships
Conflict with straight women

CHILD CUSTODY / THE CUTBACKS

To be "a fit mother" a woman is supposed to sleep with and depend financially on a man. One of the most important fights we are making is to be able to be lesbian without losing either our children or the possibility of having children.

The government cutbacks, by imposing more poverty on women, threaten to impose the status of unfit mother on any woman who is struggling for her independence, especially lesbian women, prostitutes, women on welfare, native women, and women prisoners.

How can we organize against our poverty for the power:
To have and keep the children we might want
To live where and with whom we wish
To no longer have to hide our lesbianism

We urge individuals and groups to write statements for the conference on any or all of the above areas, for the discussion which we hope will be as open and as full as possible. These papers, and any other materials, should be sent to:
Wages Due Lesbians
P.O. Box 38, Station E
Toronto, Ontario (416-466-7457 / 465-6822)

Conference details, registration forms, and a complete agenda will follow in a few weeks.

1

2

3

4

GAE'S TURRET

Halifax's Gay Alliance for Equality (GAE) formed in June 1972, published its first newsletter—entitled *GAE/Y Information Services*—in March 1973, and filed a memorandum of association with Nova Scotia's Office of the Registrar of Regulations in November of that same year. Despite an exciting and promising start to the Alliance's organizing—with regular meetings, an organized phone line, public talks at Saint Mary's University, Dalhousie University, and the Victoria General Hospital, and an appearance before the Nova Scotia Human Rights Commission—the GAE experienced a major lull from October 1974 to October 1975. Robin Metcalfe writes, in his annual secretary's report of 1976, that the organization was revived when it "adopted a less-formal, more democratic mode of operation" and vested power "in the General Membership rather than in the Executive." That same year, the GAE secured a more memorable number for its phone line: 429-6969.

The GAE held its first gay and lesbian dance party in January 1976 at 1588 Barrington Street—a space affectionately named "The Turret" because of the building's prominent spire. The GAE's dances were phenomenally successful and, as Metcalfe writes in *Out: Queer Looking, Queer Acting Revisited,* "made GAE one of the wealthiest lesbian and gay organisations on the continent" (30). The funds made from these dances were put to good use: in 1976, for example, the Alliance sent one member to the National Lesbian Conference in Ottawa, Ontario, and two to the Fourth National Gay Conference in Toronto. But the successes of the GAE's dances were more than just financial. The Turret was the first gay bar in Halifax that lesbians attended in great numbers (claiming a section of the room and naming it "Dyke Corner"), and it gave the city's growing gay and lesbian community a sense of power and collectivity. Though the tensions of gender politics challenged the GAE's cohesion—for example, the presence of shirtless dancing and, more famously, a mural painted in the Turret that some lesbian members considered misogynist—the GAE exemplifies a broader trend we see in gay and lesbian organizing in Canadian towns: because queer communities in these spaces tend to be smaller, there were often too few people to create and sustain dedicated groups separated by gender. Accordingly, social events tended to be more varied in terms of gender, age, and sexuality.

"For a time, we had in Halifax what no other place in Canada had … We had a place for the gay and lesbian community that was run by the community." **Deborah Trask, quoted in Rose, "Before the Parade," 2016**

2

GAY ALLIANCE FOR EQUALITY

P.O. BOX 3611, SOUTH POSTAL STATION, HALIFAX, N.S., CANADA B3J 3K6

1

1 Gay Alliance for Equality letterhead, c. 1970s.

2 Logo for the Turret, a community space run by Halifax's Gay Alliance for Equality, 1979. Designed by Rand Gaynor.

GAY
MONTRÉAL

Gay Montréal: Le journal d'information homosexuelle du Québec was a major weekly newspaper published from April 1976 to March 1977 that worked to challenge public perceptions about homosexuality. The publication served as a launching pad for leading authors of the gay liberation movement of Quebec and regularly featured sensational headlines, such as "Le SEXE en PRISON" ("SEX in JAIL"), "Les Travestis: bizarres ou heureux" ("Transvestites: Bizarre or Happy"), "La Sodomie: un sexologue répond à nos questions" ("Sodomy: A Sexologist Answers Our Questions,") and "L'Homosexualite: une MENACE" ("Homosexuality: A THREAT").

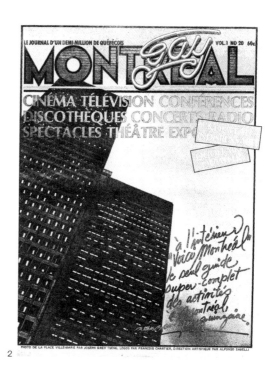

2

1

3

1 *Gay Montréal*, Vol. 1, No. 5, 1976. 2 *Gay Montréal*, Vol. 1, No. 20, 1976. 3 *Gay Montréal*, Vol. 1, No. 6, 1976.

OUT NORTH   **139**

THE VAN DYKES

On Saturday, November 26, 1977, two young lesbians from Toronto, Ange Spalding and Heather Elizabeth Nelson (also known as Brook and Lamar Van Dyke, respectively), took to the road to fulfill their dream of establishing a lesbian separatist utopia. Calling themselves the "Van Dykes," they drove their van through the U.S. and Mexico. The group added and lost members along the way: along with Brook and Lamar, the Van Dykes periodically included Skye, Judith, and Thorn Van Dyke. Brook chronicled the group's adventures in her diary, laying out the lesbian-feminist politics that motivated their separatist desires as well as the everyday obstacles the Van Dykes faced as they travelled across North America. Together, they grappled with politics, love, heartbreak, and polyamory, and strove to form strong bonds of friendship in hostile and homophobic circumstances. When they set off on their journey in 1977, Brook and Lamar came up with a theme song for the Van Dykes, sung to the melody of "Mr. Sandman":

> Would-be Van Dykes
> bring us your dreams
> make them the clearest that they've ever been
> give us a sign, like nickels and dollars
> and tell us that it's just a matter of hours
> till we find our
> land in the sun
> with killer dykes there, all having real fun
> plantin' grains and hoeing beans
> please turn on and cook up some schemes!

Lamar Van Dyke recalls the group's adventures in Ariel Levy's 2009 *New Yorker* article "Lesbian Nation":

> We found women's land in North Carolina, Florida, Texas, Arkansas, New Mexico, Arizona, a lot of Women's Land in California and Oregon. You could actually go all around the country from Women's Land to Women's Land and you met all these other women who were doing the same thing. You would run into people in New Mexico that you had seen in Texas… it was a whole world.

1

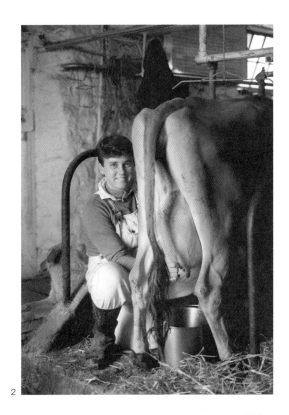

2

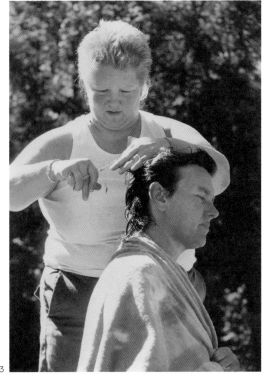

3

4

PROVINCETOWN, MASS.   WEDNESDAY NOV. 30
1977.

The purpose of this book is to keep a journal of my thoughts and visions while travelling again. We left T.O. on Saturday (NOV. 26th) late in the afternoon after an easy farewell to Pat, Lynda & Eileen and after basically a liquid farewell lunch to all at Peasants Larder. The next stop was to be Preston to say hello (after 2 months) and good-bye but over lunch, I decided I was too freaked out to face my parents so went directly to Buffalo where I fell in love with H.'s mom and her with me. Spent Saturday (w. Madelene Davis) evening & Sunday there and left on our journey at 3:00 p.m. from Lancaster (after shovelling H.'s mom's driveway - 2" snow - ugh!!) Travelled thru great little towns (RTE. 20) thru N.Y. state. Decided to stay in motel Mon. night as it was quite cold and H. & I. wanted to. Made love and talked for hours, drank wine and played watching T.V. Left next a.m.

1 Lamar Van Dyke (*left*) with Ange Spalding (*right*) next to Van-ella, the Van Dykes's VW van, 1977.

2 Ange Spalding after the Van Dykes's travels when she settled into farming, c. 1980s.

3 Ange Spalding (*seated*) with friend, c. 1980s.

4 Opening pages of Ange Spalding's diary during Van Dyke travels, 1977.

"GAY IN
THE SEVENTIES"

In December 1977, *Weekend Magazine* ran a double-page spread of gay and lesbian liberation activists. The caption accompanying the image listed the twenty-one individuals' professions: businessman, curator, author, professor, librarian, student, engineer, office worker, and teacher, among others.

The February 1978 edition of *The Body Politic* reported that *Weekend Magazine* had wanted a mix of "average gay people" to feature, no "professional homosexuals."

1

1   Feature article, "Gay in the Seventies," in *Weekend Magazine*, December 17, 1977.

While *Weekend Magazine* worked to make it look like the photograph featured average homosexuals who were only connected through their gayness, *The Body Politic* reprinted the image with their accreditations printed in *Weekend Magazine* alongside their roles in the liberation movement.

LEFT TO RIGHT, BACK ROW:

Ian Young
WM: Author, Toronto
TBP: Co-founder of Canada's first gay lib group, the University of Toronto Homophile Association; founder of gay publishing house, Catalyst Press; regular writer for *The Body Politic*

Dr. Rosemary Barnes
WM: Psychologist, Toronto General Hospital
TBP: An active member of the Lesbian Organization of Toronto

Trevor Mountford–Smith
WM: Engineer, Ontario Hydro
TBP: Member of the Gay Alliance Toward Equality; secretary of the Committee to Defend John Damien

John Alan Lee
WM: Author and sociologist, University of Toronto
TBP: Head of the Toronto Gay Academic Union

Michael Lynch
WM: Assistant professor, University of Toronto
TBP: Regular contributor to, and former collective member of *The Body Politic,* presently chairperson of the Committee to Defend John Damien

Bill Lewis
WM: Microbiologist, University of Toronto
TBP: Early member of Gays for Equality in Winnipeg, currently part of the news staff for *The Body Politic*

Edgar Z. Friedenberg
WM: Author and professor, Dalhousie University, Halifax
TBP: Writer on the sociology of adolescence

Jim Quixley
WM: Librarian, York University
TBP: Active in the Gay Academic Union; an early volunteer with the Canadian Gay Archives

David Gibson
WM: Graphic artist and civil servant, Toronto
TBP: Past secretary of the Committee to Defend John Damien; news editor and collective member of *The Body Politic*

David Garmaise
WM: Division manager, Canada Post, Ottawa
TBP: Active in Gays of Ottawa; former co-ordinator of the National Gay Rights Coalition; *The Body Politic*'s Ottawa news correspondent

Clarence Barnes
WM: Chemical engineer, University of Toronto
TBP: Member of the Gay Academic Union and an occasional news writer for *The Body Politic*

SEATED:

Ron Shearer
WM: Businessman, Toronto
TBP: An early and very active member of the Community Homophile Association of Toronto, the city's biggest and most important gay group in the early seventies

Marie Robertson
WM: Federal civil servant, Ottawa
TBP: A former member of Gays of Ottawa, presently active with Lesbians of Ottawa Now

Mark Whitehead
WM: University student, Toronto
TBP: Co-founder and still co-ordinator of Gay Youth Toronto, and a former member of the Committee to Defend John Damien

Ed Jackson
WM: Researcher, Ontario Institute for Studies in Education
TBP: Collective member of *The Body Politic* since 1972, the person who has built the "Our Image" section of the paper. Also one of those charged by the police in the current insanity

Therese Faubert
(with her baby Jody)
WM: Teacher, Toronto
TBP: Active in the Revolutionary Workers' League, a pro-gay leftist group, she was the RWL's candidate in the last provincial election, running directly against the Premier

Konnie Reich
WM: Photo lab technician, Toronto
TBP: Active with the Lesbian Organization of Toronto… and a member of the Gay Offensive Collective—they're putting together a cable TV program called "This Program May Be Offensive to Heterosexuals"

ON THE FLOOR:

Charles Hill
WM: Assistant curator, National Gallery
TBP: Another co-founder of the University of Toronto Homophile Association, and one of the people who helped start Gays of Ottawa

Debbie Parent
WM: Clerk, Bell Canada, Ottawa
TBP: A member of Lesbians of Ottawa Now

Christine Bearchell
WM: Office worker, Toronto
TBP: Dyke dynamo, busy day and night as a member of the Lesbian Organization of Toronto, the Gay Alliance Toward Equality, the Gay Offensive Collective, and, most lately, *The Body Politic* Free the Press Fund. She usually writes the "Dykes" column in *The Body Politic*

Stuart Russell
WM: Typesetter, Montreal
TBP: Very active with the Association pour les droits des gai(e)s du Quebec, and *The Body Politic*'s very diligent Montreal correspondent

THE COMING OUT SHOW

First aired on Vancouver Co-op Radio in September 1978, *The Coming Out Show* was established by a collective of twenty-two individuals from Vancouver's gay and lesbian community to establish a forum to share relevant news and culture, discuss issues of concern, provide an alternative space to bars and clubs, build community, and provide an alternative to the "straight" media outlets.

The Coming Out Show was mostly talk radio, with hosts announcing events, meetings, and services relevant to the gay and lesbian community, as well as conducting interviews (for example, with the public about attitudes toward the gay and lesbian community) and discussions about gay and lesbian issues. The show also featured short stories by gay and lesbian authors and live recording sessions with local gay and lesbian performers.

The Lesbian Show was hosted on the same radio station. This program included a weekly feature (such as family relationships, love, or breakups), announcements, news, interviews, reviews, music, a Lesbian Herstory spot, and readings of lesbian literature. Both *The Coming Out Show* and *The Lesbian Show* worked to engender a sense of community through radio broadcasting in Vancouver, providing a model for the future establishment of gay and lesbian media across Canada.

●●●●●●●●**GAY COMMUNITY CALENDAR**●●●●●●●●

Sunday	Monday	Tuesday	Wednesday	Thursday	Friday	Saturday
	1 ★ Annual Unity Wk. Picnic-ADV.tick. @ all clubs, $10. ★Gayblevision airs 10 p.m.,Cable 10	2 ★Talent Night @ Faces	3 ★Volleyball @ Nelson Pk. ★Gay t.v. meets @ WECC, 7:30 p.m. Live rock'n'roll @ B.J.'s	4 ★SPAG meets @Shaggy ★'Coming Out' 2nd Anniversary Show ★DIGNITY mass, 7:30 ★Rock 'n Roll @ BJ's	5 ★Volleyball @ Kg. George, 6:30-9:30 p.m. ★Labour Day Special @ BJ's.	6 ★Survival Benefit for KINESIS with guests Ad Hoc.Tickets/info thru Ariel & Women's bookstores.
7 ★Lesbian Mothers @ Wmn's Bookstore ★Women & Sobriety meets @People Place at 8 p.m. ★L.I.L. open phone lines - 734-1016, 7-10 p.m.	8 ★Lesbians over 40 @ Women's Bookstore ★Live entertainment @ FACES	9 ★Talent Nite @ FACES	10 ★Volleyball @ Nelson Park ★Gay TV meeting @ WECC, 7:30 p.m. ★Mixed Night @QUADRA	11 ★'Coming Out' : "Gay Community" ★Lesbian Show follows @ 7p.m. ★Gay Al-Anon @ 1811 W.16th,@ 8p.m. ★L.I.L. phoneline.	12 ★Volleyball @ Kg. George ★Stage show @ BJ's	13 ★Gay AA meets @ YMCA ★Stage show @ BJ's
14 ★L.I.L. open phoneline. ★Bowling @ Commodore Lanes, 1 p.m. ★Women & sobriety @ People Place. ★Lesbian Mothers @ Wmn's Bookstore.	15 ★Lesbians over 40 @ Wmn's Bokkstore. ★Live entertainment @ FACES	16 ★Talent Nite @ FACES	17 ★Volleyball @ Nelson Pk ★Gay TV meets @WECC ★Lesbian drop-in @ Wmn's Bookstore. ★Mixed night @ QUADRA	18 ★'Coming Out' : "Gays in the Movies" ★SPAG meets @ SHAGGY ★Lesbians Under 21, @1501 W.Broadway, 7:30-10p.m. ★Gay Al-Anon	19 ★Volleyball @ Kg. George	20 ★Gay AA meets @ YMCA ★Stage show @ BJ's ★ROCKY HORROR 12:30 a.m.@ the Ridge
21 ★Bowling @1 p.m. Commodore Lanes ★Women & Sobriety @ People Place ★L.I.L. open phoneline	22 ★Live entertainment @ FACES	23 ★Talent Nite @ FACES	24 ★Lesbian drop-in, Wmn's Bookstore ★Volleyball @ Nelson Park ★Gay TV meets @WECC ★Mixed night @ QUADRA	25 ★Gay Al-Anon ★'Coming Out' radio: "Sex Roles for Gay People", 6:30 ★Lebian Show follows ★DIGNITY mass,7:30	26 ★Volleyball @ Kg. George, 6:30 p.m. ★Stage show @ BJ's	27 ★Gay AA meets,YMCA ★Stage show @ BJ's
28 ★Lesbian Mothers ★Bowling @ Commodore, 1 p.m. ★Women & Sobriety, People Place. ★L.I.L. open phone-lines, 7-10p.m.	29 ★Lesbians over 40 drop-in ★Live entertainment @ FACES	30 ★Talent Nite @ FACES				

september '80

1

1   *The Coming Out Show* and *The Lesbian Show* Thursday listings in the Gay Community Calendar, *Vancouver Gay Community Centre*, Vol. 1, No. 8, 1980.

2   *The Coming Out Show* personnel, 1979.

The COMING OUT RADIO SHOW - 1979
DAEL KEGGLER, DOVID, DAVID MYERS, WENDY VON STATT
LYNDA FRENCHIE, JACKIE GOODWIN, RICHARD SUMMERBELL
BILL HOUGHTON, AND GREG CUTTS

2

THE FOUNDATION FOR THE ADVANCEMENT OF CANADIAN TRANSSEXUALS

Rupert Raj (under his former name, Nicholas Christopher Ghosh) formed the Foundation for the Advancement of Canadian Transsexuals (FACT) in Calgary in January 1978. Raj served as the group's president, Kyle J. Spooner as vice president, and Christopher E. Black as secretary and treasurer. Created by and for trans people, FACT provided resources on gender dysphoria and on potential surgery and medical practitioners, and organized around increasing trans people's access to health care—including access to insured sex-reassignment (now gender-confirming) surgery. Raj, through FACT, also contacted federal politicians in Ontario and British Columbia, asking for an amendment to the Canadian Human Rights Act to include "gender identity" in order to protect trans people from discrimination. In 1978, FACT began publishing *Gender Review: The FACTual Journal*, a bi-monthly newsletter that compiled these resources and documented FACT's work. *Gender Review* was the first national trans newsletter in Canada. In 1982, Raj began focusing on the specific needs of trans men at a time when very few advocacy groups for transsexual men existed, forming Metamorphosis: Counselling and Educational Services (which was incorporated in 1982 as the Metamorphosis Medical Research Foundation). Susan Huxford-Westall, who lived in Hamilton, Ontario, took over FACT and the editorship of *Gender Review* from 1981 to 1985. She reorganized FACT as a bi-national organization, renaming it the Federation of American and Canadian Transsexuals. FACT Toronto, one of the many chapters of FACT (in Ontario, Quebec, Manitoba, and western New York state), ran from 1979 to 1986, and published its own newsletter. It was succeeded in 1986 by Transition Toronto (renamed Transition Support), which is still active today (one of the longest-running trans groups in Canada). In the 2014 publication *Trans Activism in Canada: A Reader*, Nick Matte described Raj's impact:

> Ever since transitioning in the early 1970s, Rupert Raj has devoted his life to developing transsexual communities, promoting transsexuals' interests, and making trans people more socially acceptable. Raj has lived and worked in Ottawa, Calgary, Vancouver, and Toronto… He has made a lasting impact on Canadian and international trans organizing, working with activists and interested groups around the world. ("Rupert Raj and the Rise of Transsexual Consumer Activism in the 1980s," 33)

```
*research    *education
*information*law reform
*counselling*referrals
```
FOUNDATION FOR THE ADVANCEMENT
OF CANADIAN TRANSSEXUALS. F.A.C.T.

```
P.O. BOX 1238, STN. M      *newsletter
CALGARY, ALBERTA  T2P 2L2  *TS GUIDE
```

1

1   FACT business card, c. 1970s.

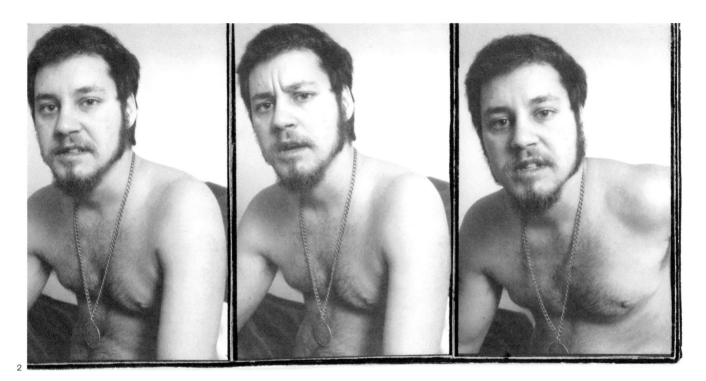

2　Nicholas Christopher
Ghosh (Rupert Raj), Vancouver,
1975. Photograph by James Loewen.

3　Nicholas Christopher Ghosh
(Rupert Raj), Calgary, 1977.

4　Portrait of Rupert Raj, 2015.
Photograph by Nigel Dickson.

DEMONSTRATIONS AGAINST ANITA BRYANT

Anita Bryant—the conservative American former beauty queen, Christian singer, Florida orange juice spokesperson, and vocal opponent of gay rights—began a cross-Canada tour to promote her evangelical anti-gay views in 1978. Her Save Our Children campaign was widely denounced by gay liberation activists who organized a boycott of the orange juice that she advertised.

Sponsored by the Canadian evangelical organization Renaissance International, Bryant's Canadian tour commenced in Toronto, where gay and lesbian activists worked to provide an alternative message to her vitriol. Activists in Edmonton, Winnipeg, and Moose Jaw organized political coalitions and demonstrations in response to Bryant, including picketing her concerts and condemning her message. In Winnipeg, the demonstration against Bryant was attended by over 350 people; in Edmonton attendees numbered over 300; and the Moose Jaw demonstration was the largest of all, inclusive of allies from progressive churches and labour movements, academics, feminists, and gay and lesbian rights activists. Activists from Calgary attended demonstrations in Edmonton, while Saskatoon and Regina activists travelled to Moose Jaw to protest Bryant. These coalitions exemplified successful cross-regional organizing within the gay liberation movement of the 1970s.

1   Protest against Anita Bryant, Toronto, c. 1970s.

2   Members of Women Against Violence Against Women (WAVAW) protesting Anita Bryant, Toronto, 1978.

3   Protest against Anita Bryant, Winnipeg, 1978.

3

BUDDIES IN
BAD TIMES

A nomadic theatre and performance company with no permanent home until 1991, Buddies in Bad Times achieved major success as a queer theatre in the 1980s, though its original intention was to bring poetry adaptations to the stage. Sky Gilbert, the now-retired director of Buddies in the 1980s, helped transform the theatre's mandate into a uniquely queer one. Over the last few decades, Buddies has produced plays that engage the queer senses and bring campy, sex-positive, irreverent, and political work to Toronto's arts and culture scene. Such work was encouraged by Gilbert, who, in addition to being a prolific playwright, is also a published author and poet. Some of his early works include *Lana Turner Has Collapsed!* (1980), *The Dressing Gown: a faery tale for adults only* (1984), and *Drag Queens in Outer Space: a dreamplay* (1990). Gilbert credits Dr. Johnny Golding, who became president of Buddies in 1985, as the person who developed queer Buddies as it currently exists.

The queerness exhibited by Buddies has drawn the ire of certain segments of the Toronto public. In 1994, for example, the *Toronto Sun*'s Christina Blizzard campaigned to restrict public funding of Buddies; in one of her most memorable articles, published shortly after Buddies opened its location on Alexander Street, Blizzard argues that the work coming out of Buddies "is not art. This is a cry for help from a sad and twisted soul." In the same article she writes, "I suspect Mr. Gilbert wants me to smack him and tell him he's a naughty boy." Buddies, a world leader in telling queer stories onstage, has produced over a thousand new works and welcomed over a million audience members. In 1994, Buddies moved to its current location on Alexander Street—in the midst of Toronto's Gay Village—taking over and renovating a theatre previously run by the politically left-oriented theatre company Toronto Workshop Productions.

1 Poster for *Queer Culture* performance by Buddies in Bad Times, 1990.

GAY ASIANS
OF TORONTO

Inspired by the 1979 National March on Washington for Lesbian and Gay Rights and by Gerald Chan's *Asianadian* magazine article "Out of the Shadows," in 1980 Richard Fung, along with Chan, Tony Souza, and Nitto Marquez, held the first meeting of what became known as Gay Asians of Toronto (GAT). According to Alan Li in "Power in Community: Queer Asian Activism from the 1980s to the 2000s," GAT's CelebrAsian in 1983 was likely "the first fundraiser for HIV/AIDS, before the AIDS Committee of Toronto was even formed. It was at that very beginning, when HIV wasn't even identified yet. People were just dying mysteriously of a gay plague" (50). In 1982, the GAT led the Toronto Pride Parade through Toronto's Chinatown (after Pride was redeveloped following the 1981 bathhouse raids), where Li delivered a speech on racial solidarity against state homophobia.

"The history of gay Asian organizing in Toronto shows that being a real visible organization in the community is critically important… I think claiming that space has been important. We didn't do that as a political gesture; we did it because we needed to, to survive." **Alan Li, "Power in Community: Queer Asian Activism from the 1980s to the 2000s," 2018** (60)

1   Poster for CelebrAsian event hosted by Gay Asians of Toronto, 1984.

2   Members of Gay Asians of Toronto, C. 1980S. Photograph by Norm Taylor.

RIGHT TO
PRIVACY COMMITTEE

On December 9, 1978, police raided The Barracks, a bathhouse in downtown Toronto. That night, twenty-three men were arrested and charged with being "found-ins in a common bawdy house." Rick Bébout recalls:

> At 1:38 AM, December 9, 1978, the police had raided The Barracks baths. With hammers and crowbars, twenty cops smashed into rooms, tore open lockers. Using only "necessary force" (as a PR flack later put it), they even kicked holes in the walls. They carted off twenty-three men, charged as "found-ins in a common bawdy house," three others, one of them George Hislop, as its "keepers." Two more were charged as keepers four days later. In a gesture not unfamiliar, the police also took The Barracks' membership list, putting some eight hundred other lives at potential risk. (rbebout.com)

After the police raids of The Barracks, a support group called the December 9th Defence Fund was established by a collective of gay men to support the men who were arrested in the raid with legal and financial assistance. Executive members included Tom Warner from the Coalition for Gay Rights in Ontario (CGRO), Brent Hawkes from the Metropolitan Community Church (page 128), and Brian Mossop from GATE Toronto. A few months later, the Fund was renamed the Right to Privacy Committee (RTPC). The organization raised funds through events, dances, and direct-mail campaigns—historian Tom Hooper notes that by May 1982, the committee had "raised almost $90,000, of which over $63,000 had been disbursed to pay legal fees, mostly for found-ins" (247). Chris Bearchell recalls:

This was unprecedented in our own community in terms of mounting this kind of defence, and there was a lot of trepidation about whether or not people would in fact rally to support the people who had been charged. So the name and the approach were chosen to maximize the possibility of actually getting support within our own community, let alone the community beyond that. (Interview with Miriam Smith, 1996)

In addition to providing legal support to found-ins arrested during the bathhouse raids, the RTPC's objectives were to reform police treatment of the gay community and to interrogate the police budget (since the RTPC understood the raid on The Barracks as a move to justify the police budgets, particularly that of the Morality Department of the Metropolitan Toronto Police). At a meeting with the Metropolitan Toronto Board of Commissioners of Police, they

1

presented a brief titled "Our Police Force Too!" that outlined ten demands for police reform, including a demand for a police liaison with the gay community. Although the Police Commission refused to concede to the RTPC's demands, the group continued to advocate for police reform. They made various submissions to government over the years and, in 1981, they established the Toronto Gay Street Patrol: a group of gays and lesbians who would patrol the streets in an attempt to protect the community from gay bashing and other homophobic violence. In 1982, the RTPC founded Gay Court Watch, a community group that would oversee gay-related trials, particularly court cases related to the bathhouse raids and the criminalization of "found-ins" and keeping a bawdy house. Hooper writes that

> countless volunteer hours spent in the courtrooms of Old City Hall and in Scarborough meant that the Legal Coordinating Committee [of the RTPC] had become familiar with the inner-workings of the legal system. This meant they became quasi-experts, but it also meant that they saw firsthand just how many indecency charges were being brought against members of the gay community… [Gay Court Watch] sought to bring the strategies used to resist the bawdy house law to cases involving the indecent act, and gross indecency sections of the criminal code. (248)

Gay Court Watch continued for nearly a decade, until the end of 1991.

2

3

1   Right to Privacy Committee (RTPC) graphic showing solidarity with the 286 men charged as found-ins during the 1981 Operation Soap raids in Toronto, c. 1980s.

2   Poster for The Barracks following police raid, 1978.

3   Locker pass for The Barracks, c. 1970s.

ORGANIZING ON CAMPUS

Much of contemporary campus organizing in Canada has its roots in the on-campus gay and lesbian organizations that started in the 1970s. The first Canadian course in Gay and Lesbian Studies, New Perspectives on the Gay Experience, was taught in 1974 at University of Toronto by Michael Lynch, and student groups sprang up all over campuses in Canada as universities began to grapple with gay and lesbian politics.

Valerie Korinek makes clear how vital campus-based organizing was to the gay and lesbian liberation movement in her book *Prairie Fairies: A History of Queer Communities and People in Western Canada, 1930–1985,* noting that "[o]ne of the most important ways that universities served to stimulate queer spaces and activism was by virtue of the fact that they attract faculty, students, and, less frequently, staff from all over, not just the urban communities in which they are based" (178). The physical distance between the university and students' hometowns, Korinek argues, often meant that individuals from away were more overt in their participation in gay politics than those who were attending university in their hometown. One primary function of campus organizations was simply to provide social support and safe meeting spaces for gay and lesbian students, faculty, and community members. The role of on-campus organizations was complex: on the one hand, student movements were effective in creating social change when mobilized; on the other hand, as Liz Millward argues in *Making a Scene: Lesbians and Community across Canada, 1964–1984,* campus-based organizations were sometimes required to de-radicalize feminist, labour, and gay politics in order to make these politics more palatable to the university itself.

1

1　Logo for Gays and Lesbians of the University of British Columbia, c. 1980s.

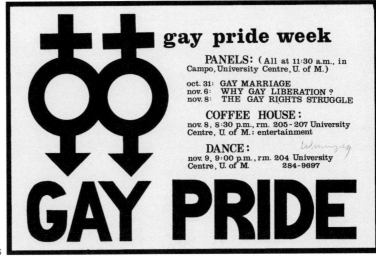

2   Poster for Gay Dance hosted
by Gay McGill, McGill University,
1979.

3   Poster for Gay Pride Week at
the University of Manitoba, c. 1970s.

4   Poster for Gays for Equality
phone line in Winnipeg, c. 1970s.

A STATE OF
OPPRESSION

While the 1970s saw unparalleled gay and lesbian liberation political formation in Canada, it also saw sustained and organized pushback from the state and its agents. Activists in Vancouver reported of local police seizing posters and various materials that gay and lesbian groups distributed around the city. Ottawa police raided Club Baths in August 1976; police in Toronto raided The Barracks in December 1978 (see also "Right to Privacy Committee," page 152). Prior to the 1976 Olympics, Montreal police coordinated "clean-up" efforts throughout the city, attempting to erase evidence of gay and lesbian communities and politics—including the infamous raids on the bars Truxx and Le Mystique, during which police arrested 146 individuals. *Gay Times*—a periodical created by members of Gay Montreal in an effort to publicize police actions against gays and lesbians in the city—reported on near-constant raids of gay spaces in 1975 and 1976: Sauna Aquarius, Le Rocambole, Le Taureau d'or, Bud's, and the popular lesbian bar Baby Face were all raided by police.

"The plan's objective is to frighten people away from places of public entertainment and to make the gay population temporarily invisible." *Gay Times*, vol. 1, no. 1, 1975

These are just a few examples of what became an ongoing and repetitive process: throughout this decade we see violence perpetrated by (and on behalf of) the state and, subsequently, more dedicated gay and lesbian organizing in its wake. The more aggressive political organizing is regularly met with increased hostility by local police forces, which often results in more politicized gays and lesbians taking part in organized movements. Catherine Nash writes that the 1978 Barracks raid, for example, marked a "decisive moment in the relationship between gay businessmen and gay activists" and the way these individuals understood the role of the "emerging 'gay ghetto'" (83). And following the raid on Truxx and Le Mystique in Montreal, more than two thousand protestors took to the streets. Especially moving and meaningful about this particular collective response is how queer activists built on the community's rage and energy to make permanent, tangible changes to the law that governs citizens in Quebec: following aggressive lobbying by activists, the Quebec National Assembly added sexual orientation to the grounds protected under the province's human rights charter. Quebec was the first province in Canada to offer such protection.

More and more members of gay and lesbian movements were identifying the connection between anti-gay violence and the forms of violence that other minoritarian communities face. A May 1980 speech by George Hislop captures this developing sentiment and shows the way some activists of the moment were articulating vulnerability shared among oppressed groups.

1   George Hislop speech cards, rally against racism and bigotry in Brampton, Ontario, 1980.

WE ARE HERE TODAY IN THE PROVINCIAL RIDING OF
BRAMPTON TO DELIVER A MESSAGE. TO THE RIDING WHICH
ELECTS WILLIAM DAVIS TO THE ONTARIO LEGISLATURE
WE COME TO LAY AT THE PREMIER"S DOORSTEP THE MESSAGE
THAT WE HOLD HIM RESPONSIBLE FOR HIS GOVERNMENT'S
FAILURE TO ASSIST US IN CURBING RACISM AND BIGOTRY
IN ONTARIO. WE ARE HERE TO LET OUR FELLOW ONTARIO
CITIZENS KNOW THAT WE ARE FRUSTRATED AND ANNOYED
BY THE CYNICAL NEGLECT OF HUMAN RIGHTS WHICH ONTARIO

2

HAS EXPERIENCED UNDER THE GOVERNMENT OF WILLIAM
DAVIS. WHEN A MEMBER OF MR. DAVIS' CAUCUS CAN
MAKE DEREGATORY COMMENTS IN PUBLIC ABOUT NATIVE
PEOPLE AND ITALIAN-CANADIANS AND STILL STAY IN THAT
CAUCUS, IT SHOULD NOT SURPRISE US THAT THE METRO
TORONTO POLICE COMMISSION SEES NO NEED TO DISASSOCIATE
THEMSELVES FROM THE ANTI-BLACK, ANTI-GAY REMARKS OF
MR. DAVIS' APPOINTEE ON THE POLICE COMMISSION, WIN
McKAY. IT IS ALL PART OF THE PATTERN OF THE DAVIS

3

GOVERNMENT"S NEGLECT OF HUMAN RIGHTS. I REMEMBER
WHEN ONTARIO SHOWED LEADERSHIP WITH ITS ONTARIO
HUMAN RIGHTS CODE, IN THE SIXTIES AND EARLY SEVENTIES.
I EVEN REMEMBER, AS LATE AS 1977 WHEN THAT HUMAN
RIGHTS COMMISSION RECOMMENDED THE STRENGTHENING OF
THE CODE AND ITS EXPANSION TO INCLUDE GAY MEN AND
LESBIANS AND THE RECOMMENDATION THAT THE CODE BE GIVEN
PRIMACY, THAT IT TAKE PRECENDENCE OVER ALL OTHER
ONTARIO LEGISLATION. I GUESS THAT WAS ALL TOO MUCH
FOR MR. DAVIS__; NOT ONLY HAS NOT A SINGLE RECOMMEND_
ATION BEEN ENACTED BUT MR. DAVIS AND HIS GOVERNMENT

HAVE ACTUALLY WEAKENED THE ☒☒☒☒ HUMAN RIGHTS ☒☒☒☒☒☒☒
COMMISSION BY GRADUALLY RETIRING ALL THE STRONG
COMMISSIONERS AND REPLACING THEM WITH WEAK SILENT
TYPES. IT WAS MR. DAVIS HIMSELF WHO APPOINTED HIS
OLD FRIEND, THE SILENT BUREAUCRAT,TO HEAD THE
ONTARIO HUMAN RIGHTS COMMISSION. HUMAN RIGHTS IN
ONTARIO HAVE BEEN ON A DOWNHILL SLIDE EVER SINCE.
WITH A RECORD LIKE THAT IT SHOULD NOT SURPRISE US
THAT MR. DAVIS' FRONT MAN MR. McMURTRY WOULD REFUSE
TO LAY MURDER CHARGES AGAINST THE POLICE OFFICERS

5

WHO SHOT ALBERT JOHNSON. APPARENTLY MR. DAVIS AND
HIS GOVERNMENT ARE QUITE PREPARED TO LET EVERYONE
ELSE TAKE THEIR CHANCES IN THE COURTS: SIMPLE JUSTICE
THEY CALL IT. BUT THEY DON'T WANT TO LET SIMPLE
JUSTICE TAKE ITS COURSE WHEN THE VICTIM IS A BLACK
MAN AND THE ASSAILANTS ARE POLICE OFFICERS. NO THEY
                                    WHY ISN'T
WANT TO STACK THE DECK IN ADVANCE./ SIMPLE JUSTICE
ISN☒T GOOD ENOUGH FOR POLICE OFFICERS ? PERHAPS ITS
FOR THE SAME REASONS THAT MR. DAVIS' GOVERNMENT
JUST PRESENTED A SO-CALLED CIVILIAN REVIEW BILL

6

WHICH IS BASED ON THE PRINCIPLE THAT POLICE OFFICERS
ARE SUPPOSED TO INVESTIGATE THEMSELVES. THAT'S
REALLY SIMPLE JUSTICE: SO SIMPLE THAT IT SEEMS ONLY
THE POLICE AND MR. DAVIS' GOVERNMENT SUPPORT THE
PRINCIPLE. NOT A SINGLE MINORITY GROUP THAT I'M
AWARE OF SUPPORTS THAT KIND OF SIMPLE JUSTICE. THANKS
TO THE LIBERAL AND NDP MEMBERS OF THE OPPOSITION
ONTARIO ISN"T GOING TO GET THAT KIND OF SIMPLE
JUSTICE. FINALLY LET ME SAY THAT WHEN BLACK PEOPLE
ARE CALLED NIGGER AND WHEN A BLACK MAN GETS SHOT AND

KILLED: OR WHEN SIKH"S AND OTHERS ARE CALLED
PAKI AND WHEN ☒☒☒☒ FAMILIES LIKE THE DINS ARE
ASSAULTED : OR WHEN THOUSANDS GATHER ON YONGE STREET
TO YELL FAGGOT ON HALLOWEEN OR WHEN QUEER BASHERS
BEAT UPON SOME GAY MAN OR LESBIAN WOMAN --- IT IS ALL
PART OF THE SAME ILLNESS IN OUR SOCIETY: AN ILLNESS
WHICH WE DEMAND THAT WE SHOULD HAVE A GOVERNMENT
WILLING TO ACT , WILLING TO SEEK A CURE.

FEBRUARY 5,
1981, RAIDS

Shortly after 11 PM on Thursday, February 5, 1981, hundreds of Toronto Police Service officers—organized by the Morality Department of the Metropolitan Toronto Police—stormed four gay bathhouses in downtown Toronto: The Barracks (at 56 Widmer Street), The Club (at 231 Mutual Street), Richmond Street Health Emporium (at 260 Richmond Street East), and the Romans II Health and Recreation Spa (at 740 Bay Street). The police manoeuvre was dubbed Operation Soap. Three hundred men were arrested—twenty employees for "keeping common bawdy houses" and the rest for "being found in at a bawdy house." The bathhouse raids resulted in the largest mass arrest in Canadian history up to that time, save for the October Crisis of 1970.

This was no routine operation. The numbers involved, the savage, vengeful treatment of those arrested, the unwarranted and systematic destruction of property by the police, all indicate that these raids were planned as a direct attack on Toronto's gay community. ("In Unity There Is Strength," editorial in *ACTION! This Is the RTPC: A Special Publication of the Right to Privacy Committee*, n.d.)

The mass arrests are striking in their sheer number and because the legislation they relied on is so archaic, conceived of and incorporated into the Criminal Code of Canada in 1892. While this section of the Criminal Code originally defined a bawdy-house as a place "kept for the purposes of prostitution," it was expanded in 1917 to refer to a place "kept for purposes of prostitution *or for the practice of acts of indecency*." This addition, which the police used to justify the raids of February 5, 1981, rests on the implication that sex between consenting adult men is only ever indecent—an interpretation also used to enter private homes and detain adult men having consensual sex in their bedrooms. (This was more than a decade after the ostensible "decriminalization" of homosexuality in Canada—a useful reminder that sustained and ongoing pressure from activists is regularly required to cause change.)

"What's wrong faggot—lost for words?"

Police officer to detained man at The Barracks, quoted in White and Sheppard, *Report of Police Raids on Gay Steambaths*, **1981**

(THIS COPY FOR ACCUSED)

APPEARANCE NOTICE ISSUED BY A PEACE OFFICER

To a person not yet charged with an offence

FORM 8.1

(SECS. 451 & 452.)

CANADA
PROVINCE OF ONTARIO }

~~HENRY DUNCAN McLAREN~~
~~121 SPRUCE ST~~
~~TORONTO ONTARIO~~

are alleged to have committed (*set out substance of offence*):

~~FOUND IN A COMMON BAWDY HOUSE~~

~~CONTRARY TO THE CRIMINAL CODE~~

you are required to attend court on ~~FRI~~day, the ~~20TH~~ day of ~~FEBRUARY~~ 19 ~~81~~, at ~~2:00~~ o'clock in the ~~AFTER~~noon,

the Provincial Courtroom ~~21 @ Old City Hall~~ at ~~60 Queen St W~~

and to attend thereafter as required by the court, in order to be dealt with according to law.

you are also required to appear on................day, the................day of ....19......, at................o'clock in the................noon,

....
(police station)   (address)

for the purposes of the *Identification of Criminals Act.* (ignore if not filled in).

You are warned that failure to attend court in accordance with this appearance notice is an offence under subsection 133(5) of the *Criminal Code.*

Subsections 133(5) and (6) of the *Criminal Code* state as follows:

"(5) Every one who is named in an appearance notice or promise to appear, or in a recognizance entered into before an officer in charge, that has been confirmed by a justice under section 455.4 and who fails, without lawful excuse, the proof of which lies upon him, to appear at a time and place stated therein, if any, for the purposes of the *Identification of Criminals Act*, or to attend court in accordance therewith, is guilty of

a) an indictable offence and is liable to imprisonment for two years, or
b) an offence punishable on summary conviction.

6) For the purposes of subsection (5), it is not a lawful excuse that an appearance notice, promise to appear or recognizance states defectively the substance of the alleged offence".

Section 453.4 of the *Criminal Code* states as follows:

"453.4 Where an accused who is required by an appearance notice or promise to appear or by a recognizance entered into before an officer in charge to appear at a time and place stated therein for the purposes of the *Identification of Criminals Act* does not appear at that time and place, a justice may, where the appearance notice, promise to appear or recognizance as been confirmed by a justice under section 455.4, issue a warrant for the arrest of the accused for the offence with which he is charged".

Signature of accused ..~~H.D. McLaren~~..

Issued at ....~~12:30~~....m. this ....~~FRI~~....day } .... ~~1981~~......at } (*Signature of Peace Officer*)

.... (No.)   (Div. or Det.)

1

2

3

1 Court appearance notice for Henry Duncan McLaren for being "found in a common bawdy house" during the bathhouse raids, 1981.

2 Photograph of Metropolitan Toronto Police at The Club, February 5, 1981. Photograph by Gerald Hannon.

3 Photograph of Metropolitan Toronto Police at The Club, February 5, 1981. Photograph by Gerald Hannon.

Pornography and Erotica

Erotica and pornographic materials—particularly those that depict gay and lesbian sex acts—were censored and confiscated by agents of the state under Canadian obscenity laws during the twentieth century. But such materials provide important insights about the history of gay and lesbian lives in Canada, including how non-normative desires have been represented, produced, distributed, and taken up. The ArQuives collects both analogue and digital formats of moving images, including 8 mm and 16 mm films, filmstrips, VHS, DVDs, and digital media with particular emphasis on collecting films and video recordings that are historically significant, document the evolution of the genre, and chronicle a unique or specialized sexual expression not commonly available through commercial or popular media distribution. The act of archiving pornography is somewhat unique to community archives— especially LGBTQ2+ collections—as such materials are typically not retained and cared for by governmental archives. The documentation of gay and lesbian pornography in particular is critical for understanding the history of gay and lesbian visual cultures, providing evidence and recognition of the divergent manifestations of queer sexualities and desires over time and chronicling the history of public health crises (for example, the emphasis on condom usage and safer sex techniques by gay men in the wake of HIV/AIDS).

T-120 **2** 94-032/19
INCH BY INCH // LIKE A HORSE . **SHA** 120 0186 16AA

~~GAY PORN~~ P F
BROTHER HUSTLERS
1999-027/09F video cassette

AGHC419 ⌖ T-120 **VHS** ~~Caroline~~ BIG MEAT **1** **04** **T-120** **SUPER AVILYN VIDEO CASSETTE** ⌖ **TDK**
P F 1999-027/06F

FUJI **T-120** **1** 94-032/18
BIGGER THE BETTER/STICKY BUSINESS/SIZING UP/ **SHA** 120 0186 16AA
A MATTER OF SIZE .

L461M
T-90 89-143 BEST OF CONTROL
(-08) STUDIO - VOLUME 3
(SPANKING)

BASF T-130 EE **VHS** Extra Quality **T130** gay porno HEARTBEAT 404 No. **BASF**
1999-027/11F P F

T-120 XAX 21 **SX** gay porno RITES of WINTER **JVC** The Inventor of VHS
1999-027/10F P F

T-120S 94-032 BIG GUNS
06 SKI FEVER
91134 NIGHT FLIGHT
STRYKER FORCE

94-053/018 FALCON #65 **SHA**
DEEP IN HOT WATER

1981–1999
NO MORE SHIT!

1

The February 5, 1981, police action on Toronto bathhouses was certainly not the first or last raid of this type in Canada, but it stands out as significant for the sheer number of police officers involved (more than 150), the number of men arrested (more than 300), the degree of violence with which individuals were arrested and detained, and the response in its wake from both right-wing and queer activists. As Tim McCaskell notes in *Queer Progress: From Homophobia to Homonationalism,* the police action in Toronto seemed to inform subsequent raids in other Canadian cities. Edmonton police, for example, learned from the experiences of the Toronto police to improve the efficacy of the arrests when they raided Pisces Spa on May 30, 1981, after a lengthy investigation by the force's Morality Department. As questions about the proper identification of the men charged as being found in a common bawdy house plagued the Toronto raids, McCaskell writes, police in Edmonton "came armed with lights and video cameras. Men were captured on tape and told to remain where they were, until they were photographed with a paper indicating name, age, and occupation. Most were photographed twice, once naked and once clothed. There would be no difficulties in identification here" (148). Over fifty men were arrested as "found-ins" that night

in Edmonton, with the majority forced to plead guilty.

Violence against gays and lesbians in Canada increased in the months following the bathhouse raids. John Burt, a member of the Right to Privacy Committee (page 152) and an individual charged as a found-in during the February 5, 1981, raids, tells *Action!* in April 1981 that "[s]ince February 20... attacks are being reported at least once a day. Nothing like this frequency occurred prior to February 20. And we are sure that many more attacks are unreported." This increase in street violence and bashing coincided with the development of far-right political blocs that took particular aim at gays and lesbians. We include some of

the materials from these groups in this chapter to give a sense of the vitriol.

Gay and lesbian collectives were certainly not the only groups that faced attacks from far-right activists—the women's movement (and, in particular, centres focused on abortion and women's reproductive rights) was also a target of both the police and far-right assailants. In June 1983, for example, Henry Morgentaler opened an abortion clinic above the Toronto Women's Bookstore; early the next month, police raided the premises, detained the doctors, and seized the clinic's files. A few weeks later, the building was firebombed. While the clinic sustained little damage, the bookstore was destroyed.

2

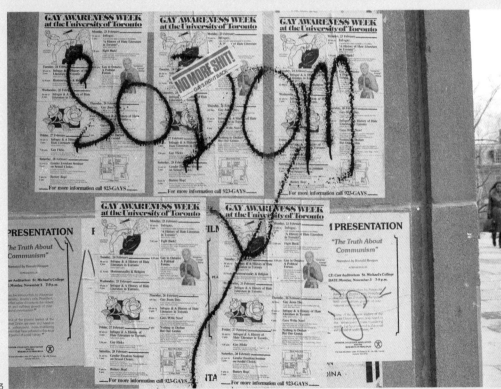

3

1 Demonstrator being arrested,
Toronto, June 20, 1981.

2 Police striking demonstrator,
Toronto, June 20, 1981. Photograph by
Gerald Hannon.

3 "SODOMY" spray-painted over a
series of posters for Gay Awareness
Week at the University of Toronto,
c. 1980s. Photograph by Gerald Hannon.

Light the Fuse (and Carry the Fire)

As homophobic far-right sentiments coupled with violence against gays and lesbians in Canada increased in the months following the bathhouse raids, public response was galvanized. Queer individuals amassed in clever and generative ways. As we show in this section, this response took many forms: political coalitions against state violence (particularly apparent in how anti-gay and anti-Black violence were linked at rallies and literature in the early 1980s), activism directly aimed at the rising far right, and myriad forms of celebrations and community building emerged. For example, the immediate collective response to the bathhouse raids in Toronto was to organize a protest rally the day following the arrests at the intersection of Yonge and Wellesley streets—where activists proclaimed, "Enough Is Enough!" and "No More Shit!"—as well as a demonstration later that month to fight against police harassment of minority communities.

Important debates among North American feminists during the 1980s resonated with gay and lesbian communities in Canada. In particular, the feminist sex wars highlighted political divisions between sex-positive and anti-porn feminists on issues including pornography, sex work, sexuality (including lesbian sexuality, sadomasochism, and BDSM), and gender identity (most notably, the inclusion of trans women in

1

Dykes in the Streets

2

women-only spaces). In 1983, the Government of Canada amended several elements of the Criminal Code to intensify the criminalization of pornography and sex work, expanding the definition of obscenity to include "degrading representations" and criminalizing the solicitation of sex in a car, which made it possible to charge and convict sex-work customers as well as sex workers themselves. The same year, the government established the Fraser Committee to collect information and solicit public input on pornography and prostitution to inform national legislation. The Fraser Report, released in 1985, ultimately advocated for the decriminalization of prostitution and the prohibition of pornographic materials that depicted physical harm or abuse.

The 1980s criminalization of "degrading representations" under obscenity laws in Canada enabled an expansion of censorship beyond pornography to include representations of sex and sexuality more broadly, particularly representations of gay and lesbian sex. The distribution of gay and lesbian visual culture and literature in Canada was also impacted by government censorship practices. While *The Joy of Sex: A Gourmet Guide to Lovemaking* (1972) circulated freely throughout the 1970s and 1980s, *The Joy of Gay Sex: An Intimate Guide for Gay Men to the Pleasures of a Gay Lifestyle* (1977) and *The Joy of Lesbian Sex: A Tender and Liberated Guide to the Pleasures and Problems of a Lesbian Lifestyle* (1977) were banned by Canada Customs. Both the straight and gay male sex manuals included anal sex, but only representations of homosexual anal sex were officially banned, with the depiction of anal sex cited as obscene. Also

targeted with bans were imported American magazines, such as the popular gay and lesbian magazine *The Advocate*. Bookstores that specialized in gay and lesbian materials, such as Little Sister's Book and Art Emporium in Vancouver, were routinely targeted as part of monitoring at the border for content being shipped from outside Canada.

Death and Heartbreak

This era also saw the profound impact of HIV/AIDS on the gay and lesbian community in Canada. Early AIDS organizations, often started by veteran queer activists who had experience and organizing skills, brought activists together with social service–focused support workers who wanted to assist dying friends and with dedicated groups of lesbians and straight allies who created networks of care for people living with HIV/AIDS.

Community response had two dimensions: first organizing and then sustaining HIV/AIDS service organizations that would, eventually, following incredible pressure from activists, receive government funding. Access to funding, Ed Jackson recalls, put these service-oriented organizations in a difficult position when it came to pressuring inactive government bodies. Accordingly, more militant organizations developed; taking no funds from the government, they were freer to criticize the government's inaction. Jackson explains that these more militant groups—for example, AIDS Action Now! (page 192), which was modelled on the New York–based organization ACT UP—learned from polarization they witnessed in New York City HIV/AIDS organizing to actively work with service organizations to avoid acrimony and wasted energy.

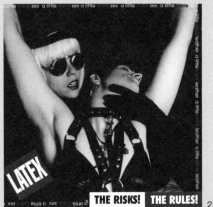

In the early 1980s, the first cases of AIDS (later understood to be caused by HIV) were diagnosed in the U.S. and Canada among gay men. Homophobic sentiment fuelled public discourse about the disease, which was first called gay-related immune deficiency (GRID) and colloquially referred to as the "gay plague" because it was believed to only affect gay men. Gaëtan Dugas, a Quebecois flight attendant widely characterized as sexually insatiable and promiscuous, achieved almost mythic status as "Patient Zero," the ostensible catalyst for the epidemic in the United States. Until very recently, Dugas's sexual behaviours were blamed for the widespread contagion of HIV and instrumentalized by conservative politicians and the religious right to condemn homosexuality. In 2016, scientists, along with historian Richard McKay (author of *Patient Zero and the Making of the AIDS Epidemic*), exonerated Dugas, citing genetic testing on preserved blood samples from the 1970s that proved HIV was present in the U.S. well before Dugas travelled there. The legend of Patient Zero exemplifies the widespread misunderstandings and lack of reliable information in the early years of the AIDS epidemic. The 1996 film *Zero Patience,* directed by Canadian activist, writer, and filmmaker John Greyson, challenges the homophobic narratives that surround both Dugas and the AIDS epidemic itself.

"The concept of Patient Zero dovetailed with a popular desire to displace the source of contagion as far as possible from white, heterosexual America… Gay, francophone, an international traveller, Dugas fit the bill in several respects." Robin Metcalfe, "Light in the Loafers: The Gaynor Photographs of Gaëtan Dugas and the Invention of Patient Zero," 2005 (70)

Misunderstandings about HIV/AIDS gripped Canadian society as much as they did Americans. Cases of Canadians contracting HIV through blood transfusions led to a form of homophobic panic that resulted in the banning of blood donations from gay men. Although all blood donations in Canada have been tested for HIV since 1985, the Canadian Blood Services began screening donors in the 1980s with the use of a questionnaire that included inquiries about sexual behaviour used to exclude sexually active gay men from being eligible to donate blood. The ban had significant political motivations and effects. As OmiSoore H. Dryden writes in " 'A Queer Too Far': Blackness, 'Gay Blood,' and Transgressive Possibilities," "Canadian Blood Services instituted a screening process that included the use of a donor questionnaire… specifically

4

designed to identify and distinguish between bodies that have
blood that gives life and bodies
with blood that brings death" (122).
Following the onslaught of the

---

1   Gaëtan Dugas, c. 1980s. Photograph
by Rand Gaynor.

2   Pamphlet on safer-sex practices
with latex aimed at queer women
audiences by the AIDS Committee of
Toronto, 1993.

3   Handbill, "Canada Needs an AIDS
Strategy," by AIDS Action Now!, c. 1980s.
Designed by Clare Meridew.

4   AIDS candlelight vigil, Toronto,
c. 1990s.

HIV/AIDS epidemic, certain
bodies—including those of gay
men—were framed as deviant and
intrinsic threats to the blood supply of the nation.

In 1997, the Royal Commission
of Inquiry on the Blood System
in Canada (known as the Krever
Inquiry) found that more than
a thousand individuals in Canada had contracted HIV from
blood transfusions. It was only
in 2011 that Canadian Blood
Services began to transform the
discriminatory policy colloquially
referred to as the "blood ban,"
allowing men who had sex with
men to donate blood if they had

not had sexual contact with men
in the preceding five years; this
time-based deferral period has
been gradually reduced to, as
of 2019, three months. Various
activist groups across Canada
have advocated over the years for
eliminating any discriminatory
blood-donation bans.

The first decade of the HIV/
AIDS epidemic was marked by
government inaction. In 1989,
activists protested at the fifth
international AIDS conference
in Montreal, demanding government funding for treatment and
prevention and for a federally
funded AIDS strategy, denouncing

travel bans for people living with HIV, and advocating for greater inclusion of people living with HIV within the framework of the conference. In response to activist pressure, in 1990 the federal government, led by Prime Minister Brian Mulroney, established an HIV/AIDS strategy that included treatment funding. In 1996, at the eleventh international AIDS conference, held in Vancouver, the scientific discovery of highly active antiretroviral therapy (HAART) for people living with HIV was announced, transforming HIV/AIDS from a necessarily fatal to chronic illness.

Leading the Charge

The coalitional politics that characterize early AIDS activism demonstrate the reach of HIV/AIDS throughout Canada. AIDS Vancouver was established in 1983 as the first HIV/AIDS service organization in the country. Concentrating initially on access to and dissemination of information on treatment and prevention, the initiative expanded into community health, focusing on health promotion, education, and support services, as well as community-based research and advocacy. Activists in British Columbia successfully advocated for access to treatment. In 1986, AIDS activists there demonstrated at the provincial legislature in Victoria to demand a viral testing laboratory in Vancouver; the lack of such a

1   LGAY TABLE CONDOM DAY 880213 (SIC)

2   HELP US ACT FIGHT AIDS
AIDS COMMITTEE OF TORONTO

facility had been cited by the government as the reason for denying the release of experimental treatment. In response, the federal and provincial health ministers announced that a lab would be constructed, making it both possible to test for HIV in western Canada and to monitor the efficacy of experimental drugs.

The AIDS Committee of Toronto (ACT) was formed in 1983 in response to the growing panic concerning AIDS, to attempt to dispel inaccurate information concerning the cause of AIDS and create spaces to share resources, information, and support among those affected. The first AIDS awareness week was established in 1984 as a result of ACT's efforts; it was recognized at a national level in 1991. In 1986, the national Canadian AIDS Society (CAS) was created as an umbrella network for HIV/AIDS community organizations across the country.

Founded in Toronto in 1988, AIDS Action Now! (AAN!) generated public pressure on the federal government to prioritize AIDS care and treatment by protesting, advocating for people living with AIDS, and participating in national and international conferences on AIDS. The next year, AAN! began publishing the bilingual *AIDS Update* to inform people living with HIV about prevention, treatment, and care, and in 1990 it established the Treatment Information Exchange (TIE). AAN! and TIE projects were renamed the Canadian AIDS Treatment Information Exchange (CATIE). By 1995, CATIE had assumed a national role in managing the national treatment registry project as a partner with Health Canada in the Canadian AIDS strategy fund.

Other organizations emerged to address the unique needs of various ethno-racial communities; these included Toronto-based

3

BAY ST. 942

NO! to QUARANTINE. SCHABAS

NO QUARANTINE DUMP SCHABAS

5

SUCER C'EST SAFE?

INFO-SIDA 282-9991

4

THE AIDS COMMITTEE OF TORONTO · OCTOBER 1991

ACT*life*

Taking it to the streets!
From All Walks of Life rains and shines

Women & AIDS
Finding our strength in real life

The Safer Sex Generation
YOUNG GAY MEN DO IT THEIR OWN WAY

6

1 Lesbian and Gay Alliance at York University promoting condom use, Toronto, February 13, 1987.

2 Pamphlet, "Help Us Fight AIDS," by the AIDS Committee of Toronto, c. 1980s.

3 AIDS Action Now! speaker, Toronto, c. 1980s.

4 Poster for AIDS information phone line in Montreal, c. 1990s.

5 AIDS Action Now! march, Toronto, c. 1980s.

6 Cover of *ACT Life*, a publication of the AIDS Committee of Toronto, 1991.

Black Coalition for AIDS Prevention (1989), the Canadian Aboriginal AIDS Network (1997), and the South Asian AIDS Coalition (founded in 1989 by queer South Asian activists and known today as the Alliance for South Asian AIDS Prevention). In 1989, Michelle De Ville, who was working at Comité sida aide Montréal at the time, formed an HIV/AIDS organization specifically geared toward trans people in Montreal.

The collective response to the HIV/AIDS epidemic did not just result in services provided and on-the-ground activism. Many Canadian-based artists—Richard Fung, John Greyson, and General Idea (A.A. Bronson, Felix Partz, and Jorge Zontal), among others—produced work that brought attention to HIV/AIDS and its effects and that intervened in the discourse surrounding the virus. Networks of care also emerged in the wake of the epidemic, formed among people living with HIV as well as with their friends, lovers, and family members. HIV/AIDS instigated new conversations about the possible constitutions of families, where the labour of care formulated new understandings of families and kinship.

1

2

1　AIDS Action Now! demonstration, Toronto, c. 1980s.

2　General Idea, *One Year of AZT and One Day of AZT*, 1991. Installation consisting of 1,825 elements of vacuum-formed styrene with vinyl, each 12.7 × 31.7 × 6.3 cm, and five elements of fibreglass and enamel, each 85 × 214 × 85 cm. Installation view from the exhibition *Fin de siècle* at the Power Plant, Toronto, 1993. Photograph by Cheryl O'Brien. Courtesy of the artist and Mitchell-Innes & Nash, New York.

1

Legislating Difference

In the 1980s and 1990s, significant legislative changes provided increasing recognition for gay and lesbian communities in Canada. In 1985, the Parliamentary Committee on Equality Rights released the report *Equality for All,* condemning the discriminatory treatment of homosexuals in Canada and recommending that the Canadian Human Rights Act be amended to outlaw discrimination based on sexual orientation. In 1986, the federal government responded to the report by stating that it would "take whatever measures are necessary to ensure that sexual orientation is a prohibited ground of discrimination in relation to all areas of federal jurisdiction." Yet it was only in 1992 that the federal court lifted the ban on gays and lesbians serving in the military, in 1995 that Ontario

2

became the first province to legalize same-sex adoption (followed by British Columbia, Alberta, and Nova Scotia), and in 1996 that the federal government passed Bill C-33, adding "sexual orientation" to the Canadian Human Rights Act. After previously ruling against Jim Egan (page 66) and

Jack Nesbit, who were fighting for the right to claim a spousal pension in 1995, the Supreme Court of Canada ruled in 1999 that same-sex couples should have equal access to the same benefits, obligations, and social programs as opposite-sex common-law couples.

In his book *On the Fringe: Gays and Lesbians in Politics,* David Rayside explains how the decentralization of governance, the Charter of Rights and Freedoms, public opinion that provided a space for equity, and the relative weakness of the religious right (compared to the United States) enabled the development of legislation around same-sex rights in Canada. He notes that a "massive realignment of partisan forces resulting from the 1993 federal election … created incentives for socially reformist Liberals to press ahead on gay rights" (106). Legislative changes in the mid- and late 1990s, Rayside makes clear, were "important" but ultimately quite "modest" (133).

The forms queer organizing took in the 1980s and 1990s also changed in light of shifting Canadian understandings of race and gender. Demographics changed drastically during the 1980s and 1990s as immigration to Canada continued to increase, transforming the cultural makeup of Vancouver, Toronto, and Montreal. In each of these cities, new immigrants tended to live in working-class and poor inner-city neighbourhoods; in those urban spaces they catalyzed new forms of queer collectivity and organizing. Cuts to immigrant services, welfare, and public health coincided with new forms of violence against queers: women of all sexualities faced restrictions on their bodily autonomy through the backlash on abortion rights, and misinformation and panic about HIV/AIDS were widespread. In other words, the misogynist and homophobic backlash converged explicitly with the xenophobic nature of the state and, as this section will show, fomented forms of collective organizing across lines of race, gender, and sexuality. Gays and Lesbians Against the Right Everywhere (GLARE) and Lesbians Against the Right (see also "Dykes in the Streets," page 184) are two examples of activists of all kinds coming together in solidarity with one another and in opposition to a common antagonist.

Intersecting Concerns

The shifting political conditions of the 1980s and 1990s saw the proliferation of organizations and collectives specifically dedicated to the liberation of gays and lesbians of colour. In 1983, on Dewson Street in Toronto, Makeda Silvera and Stephanie Martin established a Black collective house that became "ground zero for Black lesbian and gay organizing in the 1980s" (Douglas, 176). In 1985, Silvera and Martin founded Sister Vision: Black Women and Women of Colour Press. Khush—a collective of South Asian gays and lesbians— formed to address the underrepresentation of South Asians in Toronto's gay community while providing a space to reckon with homophobia within South Asian communities.

The 1980s and 1990s also marked significant developments in queer Indigenous organizing. The term *Two-Spirit* was adopted, for instance, at the third annual Intertribal Native American, First Nations, Gay and Lesbian Conference in Winnipeg in 1990. These two decades also fostered new priorities for coalitional politics between people of colour and Indigenous people. As Richard Fung recalls in Jin Haritaworn's "It Was a Heterotopia: Four Decades of Queer of Colour Art and Activism in Toronto,"

In the 1980s and 1990s when Indigenous cultural politics really blossomed, there was a tendency to create a separate space. In discussions between people of colour and Indigenous people around filmmaking, for example, Indigenous people would often say "This is not just about racism, but it's primarily about sovereignty," and make clear the difference between just an anti-racist lens and an anti-colonial one. Since that period, I think racialized activists and artists have become better at recognizing the settler colonial character of Canadian identity. (43)

1 Jim Egan (*left*) and Jack Nesbit (*right*) lead the Toronto Pride Parade, 1995. Photograph by Ali Kazimi.

2 Jack Nesbit (*left*) and Jim Egan (*right*), c. 1990s. Photograph by Ali Kazimi.

1

Gays and Lesbians of the First Nations in Toronto

ABORIGINAL WOMEN AND AIDS

F♀R♂U M

THE 519 CHURCH ST. COMMUNITY CENTRE
SATURDAY MARCH 2, 1991
1:00 P.M. TO 4:00 P.M.
AUDITORIUM
LAVERNE MONETTE , MODERATOR
SPEAKERS:

KECIA LARKIN

OTHER SPEAKERS TO BE ANNOUNCED
CO-SPONSORS:
AIDS COMMITTEE OF TORONTO
ANISHNAWBE HEALTH TORONTO
AIDS ACTION NOW
STREET OUTREACH SERVICES
INFO: 536-2507

GOING PUBLIC / KECIA LARKIN, 18, TESTED POSITIVE FOR HIV LAST YEAR AND IS NOW WARNING OTHER NATIVES THAT THEY ARE NOT IMMUNE TO WHAT HAS BEEN VIEWED AS THE "WHITE MAN'S DISEASE"

ADMISSION/CHILD CARE IS FREE

2

A DYKE WAS HERE
QUEER NATION TORONTO

3

While organizing that explicitly brings together race and sexuality is often refigured as niche by mainstreams accounts of gay life, the political work done by women and people of colour was central to the development of queer kinship in the 1980s and 1990s. A reflection of both the changing demographics of Canada under new immigration laws, the effects of AIDS on queer communities, and debilitating welfare cuts by increasingly conservative governments, queer organizing proliferated despite the supposed "tolerance" of the Canadian state post-1969. Rather, the twenty years following the violence of homophobic backlash at the end of the 1970s and early 1980s were years of remarkable cultural development among Canadian gays and lesbians. Central to this section is our worry that this period in queer Canadian history can be easily lost or re-narrated to suit the ostensibly "queer-friendly"

times in which we live. Indeed, by the end of the 1990s, gays and lesbians were recognized by the state in unprecedented and, for many, meaningful ways.

Our aim here is to resist the desire to re-narrate the active cultural and political struggles of the 1980s and 1990s. Instead, we begin this section with protests ("Enough Is Enough," page 180) and the collective dances that emerged immediately after the bathhouse raids in Toronto in 1981. We read such reactions to homophobic police violence as symbolic of the subversive spirit that animated the following eighteen years. We do our

best to capture the immensity and urgency of AIDS organizing that crosses racial and gendered categories and relies on strong bonds of solidarity. We also highlight the vast network of anti-fascist organizing led, in particular, by lesbians and women of colour: Lesbians Against the Right, GLARE, and Queer Nation (page 210) are only some of the manifestations of the political urgency of these two decades. The formation of Gay Street Patrol in Toronto, the Citizens' Independent Review of Police Activities, and the active resistance against the government's censorship of Little Sister's Book

TALKING WITH THE POLICE

1. **BE POLITE**
2. You have the right to remain silent. To avoid problems we suggest giving name, address & where you're going, if so asked.
3. You don't have to go anywhere with a police officer unless under arrest or for a breathalyzer test.
4. If you are the driver of a car, produce your driver's licence, insurance ownership, and give details of any accident.

IF ARRESTED:

1. Give your correct name. Don't resist.
2. The Charter of Rights requires the police to tell you promptly why you are under arrest.
3. Call your lawyer. If you don't have a lawyer, call 868-0720 (24 hours) and ask for duty counsel. You have a right to call a lawyer.
4. Remember: anything you say may be used against you in court and probably will.

AFTER ARREST:

1. Note names, badge #'s, licence #'s, car #'s of police officers and witnesses.
2. Write out a complete account of the incident as soon as possible under the heading: "For My Lawyer Only."
3. If abused by the police, call C.I.R.P.A.

4

and Art Emporium in Vancouver become crucial parts of the fight against oppression.

We end this section on a note of celebration. While much of these two decades' organizing took the form of active protest, it also enabled people to come together socially, based on shared desires and feelings of kinship. CODCO (page 204), a sketch comedy show that aired on CBC from 1986 to 1992, featured Tommy Sexton, who, before passing away in 1993 from complications due to HIV/AIDS, used his national platform to simultaneously poke fun at gay stereotypes and challenge homophobia. The multidisciplinary art festival Desh Pardesh (page 201), queer dance party Vazaleen (page 220), and Blockorama (page 222), a celebration of Black diasporic culture and music organized by Blackness Yes!, helped create the sense of possibility of queer life in Toronto. We hope as well that the inclusion of the AIDS memorials in Toronto, Montreal, and Vancouver will convey this sense of possibility—of kinship between queers of the past and those of the present. While the '80s and '90s were years of immense loss and struggle, they fomented forms of protest and pleasure that stay with us now, guiding us toward the future.

1 Handbill on Aboriginal women and AIDS forum by Gays and Lesbians of the First Nations, 1991.

2 Sticker indicating "A Dyke Was Here" by Queer Nation, c. 1990s.

3 Demonstration organized by the Right to Privacy Committee to celebrate the "not guilty" verdict of a teacher charged with keeping a common bawdy house in his own home, Toronto, 1981. Photograph by Gerald Hannon.

4 Public information card distributed by the Citizens' Independent Review of Police Activities, c. 1980s.

ENOUGH
IS ENOUGH

Following the Toronto bathhouse raids, activism against the state took a more urgent and aggressive tone. "No More Shit!"—a galvanizing chant that can be traced back to lesbian activist Chris Bearchell—became the refrain of the post-raid protests, when thousands of people marched on Toronto's Yonge Street to demand an end to homophobic violence.

> "They think that when they pick on us that they're picking on the weakest. Well, they made a mistake this time! We're going to show them just how strong we are. They can't get away with this shit anymore! No more shit!" **Chris Bearchell, speaking at a protest, February 6, 1981**

Protesters chanted "Enough is enough!," "Fuck you, 52!," "Pigs are shit!," and "Ackroyd out!," calling for the resignation of Chief of Police Jack Ackroyd. This response was informed by coalition politics through which the gay and lesbian community of Toronto united with other minority communities, including people of colour, who also faced police persecution. The responses to the bathhouse raids persisted for the rest of the year as Gays and Lesbians Against the Right Everywhere (GLARE) put together the June 1981 Lesbian and Gay Pride march in Toronto and Lesbians Against the Right organized Dykes in the Streets (page 184), a day of protest and visibility for lesbians in Toronto.

1

1 Poster for Gay Freedom Rally, 1981.

2 Gays and Lesbians Against the Right Everywhere (GLARE) at the International Women's Day march, Toronto, 1981. Photograph by Joan Anderson.

3 Demonstration against The Barracks verdict, Toronto, June 12, 1981.

What is GLARE?

- a group of lesbians and gay men dedicated to fighting the anti-lesbian and anti-gay attacks of the right wing through educational/political work and cultural activities to affirm the pride of our communities.

What has the group done?

- distributed 5000 Lesbian/Gay Information Sheets and currently distributing another 5000 (this is a response to a piece of hate literature called the Homosexuality Fact Sheet)
- had a speaker at a special meeting of the Board of Education who emphasized the absolute need for inclusion of sexual orientation in their policy on discrimination (Feb 23)
- marched as a contingent on International Womens Day (Mar 7)
- helped organize and marshal the picket of a pro-family rally (a "christian" right wing rally) (Mar 7)
- had a speaker in a forum on fighting the right sponsored by The International Womens Day Committee (May 7)
- formed a contingent of the counter demonstration to a pro-life rally (an anti-abortion rally - strongly endorsed by the christian right wing) (May 10)
- actively participated in a community festival opposing the Ku Klux Klan organized by the Riverdale Action Committee Against Racism (May 31)
- marched as a contingent in a demonstration opposing US intervention in El Salvador (June 20)
- presently, many members of GLARE are active in the Lesbian/Gay Pride Day Committee — organizing a celebration to mark the twelfth anniversary of the police raid on the Stonewall Tavern in New York City when the gay and lesbian communities fought back

COME OUT AND CELEBRATE - 2:00 P.M., JUNE 28, 1981, GRANGE PARK

How can you get involved?

- join us at a meeting 7:30, July 20, 519 Church St
- contact GLARE, P.O. Box 793, Station Q, Toronto, M4T 2N7

GAYS AND LESBIANS AGAINST THE RIGHT EVERYWHERE

What is GLARE?

— a group of lesbians and gay men dedicated to fighting the anti-lesbian and anti-gay attacks of the right wing through educational/political work and cultural activities to affirm the pride of our communities.

What has the group done?

— distributed 5000 Lesbian/Gay Information Sheets and currently distributing another 5000 (this is a response to a piece of hate literature called Homosexuality Fact Sheet)
— had a speaker at a special meeting of the Board of Education who emphasized the absolute need for inclusion of sexual orientation in their policy on discrimination (Feb. 23)
— marched as a contingent on International Women's Day (March 7)
— helped organize and marshall the picket of a pro-family rally (a "christian" right wing rally) (March 7)
— had a speaker in a forum on fighting the right sponsored by the International Women's Day Committee (May 7)
— formed a contingent of the counter demonstration to a pro-life rally (an anti-abortion rally — strongly endorsed by the right wing) (May 10)
— actively participated in a community festival opposing the Ku Klux Klan organized by the Riverdale Action Committee Against Racism (May 31)
— marched as a contingent in a demonstration opposing US invervention in El Salvador (June 20)
— presently, many members of GLARE are active in the Lesbian/Gay Pride Day Committee — organizing a celebration to mark the twelfth anniversary of the police raid on the Stonewall Tavern in New York City when the gay and lesbian communities fought back.

COME OUT AND CELEBRATE!
2:00 PM JUNE 28, 1981, GRANGE PARK

How you can get involved?

— join us at a meeting, 7:30, July 20, 519 Church Street
— contact GLARE, PO Box 793, Station Q, Toronto, Ontario M4T 2N7

Typesetting and layout by PinkType, 977-3883

2

1   Handwritten document "What Is GLARE?" by Gays and Lesbians Against the Right Everywhere (GLARE), 1981.

2   Typeset document "What Is GLARE?" by Gays and Lesbians Against the Right Everywhere (GLARE), 1981.

OUT NORTH   **183**

DYKES IN
THE STREETS

In May 1981, at the Lesbian Conference in Vancouver, activists organized Canada's first Lesbian Pride March, a precursor to subsequent Dyke Marches held in Canada and internationally. The conference itself, held May 16–18, 1981, at Langara College, attracted the attendance of some five hundred lesbians, offering workshops on topics spanning work, sex, spirituality, and activist organizing as well as social events, dances, musical performances, and coffee houses.

> "Look over here, look over there, lesbians are everywhere!" **Chant quoted in Chris Bearchell, "Lesbian Pride March Is a First for Canada,"** 1981

A few months later, in October of 1981, three hundred lesbians took to Yonge Street in Toronto in protest of police violence. Organized by Lesbians Against the Right, a group founded after the bathhouse raids, the amassed lesbians marched down Yonge Street carrying banners and chanting "We are the D.Y.K.E.S.!" The march aimed to make lesbians visible—an intimidating and possibly dangerous prospect given the explicit homophobia of the 1980s—and to demonstrate the possibilities for power and change when women organized as a bloc. This was a pivotal protest in the history of gay and lesbian organizing in Canada: through an anti-fascist politics, it brought together the struggles of lesbians with those of women, people of colour, and others unprotected by the state. The march also paved the way for Toronto's annual Dyke March, which began in 1991.

In her 2019 documentary *Dykes in the Streets*, Almerinda Travassos brings together footage from the 1981 march with commentary from its participants and organizers, including Amy Gottlieb:

Dykes in the streets declared our power and visibility, with many gay male allies marching along on the sidewalk. We walked down Bay Street near Old City Hall, with police escorts. There, in the middle of the street, we linked arms and chanted "Look over here, look over there, lesbians are everywhere." After more than two decades of Dyke Marches during Pride festivities, that first one reminds me how, in chilly political times, we need kick-ass radical energy. It is a reminder of the ongoing necessity of taking up public space in ways that radically reconfigure our city. ("Toronto's Unrecognized First Dyke March," 332)

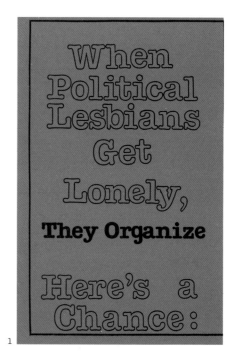

1

1   Handbill, "When Political Lesbians Get Lonely, They Organize," by the Lesbians Against the Right, c. 1980s.

2   Dykes in the Streets march of over 350 women organized by the Lesbians Against the Right in partnership with the Lesbian Organization of Toronto, October 7, 1981.

3   Brochure published by Lesbians Against the Right, c. 1980s.

COLLECTIVE
DANCE

As activism gathered speed across the country, queer social dance became an important part of collective protest. Dance events were pivotal to collective liberation more broadly, raising money to fund protests and fostering environments where queers could convene and build meaningful connections.

The Gay Community Dance Committee (GCDC), formed in February 1981, held its first dance in Toronto on March 28, 1981. The impetus was simple: the committee would encourage small, independent gay and lesbian organizations in Toronto to collaborate to host dance-party fundraisers larger than any one group could hold on its own. Volunteers from participating organizations would help organize and run the dance, and the groups would split the profits. Funds from the dances would be distributed based on the number of volunteer hours each organization provided and through dancers' direct support. By checking a box next to the name of a participating group on the back of their ticket, attendees could indicate which group they wanted the profits from their attendance to go to.

The GCDC was a coalition-building, dance-oriented liberation collective. Its work created spaces for queer individuals to come together in embodied and affectively meaningful ways, opportunities for funding for gay and lesbian liberation organizations, and a reality in which pleasure and more traditional forms of political organizing manifested together. The funds raised over its tenure are conservatively estimated to be $250,000; many of the organizations discussed in this book (including the ArQuives) received vital funding from the GCDC.

"Our monthly dances are an absolutely vital part of our lives as lesbians. They provide an important and unfortunately rare opportunity to come together collectively and share our energy—to experience ourselves as a majority group for a few precious hours each month." **Anonymous, "Protecting Our Dances," in *Womonspace News: Our Voice in the Lesbian Community*, vol. 2, no. 12, 1984**

In a 1982 issue, *Fireweed: A Feminist Quarterly of Writing, Politics, Art & Culture* published a series of lesbian-bar postcards that helped guide lesbians across Canada to these notoriously ephemeral social spaces.

1

1 Postcard of Club Déjà Vu, also known as The Blue Jay (Toronto) dyke bar, published in *Fireweed,* 1982.

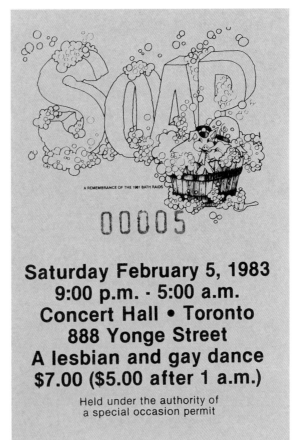

2   Poster for "Saskatchewan's Largest Gay Dance" in Saskatoon, 1984.

3   Ticket for "Soap: A Remembrance of the 1981 Bath Raids," dance organized by the Gay Community Dance Committee (GCDC), Toronto, 1983.

4   Poster for "Danse de solidarité gaie," Montreal, c. 1980s.

5   Poster for "Pink Triangle Dance," Guelph, 1981.

PUSHBACK

The backlash Toronto gays and lesbians faced intensified in the late 1970s and the 1980s partly as a result of the sexual assault and murder by a group of men of Emanuel Jaques, a twelve-year-old shoeshine boy who worked on Yonge Street near Dundas. Anti-gay groups capitalized on this violent tragedy by framing Jaques's death as evidence of homosexual depravity. For example, Positive Parents of Canada—who were at the forefront of campaigns to ban gay men from donating blood—sought to safeguard children from the "dangers" of homosexuality. The League Against Homosexuals formed with a similar aim and, as we depict here, gay activist and politician George Hislop received numerous death threats and other forms of hate mail. As gays and lesbians became more visible and more organized, so too did the pushback by homophobes:

In February [1983], Positive Parents, a Toronto anti-gay organization … demanded the banning of blood donations from homosexuals. Channelling widespread fear and echoing demands of the U.S. religious right, the group also called for the testing of restaurant employees, the closure of gay baths, and public warnings of the risk of contamination in gay-frequented places. (Tim McCaskell, *Queer Progress*, 190)

1

HELLO "SWEETY PIE" HOWS THE BOY FRIEND. DOES HE EVER SAY – NOT TONIGHT DEAR I HAVE A HEADACHE. WELL IN MORE SERIOUS MOOD I HAVE WATCHED SOME OF YOU "BROWNY" BOYS ON TV AND WHEN I SEE YOU KISSING EACH OTHER IN A LETCHEROUS WAY. I GAG AND THAT IS A FITTING TITLE FOR. THERE IS NOTHING GAY ABOUT YOUR LIFE STYLE. THERE IS NO PLACE IN A DECENT SOCIETY FOR YOU: I HAVE REASON TO DETEST YOU ALL OF YOU. TWO OF YOUR KIND TRAILED MY NINE YEAR OLD GRAND-SON BEHIND A BUILDING AND SEXUALLY ASSAULTED HIM. ALSO A BIG FAT 200 POUND HOMO SLOB ON MY STREET SEXUALLY ABUSED A FOUR YEAR

2

OLD BOY. THE WEE FELLOW POINTED OUT THIS MAL-FUNCTIONED SOFT BRAINED SLOB AS THE GUILTY FELLOW BUT THE POLICE COULD ONLY WARN HIM AS THE CHILD WAS TOO YOUNG TO GIVE EVIDENCE. LOOK AT THE HARM YOU HAVE DONE TO SOCIETY, YOU HAVE CREATED MALE PROSTITUTION AND GOD KNOWS WHAT ELSE. THESE ATLANTA MURDERS STEM FROM HOMO-SEXUALITY, SO TOO WAS THE MURDER OF THAT SHOE-SHINE BOY IN TORONTO. THE BOY WAS MIXED UP WITH THEM. YOU MUST KNOW THAT THERE HAS TO BE A MALFUCTION WITH YOUR BRAIN. THERE IS NO PLACE IN DECENT SOCIETY SO WHY DO YOU INSIST ON TRYING TO FORCE YOUR SELVES ON DECENT PEOPLE. WHY DONT YOU SEEK PROFESSIONAL

3

HELP. I FEEL SORRY FOR ANY MOTHER WHO HAS BROUGHT KINKS SUCH AS YOU INTO THE WORLD. THAT RAID BY THE POLICE WAS A TIMELY THING. THOSE PLACES YOU RAN WERE NOT BATH HOUSES THEY WERE "BAWDY" HOUSES WHERE YOU PRACTICED YOUR SLEAZY WAY OF LIFE. MORTY SHULMAN CONDEMNED. WHY DONT YOU GO TO SAN FRANSISCO. I ONLY HOPE TO GOD YOU ARE KEPT OUT OF POLITICS. JUST GET BACK INTO YOUR CLOSETS AND KEEP OFF THE STREET YOU ARE BRINGING DISCREDIT TO THE CITY AND I HOPE YOU ARE PUT OUT OF ACTION. THAT HOMO MINISTER SHOULD BE HORSE WHIPPED AND DEFROCKED I AM CONCERNED AS MANY DECENT PEOPLE ARE

HOMOSEXUALITY FACT SHEET

DON'T BE MISLED OR CONFUSED

SHEILA supports HOMOSEXUALS

SUSAN supports COMMUNISTS

SUSAN supports COMMUNISTS

SHEILA supports HOMOSEXUALS

Children

Homosexuals are more likely to molest children than heterosexuals. Remembering that only **1 to 4 per cent** of the male population are homosexuals, they therefore should account for only 1 to 4 per cent of the indecent assaults on children.

The facts are:

Cambridge study (1,026 victims) — 33% of victims under 14 were boys

Frisbies study (1959) — 29% were boys

Hammer's study (1955) — 34% were boys

Glueck's study (1955) — 41% were boys

Millbrook study — 44% were boys

Forensic Clinic study — 46% were boys

Summary

Homosexual offences consisted of 30 to 45 per cent of all sexual offences against children under 14. Put in another way, at the most, only 1 out of every 25 men (4%) is a homosexual. Yet, 1 out of 3 sexual assaults on children were committed by homosexuals.[6]

Pedophilia

A society of men (P.I.E.) already exists in England who want sex with boys and want it legally. Heterosexuals, generally speaking, can corrupt other heterosexuals, but homosexuals, very often, corrupt heterosexuals — especially in the teen-age bracket. A recent study of 1,800 students at the University of California, Berkeley, revealed that 500 had been solicited by homosexuals, and 300 of these before they were 16 years of age.

The National Coalition of Gay Organizations in 1972 called for "repeal of all laws governing the age of sexual consent."

Teachers

Teachers are entrusted with our children 5 school days each week and the best 6 or 7 hours of each day belong to these instructors. By the very nature of things, their word, opinions and values are often law. Students are affected by a teacher either positively or negatively. Some will love him, admire him and even wish to be like him. If a teacher lives in an open homosexual relationship, the students will be aware of it. The students reason that if it is okay to hire a homosexual to teach in a public institution, and if it is okay to pay a homosexual with tax money, and if it's okay to put a homosexual in charge of students, then it has to be okay to be a homosexual.

here's the story

Sheila lives in the beaches area. She was a school trustee up until Nov.10 last year when she was defeated because SHE VOTED TO ALLOW HOMOSEXUALS INTO YOUR SCHOOLS TO CONVERT YOUR CHILDREN.

Sheila has been associated with John Argue, who is head of Toronto New Democrats, and he is also the activis militant homosexual who wanted to lead homosexuals into Toronto schools to recruit children.

Susan is the on again off again communist who would like to confuse you about names. All you have to remember is THAT IT'S SUSAN WHO LIKES COMMUNISM.

SUSAN has been associated with the President of the Communist Party and in fact nominated him when he decided at one time to run for political office. I guess Susan wants your votes so she will probably deny everything I write.

SHEILA MEAGHER WAS A TRUSTEE LAST YEAR AND SHE VOTED TO ALLOW HOMOSEXUALS INTO YOUR SCHOOLS TO CONVERT YOUR CHILDREN TO A HOMOSEXUAL LIFESTYLE.

SUSAN SUPPORTS COMMUNISM. SHE WONT TELL YOU THIS BUT THEN AGAIN WOULD YOU ADMIT YOU WERE A COMMUNIST IF YOU WERE SEEKING POLITICAL OFFICE IN AN AREA WHERE MANY PEOPLE HAVE EXPERIENCED THE TERROR OF COMMUNISM?

DON'T BE MISLED OR CONFUSED

SUSAN supports COMMUNISTS

SHEILA supports HOMOSEXUALS

Stew Newton - 484-1281 ('til 8:30 p.m.)

POSITIVE PARENTS OF ONTARIO - Representing over 20,000 concerned citizens

3

1 Envelope containing hate letter addressed to George Hislop without a mailing address, directed to The Barracks' address by a postal worker (handwriting in red), 1981.

2 Hate letter sent to George Hislop, 1981.

3 "Homosexuality Fact Sheet" distributed by Positive Parents of Ontario, 1981.

ZAMI AND LESBIANS
OF COLOUR

In 1984, Black lesbians and gay men formed the organization Zami. Devoted to addressing the racism in white-dominated gay and lesbian communities and homophobia in Black spaces, Zami functioned both as a support group, meeting at the 519 Church Street Community Centre, and as a means to increase the visibility of Black gays and lesbians. Zami laid the groundwork for the formation of subsequent Black queer organizations such as the Black Women's Collective, the Black Coalition for AIDS Prevention, and Blackness Yes! Douglas Stewart recalls:

> Zami came out of a group of us sitting around the table at somebody's home one night and talking about all the different things that were not available to Black queer folk. As we're talking, somebody had the idea that we should start our own organization. We should do something about it. As was the case of the 1980s, it felt like anyway, we had an idea and we just did it. Let's plan a party. Let's do a demo. (Quoted in John Paul Catungal, " 'We Had to Take Space, We Had to Create Space': Locating Queer of Colour Politics in 1980s Toronto," 49)

Also in 1984, Lesbians of Colour was established as a community organization for Black lesbians and other lesbians of colour in Toronto. Often meeting collectively with Zami, Lesbians of Colour held potluck suppers, organized peer counselling, and facilitated discussions about topics of interest to lesbians of colour.

Central to much of the organizing of Black and women of colour lesbian organizing was the collective house on Dewson Street started by Stephanie Martin and Makeda Silvera. A community hub and the site of kinship for many kinds of queers, the Dewson Street house remains pivotal to the history of queer organizing in Toronto. Silvera recalls:

> In time, we settled in: five lesbians, and two gay men, and four children all under eight years old. Dewson spawned many political groups: sometimes the house felt like a ferris wheel; other times, a rollercoaster. We came from similar backgrounds, and had experienced rejection both by our families and many straight friends, as well as alienation from the white/gay lesbian community . . . But at Dewson we belonged; we learned to appreciate each other's food: bannock, chapattis, ugale, doubles, cou-cou. At Dewson, it was safe to laugh, to cry, to argue, to look at the different ways a lesbian might represent herself. (Quoted in "From St. Helens Avenue to Dewson Street," 178)

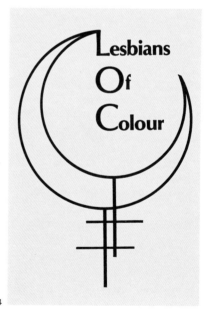

1   Newsletter for Zami, No. 2, 1985.   2   Feature article on Zami and Lesbians of Colour in *Xtra*, 1984.   3   From left to right: Carmen, Courtnay McFarlane, Anthony Mohammed, Deryck Glodon, Alex, Douglas Stewart, and Hendry Wright, 1984. Photograph by Leif Harmsen. Courtesy of the Family Camera Network.   4   Logo for Lesbians of Colour, c. 1980s.

AIDS
ORGANIZING

In the 1980s and 1990s, AIDS organizing was central to queer community building. The 1984 death of Peter Evans—a member of Ottawa's gay community who was dubbed "Canada's National Person with AIDS" in the October 1983 issue of *The Body Politic*—mobilized gay activists to advocate for people living with AIDS. Several organizations were created in Toronto: the AIDS Committee of Toronto, AIDS Action Now!, the Black Coalition for AIDS Prevention, the Gay Asians AIDS Project, the AIDS activist branch of the Gays and Lesbians of the First Nations, the Alliance for South Asian AIDS Prevention, and the Toronto People With AIDS Foundation.

The obstacles such organizations faced were immense given the persistent effects of government inaction, widespread misinformation on how HIV is contracted and spread, and ongoing stigma experienced by those living with—or assumed to carry—HIV/AIDS. Moreover, people living in rural areas had less access to HIV-informed health care, as did racialized and Indigenous communities, whose specific needs were underserved by largely white-dominated organizations. As David Rayside and Evert Lindquist argue in their article "AIDS Activism and the State in Canada," the spread of HIV/AIDS "provided a new vehicle for morally conservative homophobia and heterosexism, and created opportunities for intrusions by health officials into the private lives of gay men. The relative neglect of state health agencies in the early years of the epidemic placed burdens on local gay networks that could easily have over-whelmed them" (37).

1

2

3

1 Postcard, "Summer in the City: Explore the Possibilities Safely!" (Montreal), by AIDS Committee of Toronto, c. 1980s. Illustrated by Maurice Vellekoop.

2 Postcard, "Summer in the City: Cruise Safely!" (Toronto), by AIDS Committee of Toronto, c. 1980s. Illustrated by Maurice Vellekoop.

3 Postcard, "Summer in the City: Spread Safety Around!" (Vancouver), by AIDS Committee of Toronto, c. 1980s. Illustrated by Maurice Vellekoop.

4

5

6

4   Demonstration by AIDS Action Now!, Toronto, c. 1980s.

5   Peter Evans (described as "Canada's National Person with AIDS" in *The Body Politic*) at the inaugural press conference for the AIDS Committee of Toronto, July 1983. Evans died on January 7, 1984, at the age of twenty-eight.
Photograph by Debbie Bloomfield.

6   Douglas Stewart (*left*) with other members of the Black Coalition for AIDS Prevention, c. 1990s.
Photograph by Junior Harrison. Courtesy of the Family Camera Network.

HIGH DOSE ACYCLOVIR [prophylaxis for CMV] $820/MONTH

CLARITHROMYCIN [treatment for MAI] $190/MONTH

FLUCONAZALE [prophylaxis for fungal diseases] $295/MONTH

SEPTRA [prophylaxis for PCP] $40/MONTH

MEGACE [appetite stimulant for weight control] $350/MONTH

KETOCONAZOLE [treatment for Thrush] $135/MONTH

PEOPLE LIVING WITH AIDS AND HIV ARE SICK BECAUSE TREATMENTS ARE TOO EXPENSIVE. WE DEMAND THE MINISTRY OF HEALTH IMMEDIATELY FUND ALL THE TREATMENTS PLWA/HIVs NEED

AIDS ACTION NOW

1   Handbill, "People Living with AIDS and HIV," by AIDS Action Now!, c. 1980s. Designed by Clare Meridew.

2   Eva Halpert (*left*) with her father, Elmer, protesting the Bristol–Myers Toronto office on Bay Street, Toronto, 1989. Photograph by Dick Loek/*Toronto Star* via Getty Images.

2

1980S
PERIODICALS

Periodicals of the 1980s continued the important work of those in earlier decades, bringing information about the gay and lesbian movement to a broader audience—a feat particularly important for individuals not directly involved in the activist movement. Gay and lesbian periodicals became vitally important in producing and distributing information about HIV/AIDS at a time when, as the pharmaceuticals market and government health organizations dragged their feet and the mainstream press assigned blame to individuals living with HIV/AIDS, activists were required to become experts on the disease.

1

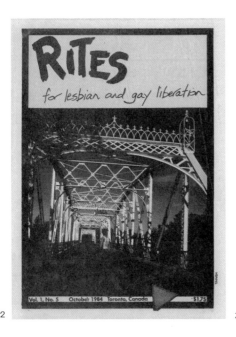

2

3

4

1 Preview issue, *Xtra*, January 27, 1984.

2 *Rites: For Lesbian and Gay Liberation*, Vol. 1, No. 5, October 1984.

3 *Angles*, January 1984.

4 *Gaezette*, No. 8, November 1989.

QUEERCORE

J.D.s, the zine written by G.B. Jones and Bruce LaBruce, sparked the queercore movement in the 1980s and 1990s. An offshoot of punk, queercore was an artistic and musical subculture that contested violence against queers and informed the work of such bands as Toronto-based Fifth Column. In their 1989 article "Don't Be Gay, or How I Learned to Stop Worrying and Fuck Punk Up the Ass," Jones and LaBruce argued that the queercore movement was necessary in the late 1980s and early 1990s because the gay movement had become preoccupied with (and co-opted by) a liberal capitalist ethos. The authors simultaneously historicize the punk movement—"it's no accident," they write, "that 'punk' and 'faggot' have a similar root"—and note the important role of "sexual delinquency" in the punk aesthetic and political stance. Jones and LaBruce argue that while it began as a radical subcultural movement with profound potential for reformulating the world in which we live, gay liberation has capitulated to consumerism and class stratification. In "Don't Be Gay," published in the punk zine *Maximumrocknroll,* Jones lists her affiliation as "Dyke Division" and LaBruce as a member of the "Fag Division" of the New Lavender Panthers.

"Short for *Juvenile Delinquents,* the zine's content was often giddily explicit and tongue-in-cheek while remaining rooted in a queer-centric moral code that railed against the very '80s, consumerist, heterosexual machismo that superseded punk's open-minded policy of embracing nonconformists in the '70s." **Eric Torres, "Queering the Pitch: On *J.D.s* and the Roots of Queercore," 2015**

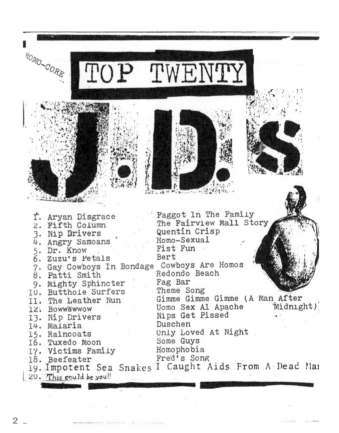

1   *J.D.s,* Vol. 8, c. 1980s.   2   "Top Twenty," in *J.D.s,* c. 1980s.

PERFORMANCE
AND COMMUNITY

Queer dances, performances, and parties proliferated in the 1980s and 1990s, especially as the
queer community banded together to raise funds
following the bathhouse raids (see also "Collective
Dance," page 186). *Fruit Cocktail,* for example, was
an immensely popular variety show that ran from
1983 to 1995 in Toronto and raised money for the
Lesbian and Gay Community Appeal, an organization
that continues to fund projects and provide grants
in the city. In 1986, Sacha MacKenzie started the
drag extravaganza *DQ,* which revived some of
the playful community spirit of the drag shows of
the late 1950s and the 1960s. As the conservative
politics of the right took hold of Canada in new ways,
it became increasingly important to look back to
the queer forms of pleasure of the past, and both
DQ and *Fruit Cocktail* enabled people to do so. Peter
Caldwell explained:

> This is one of the few occasions in Toronto where
> a large number of gay people have joined forces to
> create something. So often, we must rush around
> organizing a march or demonstration in order to
> respond to something negative which has happened
> to our community. Fruit Cocktail has afforded an
> opportunity for an extremely positive experience,
> with everyone pulling together. (Fruit Cocktail: *A Revue*
> *with Gay Appeal,* souvenir program, April 24–25, 1983, Ryerson Theatre)

1

THE LESBIAN AND GAY COMMUNITY APPEAL PRESENTS

FRUIT COCKTAIL

Newly
Renovated

FRUIT
cocktail
1 9 8 9

OCTOBER 6,7,8, 1989 ■ RYERSON THEATRE ■ TORONTO
FOR GALA INFORMATION AND TICKET RESERVATIONS CALL
THE FRUITLINE (416) 599-7960

2

1 Members of *Fruit Cocktail*
participate in Pride, Toronto, 1983.

2 Poster for *Fruit Cocktail,* 1989.

3 Sacha MacKenzie as Divine,
c. 1980s.

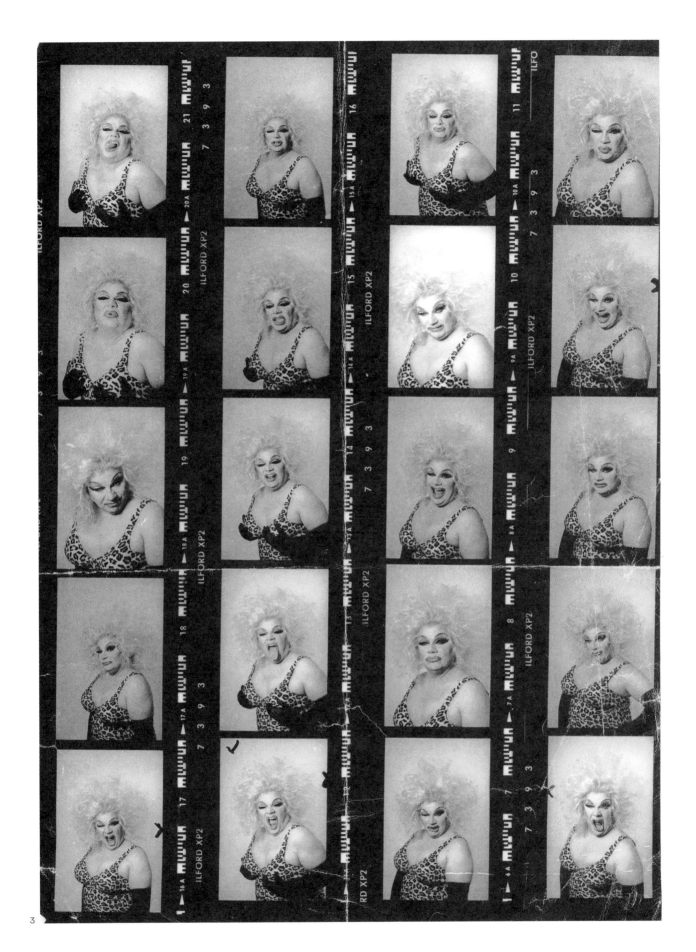

3

A DECADE OF WOMYN'S MUSIC

Womyn's music refers to a genre of music made by women and for women, often with lyrics clearly articulating lesbian politics and desires. Binding diverse music together under this label is an attention to second-wave feminist politics and the promise of women loving women. Throughout the 1980s, Canadian performers produced music that served as a soundtrack for lesbian and feminist movements more broadly. Ferron's "Testimony," for example, from her 1980 album of the same name, served as an unofficial anthem of the womyn's music movement, often sung collectively to conclude womyn's music festivals. Heather Bishop toured music festivals across North America, performing feminist and social justice–oriented music for youth and adult audiences; her 1982 album *I Love Women Who Laugh* was known by a shorter title: *I Love Women.*

Lucie Blue Tremblay's eponymous 1986 album featured songs with French and English lyrics and put her music in direct conversation with other womyn's music artists in Canada—her song "Nos belles années," for example, is a French-language cover version of Ferron's "Ain't Life a Brook." Faith Nolan's 1989 album *Freedom to Love* explored themes of sisterhood, anti-racism, and ending homophobia, building on her earlier albums *Sistership* (1987) and *Africville* (1986). These artists, among many others, provided a soundtrack for individuals to develop lesbian feminist politics and enter into a broader collective of listeners in the 1980s.

1

2

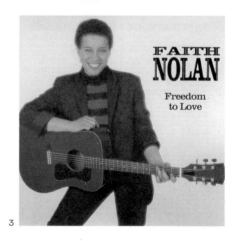

3

1   *I Love Women* album by Heather Bishop, 1982.

2   *Testimony* album by Ferron, 1980.

3   *Freedom to Love* album by Faith Nolan, 1989.

KHUSH AND
DESH PARDESH

Khush—the Hindi word for "happy"—began as the South Asian Gay Association in 1987 as a collective of South Asian gay men and lesbians. In the words of the collective, "Our goals are threefold: to create a supportive environment for South Asian Lesbians & Gays; to promote an organized, visible South Asian presence in the Lesbian and Gay Communities; and, finally, to increase awareness and appreciation of South Asian Cultures among ourselves and the community at large." The formation of Khush led to the first gay and lesbian conference for Asians in North America, Unity Among Asians. From 1988 to 2001, Khush organized Desh Pardesh ("home away from home" in Hindi), a five-day celebration of the art, culture, and politics of queer South Asians in the West. In her opening address for Desh Pardesh 1991, Punam Khosla describes one aim of the festival:

Desh tries to bring forward the voices inside the South Asian community that otherwise have no voice either within the community or in the societies in which we live. The voices of women, political organizers, feminists, and the voices of lesbians and gays who find ourselves silenced about our sexuality in the company of South Asians, or find ourselves whitewashed inside existing white dominated lesbian and gay communities. It also allows voice for those of us who are working actively and consciously against the racism that we experience in the West. And in that we have a very marked and clear historical and political difference from South Asian people living on the Sub-Continent. (*Rungh,* vol. 1, nos. 1/2, 1992)

1

Khush
South Asian Gay Men of Toronto

tel. (416) 925-9872 *ext.* 2173
P.O. Box 6172 Station A
Toronto, Ontario M5W 1P6

Confidentiality Guaranteed

We meet every third Wednesday of the month from 8-10pm at the
519 *Church St. Community Centre*
(*North of Wellesley on Church St.*)

Join us

2

3

1 Handbill promoting Khush
(*front*), c. 1990s.

2 Handbill promoting Khush
(*back*), c. 1990s.

3 Participants at a Khush
retreat, c. 1990s.

GAYS
BASH BACK!

As homophobic violence increased, queers organized for their physical safety. The Toronto Gay Street Patrol began in May 1981. Organized by a group of volunteers with self-defence training, the group patrolled Toronto's downtown and Gay Village, preventing and intervening in homophobic attacks while following principles of non-violence. The motivations for forming the group illustrate the anti-gay antagonism of both the state and its citizens: the patrol sought to protect gay people from those who engaged in bashing as a form of intimidation and recreation as well as from the indifference of the police, who refused to intervene and offer protection. Donald McLeod writes in *Lesbian and Gay Liberation in Canada: A Selected Annotated Chronology, 1976–1981* that "it was felt that the gay community's declining trust in police, combined with eleven documented street attacks between February 20 and April 10, 1981, and the unresolved murders of gay men in Toronto in recent years, made the patrol necessary" (360).

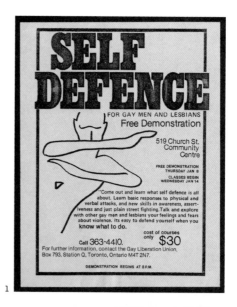

1

2

1   Poster advertising self-defence classes for gay men and lesbians at Toronto's 519 Community Centre, c. 1980s.

2   Toronto Gay Patrol self-defence training, c. 1980s.

3   Toronto Gay Patrol self–defence training, c. 1980s.

4   Button promoting gay community self–defence, c. 1980s.

5   Toronto Gay Patrol self–defence training, c. 1980s.

CODCO

CODCO (short for "Cod Company"), a comedy troupe from Newfoundland, formed in 1973 with the show *Cod on a Stick*—a send-up of Newfoundland stereotypes pervasive in other parts of Canada. Satirical, political, and hilarious, CODCO featured a shifting membership of comedians. In 1988, they developed a CBC series of the same name, which ran for five seasons. "From a gene pool the size of a pudding bowl," an announcer bellows on the show's first episode to introduce audiences to Newfoundland history, "a new breed was emerging: proud, shrewd, ready to reap the wave of astonished tourists from the rest of Canada and the United States! Once the workhorse of the British Empire, now the doormat of Canada!" Journalist, novelist, and playwright David MacFarlane described CODCO in the *Globe and Mail* as a "brilliant, inventive, and mercilessly funny comedy troupe—perhaps the most daring and influential this country has ever seen."

At the heart of CODCO was Tommy Sexton, an actor, writer, dancer, and musician born and raised in St. John's, Newfoundland. Among other recurring characters, Sexton played Duncan, the lover of Jerome (played by Greg Malone). Duncan and Jerome quipped and bickered their way into spectators' hearts—they were, as their theme song made clear, two happy homos from around the bay. That these characters were played by *actual* happy homos—like Scott Thompson's famous Buddy Cole character from *The Kids in the Hall*—resulted in comedic representations of gay men that were more complicated than most at the time.

Sexton passed away in 1993. Many who knew him—including his CODCO collaborators—worked tirelessly for HIV/AIDS education and prevention following his death. In 2006, the Tommy Sexton Centre opened in St. John's as part of the AIDS Committee of Newfoundland and Labrador, providing housing and care for people living with HIV/AIDS. Tommy's mother, Sara Sexton, was awarded the Order of Newfoundland in 2014 for her contribution to AIDS awareness in the province.

"At a time when performers were often urged to hide their sexuality, and gay men were usually the subject of punchlines instead of the ones delivering them, Sexton made sure that would never be the case on CODCO. And over [five] seasons, he did his best to use his rarefied role as a series regular on national television to further the gay agenda at every opportunity." **Andrew Sampson, quoted in Knegt, "Canada Has Had Way More Than 69 Super Queeroes," 2019**

1

GREG MALONE   TOMMY SEXTON
TWO FOOLISH TO TALK ABOUT

TOURING UNDER THE AUSPICES OF THE CULTURAL AFFAIRS DIVISION, DEPARTMENT OF CULTURE, RECREATION AND YO

2

1   The members of CODCO. Clock-
wise from left: Mary Walsh, Andy
Jones, Greg Malone, Cathy Jones,
and Tommy Sexton. Courtesy of Memorial
University Libraries, Archives & Special Collections.

2   Poster for *Two Foolish to Talk
About*, a two-person show written
and performed by Greg Malone and
Tommy Sexton, 1984. Courtesy of Memorial
University Libraries, Archives & Special Collections.

LESBIANS
TO THE FRONT!

Though the bathhouse raids are remembered as an attack primarily on gay male sexuality, lesbians were central to the immediate and aggressive response to the raids and other homophobic police violence. The Woman's Common—a meeting, organizing, and social space owned by and operated for lesbians that opened in Toronto in 1988 and ran until 1994—exemplified the remarkable possibilities created when women came together as a political and social bloc. In "Shades of Lavender: Lesbian Sex and Sexuality," Eve Zaremba outlines the different ways "lesbianism" was being taken up in feminist communities of the 1980s. She argues that lesbian identity of the moment "can be best understood in terms of three related concepts: lesbian sex, which is overt sexual activity between women, being a lesbian (or living as a lesbian), and finally, lesbian sexuality, understood as the more generalized sexual energy and attraction between women, women who may not necessarily be lesbians or have sex together" (88). Heather Ann Brown describes the history of The Common:

> A club, a restaurant and a place to hold cultural events, The Common is thought to have been the only fully women-owned and operated cooperative of its type in the world. (Certainly women from all over the world wanted information about it, hoping to replicate it in other countries.) An amazing 200 women invested $1,000 each, knowing very well that they could lose all their money, and another 250 women bought $100 memberships—all this just to get the idea off the ground! Established with the dream of "a home of our own" and the hope of providing a calmer alternative to the existing bar scene, The Common opened at 580 Parliament Street. At its height it had 1,600 paid members, but after years of tumult—and burnout—it closed its doors. ("History: The Toronto Dyke Scene")

While many of the spaces for women and lesbians founded in the 1980s eventually closed due to increasing rents and other causes of economic hardship, organizers persisted in novel and creative ways. In 1998, for instance, a group of women ran Toronto's first bathhouse for queer women. Pussy Palace (page 238), as it was known, was raided by the police in 2001, bringing to mind the social and sexual conservatism that had sparked the bathhouse raids of twenty years earlier. Despite the legal and social changes made in the name of gay and lesbian rights, the raids on Pussy Palace exemplified how the sexualities of women and queer people were regulated as forms of threat.

1 Complimentary pub pass for The Woman's Common, 1990.

2 Lesbians Making History (LMH) march, 1987. Photograph by Amy Gottlieb.

HOLA

Started in 1991, Latino Group HOLA is a political, cultural, social, and support organization for Spanish-speaking gays and lesbians of Latin American descent living in Toronto. Aside from meeting regularly at the 519 Community Centre and providing community space for Latin American gays and lesbian in Toronto, HOLA offers support and referrals regarding HIV/AIDS and immigration, participates in Pride and International Women's Day, and puts on the annual Miss Hola, Mr. Hola, and Mr. Gay Hola pageants.

1   Latino Group HOLA members participating in Toronto Pride, C. 1990S. Photograph by Rico Rodriguez.

2   Participants in the Toronto Pride Parade, C. 1990S. Photograph by Rico Rodriguez.

Buttons

Buttons have been used as consciousness-raising objects since the mid-twentieth century, allowing individuals to signal a political stance or association. William Craddock—curator of The Pin Button Project, an exhibit that shows off the ArQuives' vast collection of over 1,500 buttons—explains the continued popularity of these wearable objects, noting that "they are relatively inexpensive, easily created, and a widely distributable medium, making them an ideal form of expression for activist movements and community groups." Since the mid-twentieth century, gay and lesbian activists in Canada have been creating wearable pin buttons to promote LGBTQ+ rights, causes, and awareness and to demonstrate solidarity; accordingly, the buttons held at the ArQuives chronicle a tangible, overtly public form of queer desire and kinship.

QUEER NATION

Inspired by the forms of direct action taken up by ACT UP in the U.S. and by AIDS Action Now! in Toronto, Queer Nation comprised Toronto-based activists who worked to end homophobia, racism, and state oppression and violence. Their activism signalled the continuation of unapologetic and multi-issue queer organizing in Toronto. As Tim McCaskell writes in *Queer Progress,*

> The group began with a burst of energy. Three days after the founding meeting, it was a presence at the annual Take Back the Night march protesting violence against women. The following evening, QN joined AAN [Aids Action Now!] and the Ontario Coalition for Abortion Clinics to protest Ken Campbell … and Jerry Falwell, in town for an anti-abortion rally. (293)

Queer Nation was also active in protests against the Gulf War and adamant in its demands that Pride remain politicized under the pressure of growing corporatization. (Their slogans included, at different points, "Fight AIDS, Not Arabs!" and "We're here, we're queer, and we're not going shopping!")

"We are a QUEER NATION of unapologetic lesbian, gay and bisexual people of diverse races, abilities, ages, creeds, classes and cultures, working together to promote and celebrate the visibility of Queers through non-violent direct action. We work to eliminate homophobia, heterosexism, racism, ableism, classism and discrimination on the basis of religious or gender identity among ourselves and within society. Queer Nation is Pro-choice. We claim the dignity and the freedom which a society that breeds fear and ignorance has taken from us unjustly. We're Queer! We're Proud! We're Fabulous!" **"Queer Nation: An Introduction," handbill, c. 1990s**

When women walk down the street they are on their way to the store, or to work, or to visit family and friends, or are on an errand. **We are not here for your entertainment.**

A MESSAGE FROM THE WOMEN OF QUEER NATION TORONTO

1

2

3

PROMOTE
LESBIANISM

QUEER NATION

4

STOP
RAPE

A QUEER NATION WARNING

1　Poster by the Women of Queer Nation–Toronto, c. 1990s.

2　Anti-war demonstration organized by Queer Nation, Toronto, 1991. Photograph by Richard Lautens/*Toronto Star* via Getty Images.

3/4　Stickers by Queer Nation, c. 1990s.

GENDERTRASH

"We want complete control over our own lives and bodies and we want it now. No more shit from anyone whether lesbian, gay, straight, or feminist." **Xanthra Phillippa MacKay, typed notes in Mirha-Soleil Ross collection, c.1990s**

Gendertrash, created by Mirha-Soleil Ross and Xanthra Phillippa MacKay, was a zine "devoted to the issues and concerns of transsexuals." Four issues were published between 1993 and 1995 and, although made in Toronto, the publication had a far reach and a devoted readership all over North America and Europe. Focusing particularly on the experiences of transsexual women, *Gendertrash* also published essays and poetry on sex work and the role of transsexuals in gay and lesbian organizing and manifestos on transsexual liberation.

"Throughout her tenure as an activist and artist, Ross consistently pushed at the limits of the LGBTQ+ movement, prodding it to consider its relation to sex workers, indigenous communities and the very fate of the planet itself. As our world teeters on the brink of not only fascism but full ecological collapse, her words bear a terrible relevance for all of us today." **Morgan M. Page, "The Forgotten Legacy of Trans Artist and Activist Mirha Soleil-Ross," 2019**

1 winter 95   issue # 3 $6.00 (US/Can)

2

hey faggots

If you're going to

CALL US

TRANNIES OR TRANSIES

Then WE'LL caLL You

stupid DiCks & WEE-WEES

time for you to groW UP

3

1 *Gendertrash*, Issue 3, Winter 1995.

2 Xanthra Phillippa MacKay (*left*) and Mirha-Soleil Ross (*right*), 1993.
Photograph by Jennifer O'Connor.

3 Clipart in Mirha-Soleil Ross collection, c. 1990s.

AIDS
MEMORIALIZING

From 1988 to 1994, memorials were built in Vancouver, Toronto, St. John's, and Montreal to honour those Canadians who died from HIV/AIDS-related illnesses. In 1989, the Canadian AIDS memorial quilt was started to serve as a vivid, tangible reminder of the people who were lost. The Newfoundland and Labrador AIDS Memorial, designed by artist Don Short and created in collaboration with staff and volunteers at the AIDS Committee of Newfoundland and Labrador, features the following passage:

> We light a candle for those we have lost.
> They have shown courage in the fight against
>   HIV and AIDS.
> Their light cannot be extinguished.

1

2

1   Montreal AIDS Memorial, 2019.
Photograph by Craig Jennex.

2   AIDS quilt on display, 1993.
Photograph by Alan V. Miller.

3   Toronto AIDS Memorial, 2019.
Photograph by Lauren Kolyn.

4   Vancouver AIDS Memorial,
2019. Photograph by Jon Meade.

3

4

LITTLE SISTER'S CENSORSHIP WARS

Little Sister's Book and Art Emporium was started in Vancouver in 1983 by Bruce Smythe, Jim Deva, and Barb Thomas. Since its beginning, Little Sister's has been a bastion for feminist and queer literature. The bookstore was repeatedly the site of anti-gay bombings in 1987 and 1992.

From 1985, Little Sister's was the continued target of Canada Customs seizures of book shipments deemed "obscene." Over six hundred books and magazines were detained by Customs at the end of 1986, threatening to put the bookstore out of business. As the book seizures continued over subsequent years, Little Sister's, with support of the BC Civil Liberties Association, entered into a protracted legal battle that galvanized gays and lesbians all over the country. After filing a Charter challenge in June 1990, Little Sister's went to trial at the Supreme Court of British Columbia in 1994. Among those testifying was author Jane Rule:

> It seems to me that there is no set of rules that you can apply generally in a circumstance of this sort because literature is so various. As scholars and critics, we try to read a book and let the book dictate how we will deal with it. That is, we do not deal with what is said to be a stage drama as if it is a novel. We read it as a script for a play. If the writer makes it clear to us that it's a comedy, we don't treat it like a tragedy. We try to ascertain the intent of the novelist if we're dealing with a novel, not only the artistic intent, but often the social intent, the insights that the novelist calls to our attention. Therefore, we don't, if we're good critics, fault Jane Austen for not dealing with the French Revolution.
>
> We, on top of that, have to be very good at reading tone because writers are notorious, if you like, in delivering their message in various tones, and irony is one of the most difficult ones to deal with. It is, however, a favourite of writers. Swift's *Modest Proposal* to cook Irish babies to deal with a famine is a book, or a proposal that some people thought he was offering seriously.

1

> I think great errors in judgement can be made when a person who is judging a work for perhaps banning reasons is missing the cultural context of the book because books are not born out of nothing. They live inside the traditions of our culture and

1 Bookmark by Little Sister's Book and Art Emporium, c. 1990s.

our culture is not only a North American culture, a contemporary culture, but it also reaches back into the literatures that we have studied and modeled our own upon.

Therefore, if we are going to deal with questions of humiliation, of sexual explicitness, we would have to know that we are dealing with Dante's *Inferno,* the Marquis de Sade's work as well as dealing with writers of our own time, recognizing that there have always been writers who have been preoccupied with the darker sides of human experience, who are perhaps best equipped to give us insights into those very troubling and often horrifying things that go on in the world today where in Bosnia women are routinely raped and children are molested, where in almost every case there is a sexual component which, if we don't finally come to understand in all its complexity, we are in great danger of not knowing how to live our lives. (October 24, 1994)

In January 1996, the court ruled that Customs had the authority to apply the obscenity section of the law against the bookstore, even if it had done so in a discriminatory manner. In its December 2000 appeal ruling, the Supreme Court of Canada upheld the B.C. court's decision, albeit recognizing that Customs discriminated against Little Sister's with targeted book seizures and enforcing a requirement that Customs agents prove a seized item is obscene within thirty days. The book seizures and subsequent legal battles sparked outrage for many queers and feminists and led to frank conversations on pornography, sadomasochism, censorship, and the role of the state. Little Sister's legal battle with the state was the subject of Aerlyn Weissman's 2002 documentary film *Little Sister's vs. Big Brother.*

2 Janine Fuller, 2000. Photograph by Daniel Collins.

3 Jane Rule, 1975. Photograph by Infinity Graphics.

LESBIAN NATIONAL
PARKS AND SERVICES

The lesbian ecosystem in Canada is complex, varied, and, at times, fragile. Lesbianism does not always thrive in the Canadian wilderness without the stewardship of established, knowledgeable lesbians. With this challenge in mind, in 1997 Shawna Dempsey and Lorri Millan—the founding foremothers of the Lesbian Ranger Corps—launched Lesbian National Parks and Services. As literature for the Corps makes clear, getting into the bush and practising lesbianism in the wild takes practice and special training. Lesbian National Parks and Services is just one of the performance works developed by Winnipeg-based duo Dempsey and Millan, who have been collaborating since 1989.

"The Lesbian Ranger Corps serves and protects lesbian wildlife in all its forms. But we can't do it alone. You can contribute to the work of the Rangers in your own way…Remember that camouflage (though a useful short-term strategy) does not ensure long-term species survival. Be visible. Swell the ranks. Assert your territory. Never forget lesbian life is an essential part of any community. Whether you live in an urban centre or a small rural community, on a beach or in the outback, Lesbian National Parks and Services depends on you to help create healthier lesbian ecosystems." **Lesbian National Parks and Services Informational Pamphlet, 1997**

1

3

4

2

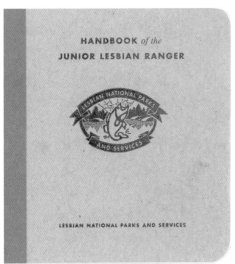
6

7

14

15

1   Lesbian Rangers Lorri Millan (*left*) and Shawna Dempsey (*right*), Banff National Park, 1997. Photograph by Don Lee, The Banff Centre.

2/7   Ephemera of the Lesbian National Parks and Services, c. late 1990s and early 2000s. Courtesy of Shawna Dempsey and Lorri Millan.

OUT NORTH   **219**

VAZALEEN

Started in 1999 by artist and legendary queer activist William Grant "Will" Munro, Vazaleen (first known as Vaseline, before a letter from Unilever threatening legal action) was a monthly queer punk and rock party in Toronto. Held outside of the Gay Village at the El Mocambo and, subsequently, at Lee's Palace, Vazaleen drew an eclectic and diverse crowd of queers, musicians, and freaks who found its raunchy atmosphere a welcome alternative to the more mainstream gay parties in the Church and Wellesley village. Several notable acts performed at the party over the years, including Crystal Castles, Nina Arsenault, Peaches, Lesbians on Ecstasy, and the Hidden Cameras. Sarah Liss recalls:

The weird, wonderful, magical thing about Vazaleen— which was also, arguably, the weird wonderful, magical thing about Will, who came up with the idea on the cusp of the millennium—was how it really and truly welcomed everyone, regardless of gender, class, race, size, sexual proclivity, culinary peccadillo, neighbourhood affiliation or musical taste. When you were there, you felt not just desired and desirable, but like whatever turned you on—fruit, feet, silk scarves, leather, bondage, bruising, baby talk, plain vanilla missionary action—was nothing to be embarrassed about. Imagine the thrill of entering a world without shame. (*Army of Lovers*, 54)

1

1   Poster for Vazaleen featuring the Hidden Cameras, June 30, 2013. Designed by Michael Comeau.

2   Series of advertisement cards for Vazaleen, c. 2000s.

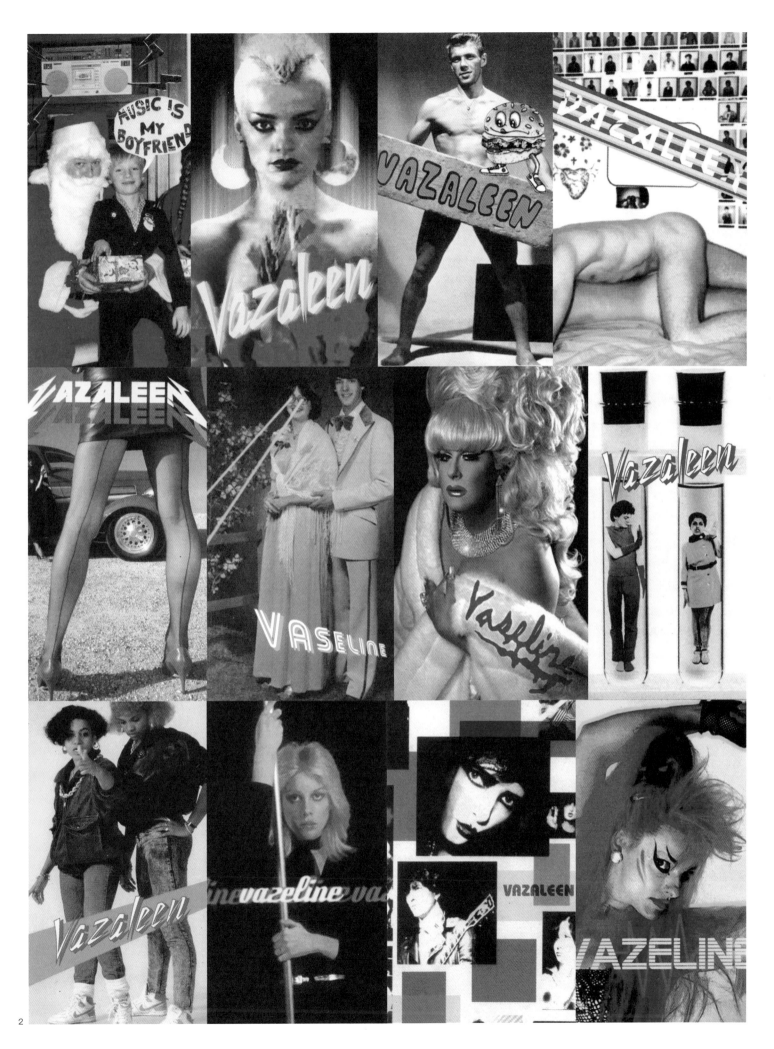

BLOCKORAMA

Organized by the Blackness Yes! collective, Blockorama began in 1998 as a day-long celebration of
Black diasporic culture and music held at Toronto's
Pride festival. As Jamea Zuberi explains to Cassandra
Lord in *Any Other Way,* Blockorama was modelled
after Caribbean block parties ("blockos") and had the
explicit aim of creating a "large presence of Black
queer people taking up and creating space for themselves" (341).

> "Blockorama was a way to create space
> for black queers in the city to find ways
> to connect what often gets disconnected.
> Our blackness gets severed from our
> queerness inside the white queer com-
> munity, and our queerness gets cut off
> and deemed an aberration inside the
> heteronormative black and Caribbean
> community." **Beverly Bain, "Fire, Passion and
> Politics," 2017** (88)

Blockorama was—and continues to be—essential
in maintaining Pride's political roots, mixing the
need for spaces of celebration with collective work
against racial and sexual violence. Its strained relationship with Pride organizers—the event was regularly moved to less than ideal spaces and received
insufficient funding and autonomy—certainly
informs the later activism of Black Lives Matter
(page 252).

1 Blackness Yes! organizers,
Toronto, 1999. Photograph by Courtnay
McFarlane.

2

3

4

2 Blockorama, Toronto,
c. mid-2000s. Photograph by Carol Camper.

3 Blockorama, Toronto, 2004.
Photograph by Carol Camper.

4 Blockorama, Toronto,
c. mid-2000s. Photograph by Carol Camper.

Oral Histories

Following the Second World War, a movement grew among academics, activists, and archivists to cultivate and chronicle histories that reflected local, public, and community realities. Oral history emerged in the late twentieth century as an interview method to document the lives, stories, and experiences of everyday people, particularly those typically neglected in mainstream historical narratives. Living historical actors assumed the role of sources, providing accounts of the recent past. The oral history movement was closely entangled with working-class and labour movements, the women's movement, and activism in other minoritarian communities. Queer oral history methods were solidified during 1970s feminist and gay liberation efforts to create new social histories (and herstories) informed by community-based research that centred on the experiences and perspectives of women and gays and lesbians. Activists and scholars began documenting queer memories, experiences, and lives through oral history interview recordings. The ArQuives collects oral histories from LGBTQ activists and community members from across Canada and beyond, documenting experiences and chronicling histories that might otherwise be forgotten. For example, oral histories collected in the mid–1980s by the Lesbians Making History collective—whose members include Rachel Epstein, Maureen FitzGerald, Amy Gottlieb, Didi Khayatt, Mary Louise Noble, and Lorie Rotenberg—inform much of the work we do in this book.

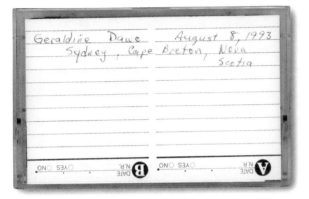

Geraldine Dawe   August 8, 1993
Sydney, Cape Breton, Nova
                            Scotia

ONO OYES N.R. B   OYES ONO N.R. A
      DATE   DATE

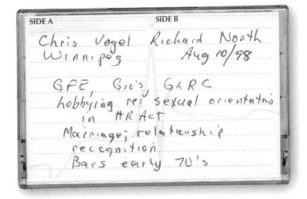

SIDE A   SIDE B

Chris Vogel Richard Noath
Winnipeg   Aug 10/98

GFE, Gio's GLRC
hobbying re: sexual orientation
      in AR Act
Marriage; relationship
      recognition
Bars early 70's

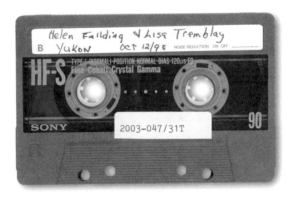

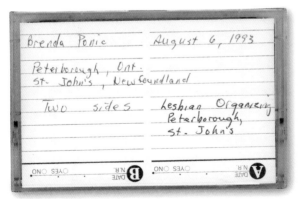

Brenda Ponic   August 6, 1993

Peterborough, Ont.
St. John's, Newfoundland

Two   sides   Lesbian Organizing
                        Peterborough,
                        St. John's

ONO OYES N.R. B   OYES ONO N.R. A
      DATE   DATE

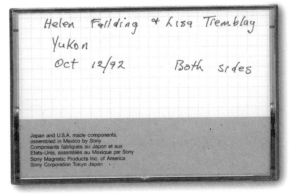

Helen Fallding & Lisa Tremblay
Yukon
Oct 12/92   Both sides

Japan and U.S.A. made components,
assembled in Mexico by Sony
Composants fabriqués au Japon et aux
Etats-Unis, assemblés au Mexique par Sony
Sony Magnetic Products Inc. of America
Sony Corporation Tokyo Japan

1999–2019
QUEER AND TRANS FUTURES

In 1999, the Supreme Court of Canada ruled that same-sex common-law couples were entitled to the same benefits and obligations as opposite-sex common-law couples, including access to benefits from Canadian social programs, such as Canada Pension Plan (CPP) spousal benefits, to which these individuals contribute. In February 2000, in response to the Supreme Court ruling, Jean Chrétien's Liberal Party introduced Bill C-23, the Modernization of Benefits and Obligations Act, which "extends benefits and obligations to *all* couples who have been cohabiting in a conjugal relationship for at least one year, in order to reflect values of tolerance, respect and equality, consistent with the *Canadian Charter of Rights and Freedoms*."

The bill, however, offered only limited tolerance of same-sex partnerships: spousal benefits were not offered to individuals whose same-sex common-law partners died before 1998, and marriage remained a lawful union of one man and one woman. Yet the passing of Bill C-23, limitations and all, is indicative of a broader shift in Canadian queer and trans political formation and strategy in the early twenty-first century as activists turned to judicial and legislative spheres to enshrine rights and responsibilities of LGBTQ2+ individuals and couples in the nation. LGBTQ2+ Canadians, the argument goes, are just like

the heterosexuals, and equally deserving of recognition and rights from the state. While this hinge to judicial and legislative spheres has been incredibly productive in Canada in the twenty-first century, it is not a wholly new approach or method in the broader queer movement; as David S. Churchill notes in "Demanding Possibilities: The Legacies and Potentials of Sex and Gender Activism," the demands made on Parliament Hill in 1971 (see also "We Demand Rally," page 120) similarly focused on "law reform and the regulatory policies of the Canadian government" (6).

In response to Bill C-23, lawyer Douglas Elliot—alongside litigants George Hislop, Brent E. Daum, Albert McNutt, Eric Brogaard, and Gail Meredith—launched a class action lawsuit, arguing that the ongoing denial of CPP benefits to gay and lesbian individuals whose spouses died before 1998 violated the Charter of Rights and Freedoms. An Ontario court ruled, in December 2003, that same-sex couples had indeed been discriminated against by the denial of spousal benefits. Benefits for same-sex couples, the court ruled, must be retroactive from April 17, 1981—the day the Canadian Charter of Rights and Freedoms came into effect. Soon thereafter, George Hislop—a founding member of CHAT, the first openly gay candidate for public office in Canada, and a long-time

gay activist in Toronto—received a cheque for unpaid survivor benefits owed him since the 1986 death of his long-time partner Ron Shearer. Hislop and Shearer had been together since 1958; they met on the ferry to Hanlan's Point (a beach that has long been a meeting place for queers) on the Toronto Islands. On October 8, 2005, less than one year after receiving the cheque, Hislop passed away in Toronto. The government appealed the earlier court ruling, but to no avail; on March 2007, the Supreme Court of Canada ruled unanimously that the denial of benefits to same-sex individuals whose partners died before 1998 was in direct violation of the Canadian Charter of Rights and Freedoms.

The rights of same-sex couples in accessing spousal benefits were not the only issues winding their way through the judiciary system in the early twenty-first century. Bill C-23 generated other questions about the rights and responsibilities of same-sex couples and the way those rights and responsibilities are understood by the state. Both the City of Toronto and the Province of British Columbia asked their respective courts, if same-sex couples and opposite-sex couples are entitled to the same rights and benefits, is Canada's ban on same-sex marriage legal? In July 2002, the Ontario Superior Court responded, ruling that the nation's

ban on same-sex marriage is, in fact, a violation of the Charter of Rights and Freedoms.

As a reactionary gesture, the Alberta government immediately passed a bill banning same-sex marriage and publicly claimed that if the federal government attempted to amend the Marriage Act, the provincial government would use the notwithstanding clause, enabling the province to override or bypass Charter rights. One year later, in July 2003, British Columbia recognized same-sex marriage. That same summer, at a meeting in Wolfville,

Nova Scotia, the United Church of Canada voted overwhelmingly to endorse same-sex marriage.

As support for same-sex marriage grew, the federal government attempted to walk a fine line; Prime Minister Chrétien publicly ruminated on "evolution in society" in support of same-sex marriage and on the vital importance for religious institutions to continue to define marriage as they see fit. In the summer of 2003, he announced legislation to legalize same-sex marriage in Canada. On July 20, 2005, Bill C-38—an "Act respecting certain aspects of legal capacity for marriage for civil purposes"—received Royal Assent and became law. By this point, Ontario, British Columbia, Quebec, Manitoba, Nova Scotia, Newfoundland and Labrador, and New Brunswick had already

recognized same-sex marriage as legal, but the passing of Bill C-38 made Canada the fourth country in the world (after the Netherlands, Belgium, and Spain) to legally recognize same-sex marriage.

Following the election of a minority Conservative Party of Canada federal government in 2006, Prime Minister Stephen Harper reopened the same-sex marriage debate in accordance with a commitment he made during the election campaign to garner the support of social conservatives. The Conservative Party was, after all, the result of a 2003 amalgamation of the Progressive Conservative Party and the far-right social conservative Canadian Alliance. While the federal Conservatives were unsuccessful in reopening the debate over same-sex marriage, they placated social conservative supporters with other methods: one famous example is their erasing of references to queer rights and political formation from the Ministry of Citizenship and Immigration's study guide for prospective new citizens.

As Tim McCaskell argues in *Queer Progress,* Harper had limited concern with same-sex rights and moved on quickly from his defeat in reopening the marriage debate: instead, he "was playing a long game to deepen the neo-liberal transformation of the economy. He had bigger fish to fry, and his social conservative allies were expendable" (390). This long game meant overseeing the neoliberal transformation of Canadian society for the twenty-first century. Neoliberalist championing of the free market and individualism had begun in the late twentieth century; it continues to erode social programs and the collective power of citizens in Canada and has resulted in increasing wealth disparity between rich and poor Canadians. In 1970, McCaskell notes, 66 percent of Torontonians were classified as middle class; in 2005, only 29 percent were. Since the start of the twenty-first century, individuals have increasingly relied on part-time, temporary, and other forms of precarious work, often without benefits or security. This is particularly true of immigrants, who are far more likely than Canadian-born citizens to be classified as low-income earners. In addition,

the Harper government's cuts to employment programs, Indigenous services, health care and funding for hospital workers, education, and climate science affected the quality of life for all Canadians—queer and straight alike.

Questioning Homonormativity

For completely different reasons than those purported by social conservatives—reasons connected to the broader effects of ongoing neoliberalization in Canada—the legalization of same-sex marriage was not celebrated by all members of the queer community. In fact, as legalization became more and more likely at the turn of the century, resistance developed among left-leaning, progressive, and radical members of queer communities. While the prospect of same-sex marriage seemed to promise equal access to the state and its services for some queer people, many others were less preoccupied with the promise of same-sex marriage and were more immediately affected by increasingly tenuous access to health care services, housing, secure and stable work, and disability benefits. In other words, poverty, class, and race remained key facts in the everyday lives of queer people, facts the celebratory rhetoric surrounding gay marriage both ignored and obscured.

Same-sex marriage also compelled many people to reckon

with the effect of marriage on the legacies and possibilities of queer community building. In an April 2001 article in *Xtra,* for example, lesbian writer, academic, and activist Jane Rule aggressively attacked the idea of same-sex marriage: "Over the years when we have been left to live lawless, a great many of us have learned to take responsibility for ourselves and each other, for richer or poorer, in sickness and health, not bound by the marriage service or model but singularities and groupings of our own invention. To be forced back into the heterosexual cage of coupledom is not a step forward but a step back into state-imposed definitions of relationship. With all that we have learned, we should be helping our heterosexual brothers and sisters out of their state-defined prisons, not volunteering to join them there."

Rule's critique of same-sex marriage resonated with what American queer scholar Lisa Duggan, in her book *The Twilight of Equality? Neoliberalism, Cultural Politics, and the Attack on Democracy,* calls the neoliberal problem of homonormativity—a gay and lesbian politics that embraces and sustains heteronormative institutions and ideals through assimilation and conformation. A critique of homonormativity continues to be shared by many queer activists and thinkers, both in Canada and globally, who see queer politics as meant to ameliorate, not mimic, oppressive conditions,

categorizations, and limitations. Rule's cynicism was prophetic. The legalization of same-sex marriage rights was heralded by many as the pinnacle and denouement of the queer political movement within Canada and attention shifted away from continuing anti-queer injustice and violence within the nation to a desire to spread a uniquely Canadian brand of same-sex rights around the world.

Queer International

Solidified in the early twenty-first century, Canada's status as a queer-friendly nation intensified with the October 2015 election of Justin Trudeau's Liberal government. A series of important international events across the

country solidified the country's gay-friendly reputation on the international stage. In the summer of 2006, Montreal hosted the first ever World Outgames, welcoming over ten thousand athletes and representatives from over one hundred countries. That same summer, the sixteenth annual International AIDS Conference took place in Toronto, with more than 26,000 delegates. The 2010 Winter Olympics held in Vancouver boasted "Pride House"—a space for queer athletes from all nations to come together under a literal rainbow banner. In 2014 Toronto hosted WorldPride, the city's largest-ever queer celebration. Events at WorldPride included a mass wedding of 115 couples and a huge headline parade with over 280 entries and over 10,000 marchers. Brent Hawkes, of the Metropolitan Community Church, and Georgian human rights activist Anna Rekhviashvili

served as grand marshal and international grand marshal, respectively. Also in 2014, the city council of St. John's, Newfoundland, voted to fly a rainbow flag at city hall during the 2014 Winter Olympics to protest Russia's anti-gay laws and state-sanctioned violence against queer individuals. The action sparked a Canada-wide campaign, and soon city councils in Halifax, Fredericton, Moncton, Montreal, Quebec City, Ottawa, Kingston, Hamilton, Guelph, London, Toronto, Regina, Saskatoon, Edmonton, Calgary, Vancouver, Victoria, Yukon, and Iqaluit joined St. John's in flying the flag. In 2016, the rainbow flag flew on Parliament Hill in Ottawa for the first time. It served as an overt symbol of the newly elected government's commitment to queer rights at home and abroad.

Under Justin Trudeau, the federal government has embraced queer rights and citizens as an overt marker of its progressive credentials. In 2016, for example, Randy Boissonnault, member of Parliament for Edmonton Centre, was appointed Special Advisor to the Prime Minister on LGBTQ2+ issues. Trudeau himself is a regular attendee at Pride celebrations across Canada—the first sitting prime minister to participate in these events. And in 2019, the government unveiled a special "Equality Dollar" to mark fifty years since the nation ostensibly decriminalized homosexuality. A conference in Ottawa in March 2019 entitled "Anti-69:

Against the Mythologies of the 1969 Criminal Code Reform" brought together activists and historians who pushed back on the government's claims that homosexuality was decriminalized in 1969. As previous chapters in this book elucidate, police and other governmental bodies continued to harass, harm, and criminalize queer individuals long after the 1969 amendments to the Criminal Code. In fact, less than two years earlier, in May 2017, Trudeau had identified the purge of gay and lesbian individuals in the Canadian Armed Forces, the RCMP, and the federal public service that took place from the 1950s to the mid-1990s as the nation's "collective shame."

Trans Canada

In March 2013, the House of Commons passed Bill C-279—An Act to amend the Canadian Human Rights Act and the Criminal Code—which extended human rights protection to trans people in Canada. The private member's bill was introduced by Randall Garrison, member of Parliament for Esquimalt–Saanich–Sooke, and passed on its third reading with unanimous support from the NDP, the Liberal Party, the Bloc Québécois, and Elizabeth May, the lone Green Party member of Parliament at the time. Bill C-279 passed with the support of eighteen Conservative members of Parliament—including *at least* one well-known and high-ranking

gay man who refused to talk publicly about his sexuality each time his party vilified queer Canadians—who did not vote in line with their 137 nay-saying colleagues. But after the bill's passing, Conservative MPs and senators framed the legislation as a "bathroom bill" that would allow predatory men access to women's washrooms and, in February 2015, the Senate amended Bill C-279 in ways that Garrison described as "transphobic" and not in the spirit of the bill supported by the House of Commons. The most problematic amendment made by the Senate exempted public washrooms and change rooms from the purview of the legislation. In May 2016, Minister of Justice Jody Wilson-Raybould introduced Bill C-16, which featured the same name as Garrison's proposed Bill C-279. The bill added the words "gender identity or expression" to the Canadian Human Rights Act and the Criminal Code; it received Royal Assent and became law in June 2017.

While legislative changes solidifying the rights of transgender Canadians are important milestones and certainly worthy of celebration, it's important to remember the broader base from which legislative and judicial alterations have developed: the long-running, steadfast, and difficult work done by queer and trans activists. The tireless work of trans activist collectives such as the Trans Lobby Group—a Toronto-based organization

spearheaded by Susan Gapka, Martine Stonehouse, Joanne Nevermann, Darla S., Michelle Hogan, and Rupert Raj, with many other participants over the years—is precisely what made these debates in the House of Commons and the Senate possible. Legislative developments did not begin with well-meaning politicians in the House of Commons—they began on the streets with the dedicated activism of queer and trans people. This activist work remains vital in the present and future. As Tom Warner writes in *Never Going Back: A History of Queer Activism in Canada,* "changing a few laws and achieving tolerance are necessary, but insufficient themselves to achieve fundamental social change" (8). And, as Michelle De Ville explains to Viviane Namaste in an interview entitled "We Paved the Way for Whatever Tolerance They Have in Their Lives" in *Trans Activism in Canada,* "progress" is a tricky thing:

> Anyone who has seen both situations—back in the late seventies and today—would say "Wow, what progress!" But I don't think it is; there's a certain progress, in the sense that you don't get shot at or arrested or beaten up on every street corner, but there are all kinds of new problems that are even more frightening than the ones that we had in the late seventies. For instance, we didn't have crack in '78; we didn't have AIDS in '78. And

today, you're given the false idea that you are accepted and tolerated—more tolerated than accepted, first of all. The fact that doctors give hormones away freely, that it doesn't seem to be a problem, but they still don't offer you a job. We still pretty much have to work as sex workers. Now it just has a different face: instead of working on a street corner, they work out of apartments or really badly concealed bordellos or massage parlours. So it's basically, I don't want to be vulgar, but it's basically "same shit, different smell." I guess it bothers people less today because it's hidden away. You call that progress? I don't think so. (24)

Continued Violence

Concurrent within Canada with these legislative and judicial changes and public performances of queer support, however, is ongoing violence against queer individuals. In fact, anti-gay violence during the early twenty-first century is too commonplace to exhaustively chronicle here. Among the more widely recognized crimes against queer individuals during this era are the murder of Aaron Webster in Vancouver's Stanley Park in November 2001 and the stabbing of Scott Jones in New Glasgow, Nova Scotia, in October 2013. While Jones survived the attack, his assailant left him paralyzed from the waist down. In 2008, a lesbian couple was attacked by another parent as they waited to pick up their son from school in Oshawa, Ontario; in 2010, a gay couple's home in Little Pond, Prince Edward Island, was firebombed; in 2013, a lesbian couple in Kingston, Ontario, went public with a series of homophobic letters they had received from other Kingston residents. In January 2018, Bruce McArthur was arrested in Toronto and plead guilty to eight counts of first-degree murder; his victims were Skandaraj Navaratnam, Abdulbasir Faizi, Majeed Kayhan, Soroush Mahmudi, Kirushna Kumar Kanagaratnam, Dean Lisowick, Selim Esen, and Andrew Kinsman. One year after McArthur's arrest, far-right extremists and white supremacists attacked attendees at Pride festivities in Hamilton, Ontario. Hamilton police chief Eric Girt, who was widely criticized for his officers' slow response to the violence, suggested that if the LGBTQ community made uniformed officers feel more welcome at the event, they would have responded to the anti-gay violence more quickly. Girt's claim that police would have better served and protected participants if they were invited is astounding in its insincerity but not an uncommon type of blame when it comes to policing and the LGBTQ community. In 2018, for example, despite all evidence to the contrary, Toronto police chief Mark Saunders claimed that the investigation into McArthur's killings was hampered because the community wasn't helping enough—he told the *Globe and Mail* that "nobody was coming to us with anything." As Justin Ling shows in the podcast *Uncover: The Village*, this is clearly untrue: friends of disappeared men identified McArthur to police in 2013. Between then and his arrest in early 2018, McArthur murdered five more men.

Violence at the hands of the state plagued, and continues to plague, queer and trans communities in the twenty-first century. Aggressive and violent bathhouse raids targeted Goliath's Bathhouse in Calgary, the Warehouse Spa in Hamilton, and the Pussy Palace in Toronto, among many others. Queer people of colour face harassment at the hands of the police through carding and other tactics of control that have long been used against queer and trans individuals and communities of colour. The work of Black Lives Matter (page 252) and Idle No More—the latter catalyzed by the challenge to Indigenous communities and environmental protections under the Harper government's omnibus Bill C-45—show us how the struggles for Indigenous sovereignty, access to resources, safety from state violence, and freedom from poverty are also a part of the struggles of many queer people.

The criminalization of people living with HIV—which stemmed from a 1998 Supreme Court of Canada decision that failure to

1

(and some convicted) for not disclosing their HIV-positive status before sex with a condom and others charged for non-disclosure before condomless sex with a low or undetectable viral load. Criminalization of HIV non-disclosure contributes to increased stigma and discrimination for people living with HIV, particularly in already marginalized communities. According to the Canadian HIV/AIDS Legal Network, half of all people charged for HIV non-disclosure between 2012 and 2016 were Black men, while Indigenous women are disproportionally represented in women charged.

The Past in the Present

In this chapter, we feature contemporary examples of a collective reassessment of queer pasts. There is a re-evaluation of forms of political formation, performance, and activism that might, at first glance, seem antiquated: a return to forms of sociality enabled by public sex and bathhouse cultures and an embrace of historical music-making, public lesbian actions, and queer and trans burlesque, among other performance projects. Alongside these collective projects of remembering, we identify and celebrate diverse forms of queer experience and kinship that are articulated in this era, including the work across Canada of Unity Mosques (page 262), which create spaces for Muslims to embrace

disclose one's HIV-positive status to a sexual partner essentially invalidated a partner's ability to give consent—intensified in the twenty-first century; in 2012, the Supreme Court of Canada ruled that HIV-positive individuals have a duty to disclose their status to sexual partners unless they exhibit a "low" HIV viral load (1,500 or fewer copies of the virus per millilitre of blood). The Canadian HIV/AIDS Legal Network notes that many people living with HIV "are being convicted of serious criminal offences and sentenced to years in prison for not disclosing their HIV status to their sexual partners—even when there is little to no risk of transmission." The criminalization of individuals with HIV plays out differently across Canada—while at least 197 people have been charged with criminal offences for

failing to disclose their HIV status, the offences range from assault, nuisance, and negligence to attempted murder, with the most common charge being aggravated sexual assault. McCaskell writes in *Queer Progress* that the criminalization of HIV stemmed not only from misguided public health concerns but also from "irrational fears of HIV" (400). In a 2008 policy brief, the Joint United Nations Programme on HIV/AIDS highlighted that there is no evidence that the criminalization of HIV is effective in acquiring justice or preventing HIV transmission. Although since 2012 Canadian law criminalizes only non-disclosure of HIV status before sexual activity that poses a "realistic possibility of transmission"—a clause that takes into consideration condom use and viral load—several people have nonetheless been charged

2

3

both their faith and their queer and trans politics, as well as the production and distribution of trans and Two-Spirit literature by trans and Two-Spirit people. What we hope to indicate, in this final temporal chapter, is that queer life in Canada remains complicated and disparate and difficult to capture in a single narrative.

As anti-queer and transphobic violence continues, we also see the development of an ostensibly more benevolent state when it comes to government relations

1 Participants in Montreal Pride Parade, August 2018. Photograph by Martine Doucet.

2 Two-Spirited People of the First Nations members participate in Toronto Pride Parade, c. 2000s.

3 Drag legend Chris Edwards performs onstage, Toronto, c. 2000s.

with queer and trans individuals. In June 2016, for example, Toronto police chief Mark Saunders issued an official statement of regret (*not* an official apology) for Operation Soap, the 1981 violent police raids of Toronto bathhouses (see "February 5, 1981, Raids," page 158). In November 2017, Prime Minister Justin Trudeau offered an apology for the twentieth-century federal government–led purge of gay and lesbian members of the federal government and military.

While these statements are often well-meaning and a potentially productive way of moving forward, they are sometimes difficult to take seriously as sparking tangible change. A few months after Chief Saunders's statement of regret, for example, plainclothes Toronto Police officers charged seventy-two people as part of Project Maria—an

undercover sting operation targeting gay-male cruising in Marie Curtis Park in suburban Etobicoke. Regardless of the sincerity of these attempts at apologies, they indicate a need to re-assess the queer pasts we chronicle in this book from the vantage point of the present.

Narratives of queer life that focus exclusively on progress— that claim everything is constantly getting better—are incomplete, as are narratives of loss that emphasize the so-called good old days to the point that they foreclose the possibilities of contemporary activism in the age of state recognition of queer and trans rights. We hope that in this chapter the beginnings of an alternative possibility emerge, one in which we look to the past for guidance in the political struggles of the here and now.

RAINBOW
REFUGEES

In the first decades of the twenty-first century, legal changes pertaining to LGBTQ2+ communities were happening swiftly in Canada. Many of these legislative changes affirming LGBTQ2+ rights have been celebrated both in Canada and internationally. During this period of rapid change in Canada, however, seismic shifts on a global scale have required LGBTQ2+ Canadians to reckon with our role in the larger political landscape.

As Tim McCaskell writes in *Queer Progress,* "in a world ever more awash with political, economic, and climate refugees, a new category of sexual refugees was emerging. Countries like Canada were considered a safe haven. Faced with individual emergencies, groups with a liberal human rights approach emerged to fill the gap" (411). The refugee crisis, in other words, mobilized a number of groups to work toward the resettlement of sexual minorities as refugees in Canada. Rainbow Refugee in Vancouver, for example, was founded in 2000, Toronto's Rainbow Railroad in 2006, Ottawa's Capital Rainbow Refuge in 2010, and The Rainbow Refugee Association of Nova Scotia (RRANS) in 2011. Toronto's 519 community centre hosts Among Friends, a weekly program for LGBTQ2+ refugee claimants designed to ease resettlement in Canada, running since 2005. These are just some of the groups in Canada committed to providing safer immigration and settlement support for LGBTQ2+ newcomers as they navigate the bureaucratic and often hostile immigration system.

The landscape of LGBTQ2+ refugee settlement in Canada is shifting. In April 2019, the Progressive Conservative government of Ontario, under Premier Doug Ford, cut funding to Legal Aid Ontario, a non-profit program that assists low-income individuals with access to justice in Ontario. These cuts have decimated legal support programs for immigration and refugee cases—legal aid services that have been in greater demand in recent years. Two months later, the federal Liberal government announced an initiative to support LGBTQ2+ refugees: the Rainbow Refugee Assistance Partnership provides support for Canadians in privately sponsoring refugees who are fleeing violence because of their gender presentation or sexual orientation.

Yet as journalist Declan Keogh notes in his article "Pride to Survive: Queer Refugees Look to Toronto for a Lifeline," the same federal government is working to "bar refugees from making claims at the Canadian border if they had already made a claim in another country or had a previously unsuccessful claim in Canada." Organizations committed to LGBTQ2+ refugee support do crucial work of assisting individuals in arriving and settling in Canada and challenging the Canadian government by organizing against restrictive immigration policies.

1

You Can Save Lives.

RainbowRailroad.ca

Rainbow Railroad helps LGBT individuals escape imminent danger in countries where governments tolerate or support violence against them.

The individuals we help have been ostracized and attacked by their communities, fired by their employers, and sometimes even tortured by their families, leaving them homeless and without resources. A plane ticket issued quickly or a bed in a safe house can make the difference between life and death for these individuals.

We are a registered Canadian charity made up of entirely of volunteers. Since 2006 we have provided financial support to over 30 individuals and advice and support to countless others.

You can save LGBT lives. Visit **www.RainbowRailroad.ca** to find out how to help.

1 Cover of *NOW* magazine, Issue 1941, Vol. 38, No. 40, June 20, 2019. Published by NOW Communications Inc. Photograph by Samuel Engelking.

2 Pamphlet advertising Rainbow Railroad (*front*), c. 2010s.

3 Pamphlet advertising Rainbow Railroad (*back*), c. 2010s.

THE PUSSY
PALACE

Reformulating the gay male bathhouse tradition, the Pussy Palace—a women's bathhouse night hosted at gay-male bathhouse spaces in Toronto—rethinks who has access to public space, public intimacy, and public sex cultures. The inaugural Pussy Palace event took place in the fall of 1998 following sustained activism by a handful of queer women activists. Unlike male-oriented bathhouses in the city, the Pussy Palace offered a space for queer *women* to meet as a collective group for communal experiences of intimacy—it worked against the ways that queer women's sexuality is often rendered invisible. On September 14, 2000, under the pretence of a liquor-licence violation, a group of male Toronto police officers raided the Pussy Palace event, where many participants were nude, and proceeded to question participants and organizers. Community response was swift: a few days later, following a meeting at the 519 organized by the Women's Bathhouse Committee, nearly four hundred people marched to police headquarters. One month later, demonstrators met in front of 52 Division headquarters for the Pussy Palace Panty Picket Protest and waved panties and underwear in the air chanting, "Keep your hands off our panties!" Ultimately, the charges against the Pussy Palace organizers were stayed and the Toronto Police were ordered to issue an apology and commit to sensitivity training. In their article "Pussies Bite Back: The Story of the Women's Bathhouse Raid," Chanelle Gallant and Loralee Gillis (two members of the Toronto Women's Bathhouse Committee) argue that the Pussy Palace "changed women's sexual culture in Toronto. It created new possibilities for how women could think about, organize, and enact their sexual desires. Whether or not women attended the Pussy Palace, it existed as an option, as a possibility, as a problem for how women think of themselves as sexual beings" (153).

1

2

3

YOUTH SUPPORT

Central to queer organizing in Canada has been the important work done by and for queer and trans youth. Prior to the creation of online support groups and the proliferation of queer content on social media, in-person youth organizing enabled young queer people to meet and build connections with each other. There is a long history of this in Canada: Gay Youth Toronto, a support group for people under twenty-one years of age, was formed in 1972.

While more youth now have access to alternative methods of support at school and online, hotlines and drop-in programs remain important. The LGBT Youth Line, for instance, provides support for queer and questioning youth across Canada over the phone and by text; GAB Youth in Vancouver—run out of Qmunity, a resource centre for queer, trans, and Two-Spirit communities—is a drop-in group for youth under the age of twenty-five years. Parents and Friends of Lesbians and Gays (PFLAG) supports LGBTQ youth and their families through leadership trainings, queer camps, and mental health counselling. Similarly, Gay–Straight Alliances (GSAs) are becoming increasingly common in schools, though they are by no means unchallenged. In Alberta, Bill 24—which compels schools to create GSAs if requested by students—is currently being challenged by faith-based schools and some parents. Yet the history of youth advocating for themselves and for queer and trans rights is strong.

In 2002, for instance, Marc Hall won a case against Ontario's Durham Catholic School Board, which had barred him from taking a same-sex date to his high school prom. While some queer students choose, like Hall, to petition their schools to make queer-positive changes, other youth organize spaces for themselves outside of school. Queer proms occur annually all over Canada. "Over the Rainbow," held in May 2019, was, for example, organized by the Prince Edward Island Queer Youth Collective and was the first queer prom for youth in the province.

1

1   Poster for "Supporting Youth-In-Transition" program to assist young people in accessing housing, income, jobs, education, health care, and life skills, by Supporting Our Youth (SOY), 2015.

2   Members of the Gay–Straight Alliance at Millwood High School participate in the Pride Parade, Halifax, 2012. Photograph by Shaunl.

2

'Cause sometimes you just need someone to talk to.

3

4

5

6

7

3/4 Promotional material for Lesbian Gay Bi Trans Youth Line, c. 2010s.

5 Promotional material for Lesbian Gay Bi Trans Youth Line, c. 2000s.

6 Promotional material for The Youth Project, Halifax, c. 2000s.

7 Promotional material for Outline, a youth phone line by The Youth Project, Halifax, 1996.

PRIDE

The proliferation of Pride festivals across Canada exemplifies the rapid changes to queer life in the twenty-first century. Since the early 1970s, Pride festivals have developed across Canada in big cities and small towns alike, but it is in recent decades that Pride festivals have become mainstream cultural events. As Pride has become an increasingly visible part of life for all Canadians, the politics of these festivals has changed. For many, the danger of being outed through participation in overtly queer events has decreased. As a result, Pride events are increasingly participated in by allies and thought of by many as a celebratory event rather than a political action.

Some queer activists argue that while Pride began as a way for queer people to register their opposition to the state and its homophobia, it has been sanitized and depoliticized in the era of gay rights. Recent conversations about the role of police in the marches exemplify these tensions, as do the attempts to ban Queers Against Israeli Apartheid from the Toronto Pride march in 2010 and the frustrations with the increased corporatization of Pride in general. While the debates about the nature of Pride continues, collective marches and celebrations can still do crucial political work, opposing anti-gay violence and imagining alternatives to state homophobia.

1

1 Participants march in Winnipeg Pride Parade, 2014. Photograph by eddi9.

2 A participant in the Montreal Pride Parade, 2017. Photograph by Nicolas McComber.

3 Participants march in the Ottawa Pride Parade, 2012. Photograph by Paul McKinnon.

4 Participants march in the Halifax Pride Parade, 2012. Photograph by tomeng.

5 Participants march in the Vancouver Pride Parade, 2018. Photograph by edb3_16.

6 Participants raise their fists during one minute of silence honouring the victims of HIV/AIDS and homophobia at the Montreal Pride Parade, 2018. Photograph by Martine Doucet.

7 Participants at the Montreal Pride Parade, 2018. Photograph by Martine Doucet.

2

3

4

5

6

7

Gay Guidebooks

Guidebooks published specifically for gay and lesbian travellers helped roaming queers find potentially safe and welcoming bars, restaurants, hotels, and cruising spots, among other spaces. Prior to the internet, to social media, to cruising apps that can geographically situate a user, these guidebooks served as indispensable collections of information and tips to stay safe when spending time in unfamiliar cities.

In 1964, Bob Damron began publishing a guide to gay bars he visited as he travelled across the United States on business. His guide—*Bob Damron's Address Book*—quickly became a trusted source for gay listings. A few years later, the publication began including Canadian cities and sites. The 1972 edition added "Cruisy Areas" to the listings, including "parks, beaches, and other public grounds which may or may not be active depending on the season, weather, and time of day." One particularly promising cruising location featured in the Canadian section is "The Green" in Fredericton, New Brunswick. Canadian guidebooks developed in the 1970s and 1980s as an established gay liberation network grew across the nation and businesses worked to attract gay and lesbian patrons.

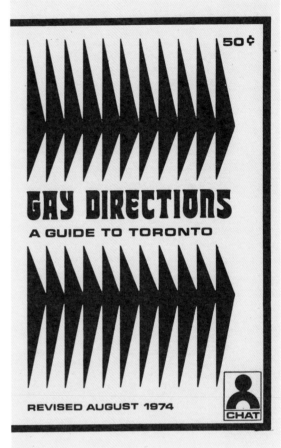

THE POLITICS
OF PARENTING

Political organizing around queer parenting has long been a force in Canada, with many organizations emerging out of Toronto beginning in the 1970s. The Lesbian Mothers' Defense Fund was organized in 1979 by lesbian members of the Wages for Housework campaign (see also "Lesbian Organizing," page 136) to provide information, resources, and legal advice for women fighting for custody of their children. In the 1980s, groups like Gay Fathers of Toronto (founded in 1978 by Michael Lynch) and Gays & Lesbians Parenting Together held meetings at the 519 Church Street Community Centre to discuss the politics of gay and lesbian parenting. In the late 1990s, the first Dykes Planning Tykes session (later known as Mommies & Mamas 2B) was sponsored by the Toronto Centre for Lesbian & Gay Studies at the University of Toronto. Soon thereafter, Rachel Epstein was named the coordinator of the newly formed LGBT Parenting Network—a program of the Family Service Association of Toronto.

Other courses have been developed by activists in Ontario: Chris Veldhoven hosted Daddies & Papas 2B in 2003 at the 519; Robin Fern started Trans Fathers 2B in 2007 at the Central YMCA. In 2007 the LGBT Parenting Network moved to the Sherbourne Health Centre (where it remains today) and added a Q to its name, becoming the LGBTQ Parenting Network. In 2011, Epstein, Veldhoven, and j wallace skelton organized the first Queer & Trans Family Planning course at the 519. An attention to the particular needs and legal oppression of trans people at the LGBTQ Parenting Network led in 2010 to the development of the Transforming Family Project, and in 2014 to the Trans Family Law Project. In 2016, the All Families Are Equal Act became law in Ontario. Among other important developments, the Act de-genders the language used to talk about parents in Ontario, eschewing the terms *mother* and *father* for the more capacious *parent*.

Such legal changes have the potential to shift the terms of what constitutes a family in Canada. British Columbia's Family Law Act, for example, came into effect in 2013 and allows up to four people to be listed as parents on a child's birth certificate. In 2014, an infant in Vancouver became the first to have three legal parents: a lesbian couple and their male friend and co-parent.

"In Canada, early grassroots LGBTQ+ parenting groups as well as institutional programs like the LGBTQ Parenting Network in Toronto, combined with the work of activists, lawyers, artists and others, plus the sheer numbers of LGBTQ parents, have changed the landscape for queer and trans people who are or want to be parents. Our victories and claims to space are fragile—we cannot take for granted the right to create family as we choose, and we must always, always stand up for those who are being denied this right." **Rachel Epstein, former coordinator of LGBTQ Parenting Network**

1   Poster for "Fabulous Fathers" by the LGBTQ Parenting Network, C. 2010S.

2   LGBTQ Parenting Network valentine, C. 2000S. Artwork by Shira Spector; design by Sue Goldstein.

3   Promotional material for LGBTQ Parenting Network, C. 2000S. Illustration by Maurice Vellekoop.

4   LGBTQ Parenting Network valentine, C. 2000S. Artwork by Shira Spector; design by Sue Goldstein.

NOMOREPOTLUCKS

Nomorepotlucks (NMP) developed in the early 2000s when Mél Hogan, Dayna McLeod, and M-C MacPhee took over CKUT's long-running *Dykes on Mykes* radio show in Montreal. Community announcements and events described on the show were put online in 2003 as an events calendar providing information about queer and feminist happenings in Montreal. On January 1, 2009, these collective projects launched as an online and print-on-demand queer/feminist journal of scholarship, activism, politics, and artwork in Canada.

Informed by feminist politics of access, all issues of *NMP* are available for free at nomorepotlucks.org. The publication is a collectively produced, not-for-profit journal that rivals queer and feminist academic journals in its content. Curated by Hogan, MacPhee, and Andrea Zeffiro, *NMP* is made possible by a community of dedicated volunteers. Issues feature contributions from writers, artists, academics, and activists from across Canada and beyond, all of whom create work related to an overarching theme. The journal breaks down barriers that too often silo diverse queer and feminist projects, creating space for seemingly disparate conversations—about the arts, activism, politics, and culture—to come into contact with one another and generate new possibilities for queer kinship and politics. Hogan explained its goals this way:

> We really encourage people to publish stuff they can't see being published anywhere else. For academics in particular this can mean work that isn't accepted by more traditional peer-reviewed journals that normally have a very long turnaround, and works that are presented as video, audio, or any combination of these things… For artists, *NMP* is a great place to not only showcase their work but to have it reviewed and written about, either by being matched to a curator or an *NMP* editor… For activists, we think *NMP* is a place to be heard—it's definitely an alternative to a newspaper or a blog, in part because it's within the context of an arts and culture journal. (melhogan.com)

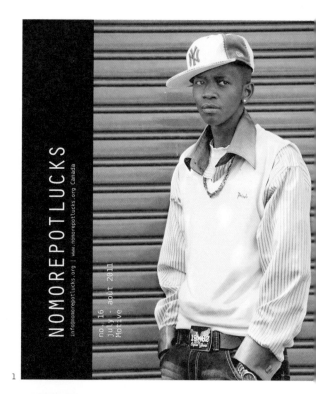

1

2

1   "Motive," *Nomorepotlucks*, No. 16, July–August 2011. See, in this issue, "Captured and Seen: A Conversation with Zanele Muholi by Michèle Pearson Clarke." Photograph by Zanele Muholi.

2   "Interview," *Nomorepotlucks*, No. 50, May–August 2018. See, in this issue (guest edited by Dayna McLeod), "Shame: Thinking with Chun Hua Catherine Dong by Lily Cho." Photograph by Chun Hua Catherine Dong.

VIDEOFAG

Launched in October 2012 by William Ellis and Jordan Tannahill, Videofag was an art space in Toronto's Kensington Market that served as an incubator for queer art and performance until the June 29, 2016, party RIP Videofag marked its closure. Ellis and Tannahill write in *The Videofag Book* that "the entire space was barely eleven feet wide. It wasn't much to look at, but over four years it played host to a revolving door of artists and outcasts" (8). Building on a long genealogy of spaces in Toronto that embrace collaborative performance and art-making as generative methods of queer community building—including, among others, General Idea, the JAC Collective, Buddies in Bad Times (page 150), and Vazaleen (page 220)—Videofag provided many queers a space to imagine and create.

The venue hosted a multitude of performers—Kids on TV, the Hidden Cameras, Keith Cole, Rae Spoon, Vivek Shraya, Will Munro, R.M. Vaughn, Jess Dobkin, G.B. Jones, and Lido Pimienta, among so many others—showing the continued importance of spaces in which queers can amass and imagine and create alternative worlds.

1

1   Poster for the first anniversary of Videofag, 2013. Designed by Adrienne Crossman.

THE QUEER SONGBOOK ORCHESTRA

The Queer Songbook Orchestra, a Toronto–based chamber music ensemble comprising twelve members and a developing array of queer and trans guest performers, is dedicated to revisiting and reassessing queer music histories of the past—many of which are too often erased or overlooked—within the political parameters of the present moment.

Founded in 2014 by artistic director Shaun Brodie, the Queer Songbook Orchestra draws from a variety of popular music genres to reinterpret past queer musical moments and offer contemporary listeners new entry points into queer music and community.

The group uses personal stories and narratives provided by LGBTQ2+ individuals across Canada to build their performances.

For their Tour of Heart & Mind, for example, the orchestra solicited stories from LGBTQ2+ people that provided the framework for the show. The tour stopped in Whitehorse, Regina, Winnipeg, Charlottetown, and St. John's. Other shows include Anthems & Icons, Songs from In and Around the Closet, and Songs of Resilience; the stories that inform each performance—and materials related to the performances themselves—are held at the ArQuives.

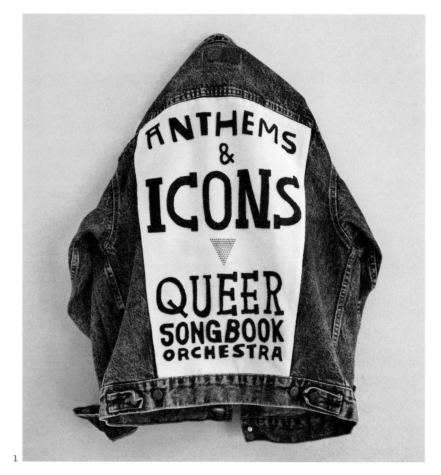

1

2

1 *Anthem & Icons* album by the
Queer Songbook Orchestra, 2018.
Design by Hazel Meyer.

2 The Queer Songbook Orchestra with guests Cris Derksen
(*front, centre, sitting*), Reg Vermue
(Gentleman Reg) (*middle row, left,
sitting*), Beverly Glenn–Copeland

(*far right, standing*), and Vivek
Shraya (*back row, far right,
standing*) at Buddies in Bad Times
Theatre, Toronto, 2017. Photograph by
Colin Medley.

BLACK LIVES
MATTER

On Sunday, July 3, 2016, Black Lives Matter–Toronto (BLM) halted the Toronto Pride Parade for about thirty minutes. At the intersection of Yonge and College streets in downtown Toronto, BLM (the parade's "honorary group") stopped marching, invited Indigenous activists and drummers to join them in the intersection, and sat in protest to call attention to anti-Black violence within the LGBTQ2+ community and in the city of Toronto more broadly. During their protest, BLM made multiple demands of Pride's organizers.

One of the protest's most radical functions was to claim space for Blackness and emphasize the ways race and sexuality have long been constitutive of each other—to remind parade spectators and participants of the Black politics, labour, and energy that have gone into the formation of contemporary LGBTQ2+ identity and experience, as well as the importance of histories of radical activism. After the protest action, queer scholar Gary Kinsman argued that "Black Lives Matter… carried with it the spirit of Stonewall and the activist roots of Pride." Queer scholar Rinaldo Walcott argued that Black Lives Matter's protest shows that "political organizing, direct action and community building could be immediately complex, queer-centered, trans-centered." A letter signed by a collective of scholars and activists in Ontario argued that BLM's action at Toronto Pride "modelled what queer inclusion really means."

"Black Lives Matter is important because we're challenging a police system with a belief system. We're bringing forth a set of ideas. A vision, an idea that says that Black people are the fulcrum of liberation, are the fulcrum of white supremacy, that if we centralize the experiences of Black people, that if we give the most marginalized what they need, then we all have what we need. Because there is no one more equipped to fight for freedom for all than those at the very bottom… how do we know who's at the bottom? We need only look to our prisons. We need only look to who is dying at the hands of police. We need only look at the most disenfranchised. Because even within the narrative of Blackness, we know it is queer Black people. It is trans Black people. It is poor Black people. And disabled Black people. We are an organization that is deeply invested in a Black, trans, feminist politic… We recognize and build capacity around that type of leadership. So if you want to be part of this movement, then we need to learn together. To love together. To create space for that beautiful plurality together."

Janaya Khan with LeRoi Newbold, "Black Lives Matter

Toronto Teach–In," 2018 (147)

---

1 Members of Black Lives Matter—Toronto (BLM) march in the Toronto Pride Parade, 2016. Photograph by Steve Russell/*Toronto Star* via Getty Images.

2 Participants at the Montreal Pride Parade, 2018. Photograph by Martine Doucet.

BLM Demands at Pride 2016:

- Commit to BQY (Black Queer Youth) continued space [including stage/tents], funding, and logistical support.
- Self-determination for all community spaces, allowing community full control over hiring, content, and structure of their stages.
- Full and adequate funding for community stages, including logistical, technical, and personnel support.
- Increase funding for Blockorama (to $10,000 + ASL interpretation & headliner funding).
- Removal of police floats in the Pride marches/parades.
- Reinstate and make a commitment to increase community stages/spaces (including the reinstatement of the South Asian stage).
- A commitment to increase representation amongst Pride Toronto staffing/hiring, prioritizing Black Trans women, Indigenous folk, and others from vulnerable communities.
- A public townhall, organized in conjunction with groups from marginalized communities including, but not limited to, Black Lives Matter–Toronto, Blackness Yes, and BQY to be held six months from today. Pride Toronto will present an update and action plan on the aforementioned demands.

1

2

FAMILY CAMERA
NETWORK

A collaborative project meant to interrogate and explore the connections between photography and notions of biological and/or chosen family, the Family Camera Network chronicles LGBTQ2+ experiences of family, community, and kinship. From 2016 to 2019, the Family Camera Network built a public archive of more than 17,000 family photographs (and dozens of oral history interviews) chronicling the lives LGBTQ2+ people and their individual and familial experiences of diaspora and migration.

With public programming at the Royal Ontario Museum and The ArQuives, among other venues in Toronto, the Network's collection demonstrates the richness of queer life through which we can trace broader Canadian histories of migration, social and political change, and kinship within and between communities of colour and other minority communities.

The Family Camera Network is organized by Thy Phu and co-organizers Sarah Bassnett, Deepali Dewan, Sarah Parsons, and Elspeth Brown—the latter of whom also serves on the Board of Directors of the ArQuives. The photographs we include here document chosen queer families and reveal the persistent desire to create and expand family outside and including biological bonds.

1

1 Sajdeep Soomal (*left*) with jess sachse (*right*), 2017. Photograph by Nate Sachse. Courtesy of the Family Camera Network.

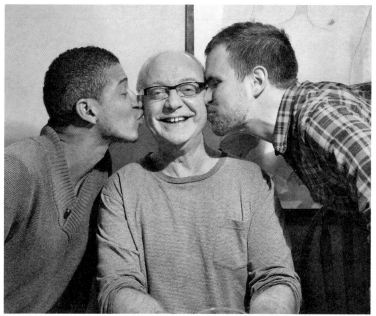

2   Luong Thai Lu at Thap Ba Ponagar (Ponagar Tower), Nha Trang, Vietnam, 1962. Photograph by Sang Thai Luong. Courtesy of the Family Camera Network.

3   Cecilio Escobar (*middle row, left*) and friends, 2015. Photograph by Anna (last name unknown). Courtesy of the Family Camera Network.

4   From left to right: Dionne Falconer, Courtnay McFarlane, Douglas Stewart, Angela Robertson, and Junior Harrison, Toronto, 2012. Photograph by Rose-Ann Marie Bailey. Courtesy of the Family Camera Network.

5   Dennis Findlay (*centre*) with Akim Larcher (*left*) and Ian Cummins (*right*), Toronto, 2011. Courtesy of the Family Camera Network.

INDIGENOUS
ORGANIZING

The organizing work of queer, trans, and Two-Spirit Indigenous people has been central to the progressive changes within LGBTQ2+ organizing in Canada. Following the development of the term *Two-Spirit* in Winnipeg in the 1990s, many organizations emerged and advocated on the behalf of queer, trans, and Two-Spirit communities. The Two-Spirited People of Manitoba, the Two-Spirited People of the First Nations (based in Toronto), the Two-Spirit Collective that grew out of the Urban Native Youth Centre in Vancouver, and the Saskatoon Two Spirit Society are just some of the organizations that work toward the recognition and safety of Indigenous Two-Spirit queer people. While such organizations aim to address the concerns of queer and Two-Spirit people within Indigenous communities, they also provide the opportunity for the broader LGBTQ community in Canada to challenge its anti-Indigenous racism and to reckon with its complicity in the settler colonial state.

"The determination of gender comes in large part through our sense of spirit. We maintain the belief that those among us who are different are the way they are as a result of a special gift from The Grandmothers. It matters not whether that difference is from birth or brought about through a revelation, or in a vision."

Aiyyana Maracle, "A Journey in Gender," 2000 (40)

Albert McLeod, founder of the Two-Spirit Archives in Winnipeg, argues that both the specific histories of Two-Spirit people within Indigenous communities and the broader political goals of Two-Spirit organizing are easily misunderstood and co-opted. On behalf of the Two-Spirited people of Manitoba, he writes,

The Two-Spirit Identity and human rights movement is specifically about indigenous people who self-identify as lesbian, gay, bisexual, transgender, queer and questioning. Our movement has evolved over the past forty-one years since the Gay American Indians (GAI) organization was founded in San Francisco in 1975. During the 60's and 70's many indigenous LGBTQ people found varying degrees of acceptance in the broader LGBT community. In response to the growing HIV epidemic in North America, the first international gathering of Native American gays and lesbians was held in Minneapolis in 1998. Subsequent gatherings have been held across the continent since then… Our travels to various locales have been intentional and serve to create safe spaces for local Two-Spirit people. (2spirits.com)

The photographs and documents we include here cover only a few of aspects of queer, trans, and Two-Spirit organizing. While our examples are from the Canadian context, Two-Spirit organizing regularly traverses national boundaries drawn by settler colonial states and speaks to the concerns of Indigenous people within and outside of the Canadian state.

1 Photoshoot in the park, likely in Toronto, c. 2000s. Gift of the Two-Spirited People of the First Nations.

2/3 Two-Spirited People of the First Nations at Toronto Pride, c. 1990s/2000s.

1 Two-Spirited People of the
First Nations at Toronto Pride,
c. 1990s/2000s.

2 Condom packets distributed
by the Two-Spirited People of the
First Nations, c. 2000s.

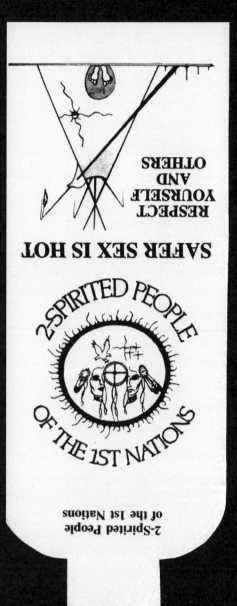

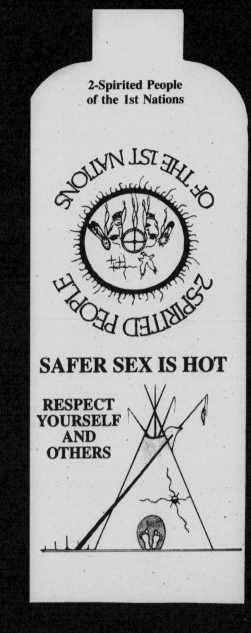

2-Spirited People
of the 1st Nations

2-SPIRITED PEOPLE
OF THE 1ST NATIONS

SAFER SEX IS HOT

**RESPECT
YOURSELF
AND
OTHERS**

MONSTROUS
LESBIANS

KillJoy's Kastle: A Lesbian Feminist Haunted House is a large-scale, site-specific, immersive performance created by Allyson Mitchell and Deirdre Logue and brought to life by an array of collaborators. The performance opened in Toronto in October 2013 and has subsequently been staged in London (2014), Los Angeles (2015), and Philadelphia (2019). *KillJoy's Kastle* recalls and restages lesbian-feminist histories and stereotypes (in all their ostensible terror) so that participants might reassess these histories and the ways they are remembered in the present moment.

The performance, animated by lesbian feminist movements of the 1960s and 1970s, is a public performance of feminist politics—an act of claiming space and evaluating representations of gender and sexuality in a heteronormative and patriarchal reality. It builds on another well-established, though much spookier, method of performance: evangelical hell houses—immersive performance spaces built to scare young people from the "sins" of homosexuality, premarital sex, and abortion. Visitors to *KillJoy's Kastle* are welcomed by a tour guide—a "Demented Women's Studies Professor"—and guided by other ghostly characters as they make their way through interactive, live-action scenes that each serve as a spectre of lesbian-feminist activism and political formation.

"[*KillJoy's Kastle*] seeks not to convert but to deconstruct; its goal is to process the fragments of information, histories, and bodies that render the queer woman abject and monstrous." **Moynan King, "Playing Demented Women's Studies Professor Tour Guide, or Performing Monstrosity in Killjoy's Kastle," 2019** (86)

Visitors to *KillJoy's Kastle* encounter a variety of performers including, among many others:

The Lesbian Zombie Folksingers

Da Carpet Muncha

The Polyamorous Vampiric Grannies

The Marvelous Emasculator

The Ball Bustas

Undead Pro-Choice Activists

The Menstrual Trans Man with Diva Cup

The Lesbian Art Dealer

The Gaybourhood Watch

The Crypt of Dead Lesbian Organizations, Businesses, and Ideas

1   Entrance to *KillJoy's Kastle* during opening night in Toronto, October 16, 2013. Photograph by Lisa Kannakko. Courtesy of the artists.

2   Inside *KillJoy's Kastle*, Toronto, 2013. Photograph by Lisa Kannakko. Courtesy of the artists.

3   Inside *KillJoy's Kastle*, Toronto, 2013. Photograph by Lisa Kannakko. Courtesy of the artists.

1

2

3

UNITY MOSQUE

Founded in 2009, the El-Tawhid Juma Circle (ETJC) is a mosque network that strives for equity and parity in its prayer space—among all genders, sexualities, religions, races, and other forms of difference. ETJC, also known as Unity Mosque, has locations in Montreal, Toronto, Ottawa, and Calgary. Many services are also available to access via Skype for the ease of participants who may be unable to attend due to health, geography, or other complicating factors. In each of these mosques—often with no set physical address—participants take turns giving the call to prayer, providing a sermon, and leading the group in prayer.

El-Farouk Khaki, the imam of the ETJC, has long been creating space for queer Muslims in Toronto. He founded Salaam: Queer Muslim Community in 1991.

"I am clergy who has risen to meet a need that is unmet by others. I try to bring to my ministry my politics, my human rights activism, and an anti-colonialist political and feminist narrative." **El-Farouk Khaki,** **"Building the Unity Mosque," 2017** (322)

1

1   El-Farouk Khaki (*left*) during prayer in Toronto, 2016. Photograph by Richard Lautens/*Toronto Star* via Getty Images.

TRANS AND
TWO-SPIRIT LITERATURE

The first decades of the twenty-first century saw the burgeoning of literature by and for trans people. An intervention in and expansion of the gay and lesbian literature genre of the twentieth century, trans literature helped bring questions about gender and the gender binary to the forefront of queer life. Trish Salah's *Wanting in Arabic,* for instance, was published in 2002 and, after its re-issue in 2013, won a Lambda Literary Award. Salah traces through poetry the complex pathways between sex and gender, language and race, and theory and practice.

In 2018, Billy-Ray Belcourt won the Griffin Poetry Prize and the Indigenous Voices Award for his poetry collection *This Wound Is a World.* In this collection, Belcourt—a writer and academic from the Driftpile Cree Nation—brings together the traumas of colonial violence with the forms of love and joy made possible by Indigenous resilience, themes that also inform Arielle Twist's collection of poetry *Disintegrate/ Dissociate* and Gwen Benaway's 2019 Governor General's Literary Award–winning collection *Holy Wild.* Novels and anthologies of both fiction and non-fiction have become ways for writers to articulate the realities of contemporary trans experience, as we see in Tom Cho's *Look Who's Morphing,* Joshua Whitehead's *Jonny Appleseed,* and Casey Plett's *Little Fish,* among others.

Ivan Coyote and Rae Spoon's *Gender Failure,* Kate Bornstein and S. Bear Bergman's *Gender Outlaws,* and Vivek Shraya's *I'm Afraid of Men* encourage readers to reassess the gender binary and its inability to adequately capture the complicated lives many of us live. Imagined worlds and collective methods of resistance to transphobic violence come to life in Kai Cheng Thom's *Fierce Femmes and Notorious Liars.* Trans literature, while taking the form of traditional publishing, also draws from the DIY publishing cultures of earlier

1

trans and feminist movements. Chapbooks such as Morgan M. Page's *At Land* and Estlin McPhee's *Shapeshifters* bring together the new and the old worlds of publishing, and remind us how early zines like *Gendertrash* (page 212) remain crucial to trans literature today.

The new landscape of trans literature is also exciting because it articulates both the unique and the ordinary aspects of trans experience. As Casey Plett writes in "Rise of the Gender Novel," "there are people out there writing good trans characters; many of those writers happen to be trans." Contrary to a literary history that has fetishized trans people as "curiosities" and articulated trans experiences primarily for cisgender readers, new forms of literature attempt to account for the vast array of trans lives and, as such, produce complex, realistic, and multidimensional characters.

1   Casey Plett's *Little Fish,* Kai Cheng Thom's *Fierce Femmes and Notorious Liars,* Joshua Whitehead's *Jonny Appleseed,* and Gwen Benaway's *Holy Wild.*

UNAPOLOGETIC
BURLESQUE

Queer burlesque gained new life in the twenty-first century, building and expanding on the already rich and provocative history of burlesque in Canada. Historically a means through which women could perform while also challenging restrictions on femininity, sexuality, and the female body, burlesque became a method of expression and resistance for a new generation of queers. In Toronto, the Scandelles, created by Sasha Van Bon Bon and Kitty Neptune, delighted audiences with their provocative and enlivening shows, such as *Who's Your Dada?* and *Under the Mink*. Other troupes, such as Unapologetic Burlesque, Boylesque, and Les Femmes Fatales, created spaces for not-your-typical performers: men, women of colour, trans people, and people with disabilities took the stage both to entertain and to reinvigorate our ideas of sex, pleasure, and bodily autonomy.

As T.L. Cowan writes of the recent history of cabaret, grunt gallery in Vancouver was a place in which the pleasurable and political nature of burlesque converged and enabled new possibilities of community. The gallery hosted cabaret for a variety of communities who may not perceive cabaret as part of their history, including a First Nations Performance Series and Queer City, a performance series featuring LGBTQ2+ individuals. *HalfBred*, performed in 1995, focused on the "in-between" spaces of existence—miscegenation, bisexuality, and gender transgression—and brought these spaces into conversation with each other. While Cowan focuses on the 1990s at grunt, performances in the twenty-first century remind us of the liberatory potential of burlesque and similarly encourage us to imagine ourselves outside the limitations of our racialized and gendered bodies and to form bonds with others within and outside of felt identities:

The magic of the cabaret, while it can engender tokenism and cliquishness in the name of *diversity,* is that, even if it is motivated by an identity political praxis, the variety format can usually not help but to consolidate and expand their subjects and subject matter simultaneously… there is no such thing as a *single way* to be bisexual, no such thing as a *unified* transgender or Indigenous or Two-Spirited positionality. Even while individual performers may attempt to articulate their own understandings of what it means to be Two-Spirited, Indigenous, trans, multi-racial, or queer, the variety format reveals the impossibility of framing a singular identity under the banner of these identity categories. (performance.gruntarchives.org)

1

---

1 From left to right: James & the Giant Pasty, Dew Lily, El Toro, and Wrong Note Rusty, c. 2010s. Photograph by Ruth Gillson.

2 From left to right: James & the Giant Pasty, Ginger Darling, Newfound Lad, Wrong Note Rusty, and El Toro, c. 2010s. Photograph by Lee Vandergrift.

3 From left to right: James & the Giant Pasty, Newfound Lad, Shagina Twain, and Wrong Note Rusty, c. 2010s. Photograph by James Monette.

4 From left to right: James & the Giant Pasty, Dew Lily, El Toro, and Wrong Note Rusty, c. 2010s. Photograph by James Monette.

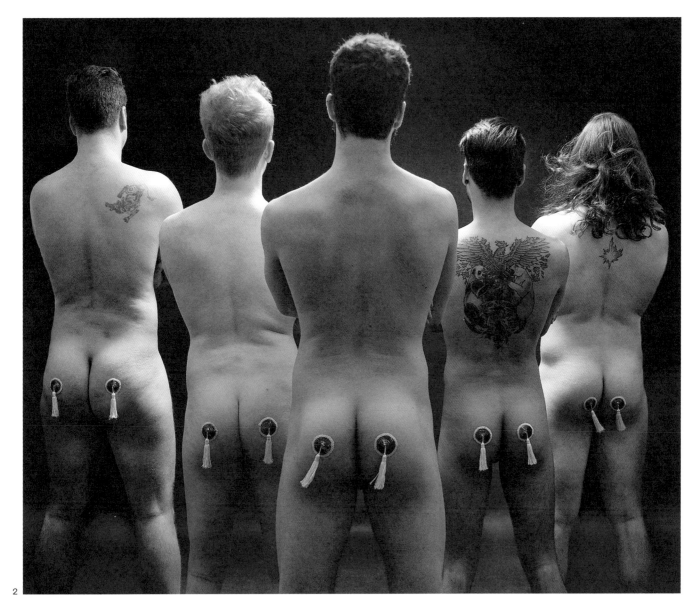

2

3

4

National Portraits

The National Portrait Collection launched in 1998—on the twenty-fifth anniversary of the Archives' forming—to celebrate twenty-five individuals who participated in the building and nurturing of the LGBTQ2+ community. The first twenty-five inductees included activists, artists, authors, politicians, filmmakers, and others whose work was important to a sense of queer Canadian collectivity.

In 1999, the collection toured Western cities and was displayed in Saskatoon, Edmonton, and Regina. In 2002, a nomination process was developed and nominations were solicited from across Canada. That same year, the collection was digitized for ease of access from across Canada. The collection continues to grow, with three inductees being added each year. The committee charged with developing the National Portrait Collection continues to encourage portraits in variety of media, including photography, oil, watercolour, and mixed media.

National Portrait Collection inductees

Elmer Bagares	Amy Gottlieb	Mary Meigs	Marie Robertson (6)
Chris Bearchell	John Greyson	Billy Merasty	Svend Robinson
Rick Bébout	Brent Hawkes	Robin Metcalfe	Gerry Rogers
Anne Bishop	Gens (Doug) Hellquist	Peter Millard	Mirha-Soleil Ross
Persimmon Blackbridge	Tomson Highway	Bonte Minnema	Jane Rule
Nicole Brossard (9)	Charlie Hill	Jearld Moldenhauer	Craig Russell (2)
Alec Butler	George Hislop	Shani Mootoo	Kyle Scanlon
Bernard Courte	Richard Hudler	Alex Munter	Shyam Selvadurai (5)
Harold Desmarais	David Kelley	Pat Murphy	Makeda Silvera
C.M. Donald	El-Farouk Khaki	Glen Murray	Mary-Woo Sims
Michelle Douglas	Robert Laliberté	Nancy Nicol	Tim Stevenson
John Duggan	k.d. lang	Richard North	Douglas Stewart
Sara Ellen Dunlop	Denis LeBlanc	Keith Norton	Barbara Thornborrow
Jim Egan	John Alan Lee	Carmen Paquette	Shelley Tremain
Gloria Eshkibok (4)	Bev Lepischak	Carole Pope	Susan Ursel
Lynne Fernie	Alan Li (8)	Ken Popert	Chris Vogel
John Fisher	Michael Lynch (7)	Kyle Rae	Delwin Vriend
Janine Fuller	Ann-Marie MacDonald	Rupert Raj (3)	Tom Warner
Richard Fung (1)	Jovette Marchessault	David Rayside	Douglas Wilson
Sky Gilbert	Tim McCaskell	Neil Richards	Eve Zaremba

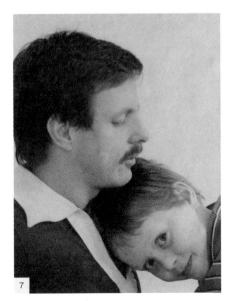

EPILOGUE: COLLECTIVE REMEMBERING

We (the authors) began this book as a way of better understanding our persistent attachments to queer pasts and to archival projects that keep these pasts alive. As two individuals who came into our queer politics at the cusp of liberal gay rights, we feel a great sense of kinship with queer people who came before. This kinship stems in part from gratitude to those who led the movements against state homophobia and everyday violence; but it also stems from our desire to learn from those older than us, those who lived and organized for their—and others'—sexual freedom in times more precarious and immediately violent than our own. One of the most meaningful results of writing this book is the intimacy we have built with older activists—sometimes through meetings in person, but often through our reading of published texts, and research in and time spent at queer archives and special collections in Canada.

We are drawn to the ArQuives in Toronto for its persistent work in memorializing the history of queer community, organizing, and kinship in Canada. But the ArQuives is only one small part of a larger network of projects that preserve these pasts and bring them into the present. Projects that chronicle and archive queer pasts can be found throughout Canada. The Transgender Archive housed at the University of Victoria is the largest trans archive in the world. The Two-Spirit Archives at the University of Winnipeg began with a series of donations by Albert McLeod, director of the group Two-Spirited People of Manitoba; it is the most comprehensive collection of materials on LGBTQ2+ Indigenous people in Canada. The Archives gaies du Québec/Quebec Gay Archives has, since 1983, collected materials related to the history of the LGBTQ2+ communities of Quebec. The Queer Media Database Canada-Québec Project (also known as Media Queer) continues to develop a phenomenal archive and online catalogue of LGBTQ2+ Canadian film and video work. The University Archives and Special Collections at the University of Saskatchewan houses a huge collection of LGBTQ2+ materials that chronicle political formation in the province and elsewhere. Housed at Simon Fraser University, the Archives of Lesbian Oral Testimony (ALOT) collects and digitizes oral testimonies, bringing evidence of queer women's lives to a broader audience.

Municipal and provincial archives also hold sizeable collections, including the BC Gay and Lesbian Archives at the City of Vancouver Archives and the Nova Scotia LGBT Archives project—a collaboration between Halifax Public Libraries, Dalhousie University, and the Nova Scotia Rainbow Action Project (NSRAP)—as well as exciting special projects within these institutions, such as the New Brunswick Queer Heritage Initiative. The Family Camera Network (page 254) asks questions about (biological and chosen) family and chronicles queer individuals' experiences of diaspora. The AIDS Activist History Project, hosted at Carleton University, captures and archives personal narratives of Canadian AIDS activists in Halifax, Montreal, Ottawa, Toronto, and Vancouver alongside ephemera from activism in Canada more broadly.

Many archival projects in Canada implicitly or explicitly address the absences in the ArQuives' collection. For instance, Marvellous Grounds, an archival collective based in Toronto, brings to the fore the invisibilized histories of racialized queer, trans, and Two-Spirit communities. The Canadian Women's Movement Archives in Ottawa and Rise Up! A Feminist

1   Gary Kinsman (*left*), with other participants at Toronto Pride, 1984.

Digital Archive preserve and make available materials from the history of women's organizing in Canada. Queer history projects in Calgary and Edmonton, among many others in cities across Canada, do important work of decentring Toronto in the narratives of queer life in Canada.

Queer practices of archiving and remembering have the potential to push back against the erasure of LGBTQ2+ lives and to refute simplistic narratives of the past. While we have focused here on the collection of the ArQuives, we hope this book becomes part of this broad network of queer remembrance projects. This book is an opening gesture—a scratching of the surface of complicated and diverse histories of queerness in Canada. We are honoured to participate with so many others in this ongoing, collaborative, and necessarily collective work.

Canadian Gay Liberation Movement Archives

The Canadian Gay Liberation Movement Archives were founded to act as a resource center to collect, preserve and make available all materials relating to the Candian gay community, so that our past and present history and culture, up till now denied us by straight society, might be maintained in its entirety. Such an archives will, it is hoped, make Canadians, both homosexual and heterosexual, more aware of our role and importance in Canadian society, and encourage and facilitate research and studies into all aspects of gay life in Canada. One of the primary aims of the Archives is to trace the history of the gay liberation movement in Canada by collecting copies of all documents relating to the development of the movement in this country such as books, newspapers, magazines, booklets, pamphlets, newsletters, posters, leaflets, articles, personal accounts or any other relevant materials. Though the primary concern of the Archives is the establishment of a complete Canadian collection, the scope is international.

The Canadian Gay Liberation Movement Archives whose founding was first announced at the first National Conference in Quebec City last October has now been in existence for 10 months. The first task of the Archives was to organize and file the extensive material from the Body Politic files, under whose sponsorship the Archives were established and remain. Secondly, gay organizations across Canada were contacted to request their support in the form of contributions of materials and funds. Most groups responded in a very favourable manner, sending materials and letters of support. Contributions of funds were gratefully received from GATE Toronto, GATE Vancouver, the University of Western Ontario Homophile Association, the Zodiac Friendship Society and Gay Montreal. With these funds 2 file drawers, stationery, postage and a few minor acquisitions were purchased. A Canada Council "Explorations" grant was applied for but refused. All Canadian gay publications and most major American publications were also contacted to request back issues and to request being put on their mailing lists. Most have been very co-operative. Most equivalent American archival projects- the Institute for Social Ethics in Hartford, Conn., the American Gay Liberation Movement Archives at Northwestern University, the Homosexual Information Centre in Los Angeles, the Stonewall Library in Florida, the Chicago Gay Archives, the Boston Gay Archives Project and the Mattachine Library in New York- have been contacted to exchange ideas and to discuss the possibility of exchanging materials. The Archives has already served on several occasions to provide documentation for individuals and organizations doing both academic and gay liberation research. Copies of documents and briefs concerning the human rights code struggles of the various organizations were forwarded to Gay Montreal which is commencing a similar campaign, for example.

For those interested in the file system of the Archives, there are 2 separate files- one for Canadian groups, each Canadian gay organization is filed alphabetically according to city- and a second for publications, both Canadian and foreign.

Materials are now being received on a daily basis, through the regular mailing of most publications and organizational documents and through the donations of organizations and individuals. As the collection becomes more and more significant, its value as a resource centre for documentation on gay liberation will increase. Contributions of any sort, particularily of pre 1973 materials is desperately sought. Early 1960's Canadian material, such as copies of Two have still to be found. Donations of money are also needed, since a great deal remains to be purchased, the basic gay lib literature, for example, and other more rare items. A great deal also remains to be filed, a painstaking and timeconsuming work.

(416) 465-1403   203 Boulton Avenue Toronto, Ontario M4M 2J8

AFTERWORD: THE LABOUR OF QUEER ARCHIVING

PHANUEL ANTWI
AND AMBER DEAN

Amassing a history of the present is *work*. It is labour-intensive and, as the writers of the first Canadian Gay Liberation Movement Archives leaflet insisted, it is "painstaking and timeconsuming work" (page 270). The painstaking labour that authors Craig Jennex and Nisha Eswaran invested in digging through the ArQuives' holdings and collecting the broad range of materials that appear in these pages accomplishes at least two important things: it allows us to feel a sense of excitement and possibility, by recognizing the ways in which LGBTQ2+ people have asserted that our lives and histories matter, *and* it invites us to read across decades to consider how the past matters *now*. What they have accomplished is a form of what queer theorist Ann Cvetkovich calls "queer archive activism," because this book insists "that the archive serve not just as a repository for safeguarding objects, but also as a resource that 'comes out' into the world to perform public interventions" (32). More than this, Jennex and Eswaran's labour foregrounds

what queer theorist José Esteban Muñoz calls "ephemeral evidence," as they "grant entrance and access to those who have been locked out of official histories" (9).

By reflecting here on the labour of Jennex and Eswaran and of all those who contributed to the archiving of the materials collected in this book, as well as on the labours of those members of queer and trans communities whose histories are generally archived in less conventional forms, we aim to tease out some of the stakes of this kind of work. What does an archive *do*? What does it mean to attempt to document a history of radical struggle? What *acts* does an archive form or inspire? In his recent essay "All Power to All People? Black LGBT-TI2QQ Activism, Remembrance, and Archiving in Toronto," Syrus Marcus Ware prompts us to remember that when we assess the versions of history documented in an archive, we must consider "how power and privilege influence what is allowed to be remembered, and what is considered archivable" (170). Because we live in a world shaped by white privilege, archives—even independent, radical archives, he suggests—tend to "create and inscribe a narrative of struggle

and resistance that always begins with whiteness" (171).

This tendency to begin with whiteness is as true of the collections of the ArQuives—from which most of the materials in this book are drawn—as it is of most mainstream or state-sponsored archives. And yet we remain hopeful that by attending to the labour of amassing such an archive, it is possible to locate and mobilize moments of complex solidarities that can challenge this re-centring of whiteness. This book archives queer memory and history not readily available; it emphasizes the ephemerality of queer archives; but it also invites us to ask, How can the archives assembled here have "powerful worldmaking capabilities" (Muñoz, 11) for a wide range of publics and not simply white, homonormative publics? Following queer and Black diaspora cultural studies scholar Rinaldo Walcott, the archival material collected in this book has the potential to "constitute conversations that work at the level of the ephemeral so as to produce communities of sharing and political identifications across a range of local, national, and international boundaries of desire and sex" (140–41). We hope that as we labour to

1 Leaflet by the Canadian Gay Liberation Movement Archives, 1974.

mobilize conversations across the archival ephemera assembled here, we can, to borrow from Walcott again, "make the political appear" (141).

The authors of this book have argued that "memory work," or the work of attending and connecting to past queer lives and queer struggles, remains essential to queer life in the present (page 11). But what does it mean to connect to the past? Most often, history is framed in a way that encourages learning *about* the past but not *from* it (Britzman 1998; see also Simon, Rosenberg, and Eppert 2000), in the sense that we take in events, facts, and figures as history but are less often provoked to reckon with any implications these things might have for our lives now. We are mostly encouraged to think about the past as *past*—interesting to learn about perhaps but not really pressing on our contemporary lives today. This conventional way of thinking about what the past is and how it becomes relevant to our everyday lives is an enormous political problem, and too often a barrier to building meaningful solidarities across differences. For if the past is *past,* then whatever violence or injustice may have happened in that past is really just history—possibly deemed worthy of a government apology or two following enormous political struggle, but still over and done with, events from which we have collectively moved on or "progressed." People who take this

view of the past are most often the "victors" of history: those who wield power and privilege to secure their own dominance and relative protection from precarity. Marginalized and oppressed communities tend to understand and live (with) the past quite differently. For us the past is ongoing, the past is *now,* the past does not go away because someone has apologized for it, and the past profoundly shapes our sense of who we are and what we are doing in the present.

This very different way of understanding and relating to the past helps explain why, though we can flip through the decades of activism the book documents and still feel hopeful, Jennex and Eswaran have avoided representing LGBTQ2+ history in Canada as a straightforward march toward ever-greater progress (as far too many people today seem to assume it is). We suggest that this book asks us to read both along and against the grain of the archive: it invites us to read *along the grain* by highlighting significant moments archived decade by decade, and it challenges us to read *against the grain* by refusing to represent these decades as a linear march toward progress.* Cultivating the ability to read both along and against the grain of an archive is essential work for those invested in critical histories of the present. There is no march toward seemingly inevitable rights and freedoms for LGBTQ2+

communities living north of the 49th parallel on offer here, nor should there be. What is obvious, especially when we survey the ongoing violence experienced by LGBTQ2+ people today, is that legalized rights and freedoms do not translate into liberation from oppression and violence—at least not for most. Black lesbian poet, writer, and activist Audre Lorde's now widely cited warning continues to ring true: *"For the master's tools will never dismantle the master's house.* They may allow us temporarily to beat him at his own game, but they will never enable us to bring about genuine change" (112).

What runs like a connecting thread throughout the decades of queer struggle archived in this book is the persistence of state-sanctioned violence against LGBTQ2+ people. The examples we can read across this book map a long durée of state violence toward queer subjects (see "Queer Happenings Pre-1939," page 16), reminding us that despite the structures that produce queer absence in the nation, we are still *here.* But "here" is a complicated ground: historian Lorenzo Veracini argues that "archives are

---

*In *Along the Archival Grain: Epistemic Anxieties and Colonial Common Sense,* Ann Laura Stoler argues that we must learn to read *along* (and not just *against*) the grain of an archive in order to understand the versions of reality and history that the archive aims to cement.

by definition settled places"; he goes on to insist that "thinking about archives and their constitution and operation is also a reflection on settler colonialism as a specific mode of domination" (269). In a settler colonial nation, Indigenous Studies scholar Chris Finley reminds us, "the bodies of Native women and men are queered and racialized as disordered, unreproductive, and therefore nonheteronormative. By making Native bodies 'disappear,' the colonial logic of Native nonheteronormative sexualities justifies genocide and conquest" (37). In other words, the practice of identifying what is "queer" is intimately entwined with the formative violence of settler colonial states such as Canada. The archival materials collected here teach us that the formation of a settler colonial state, one that aims to disappear Indigenous subjects, also requires other forms of violence—racist, sexist, homophobic, and gendered violence—to prop up its legitimacy. But archives can also be *unsettled*. This unsettlement happens through the labour of attending to an archive's seemingly settled places—as Jennex and Eswaran have—in the interests of challenging the "finished" representations of history that these settled places might suggest.

In conjoining the labour of unsettling the archive to the work of resisting this ongoing state-sanctioned violence, we find evidence in the book of complex solidarities across differences and of missed opportunities to build or sustain such solidarities. For instance, in response to the 1981 police raids of several gay men's bathhouses in Toronto, the authors found ample evidence in the archives of solidarities formed between Black and queer community members resisting police violence (page 168; see also Jennex 2015). The need for these solidarities echoes in the ongoing resistance to police violence organized by groups like Black Lives Matter (page 252). BLM's resistance to racism within the queer and trans community demonstrates how queer and trans Black, Indigenous, and people of colour are still too often identified by white queer and trans people as racialized first and as queer and trans second or not at all. We can read this problem of (mis)identification as what Dionne Brand calls "signs of exits" (204), or the evacuation of certain bodies from certain categories at certain historical moments. Through this critical reading practice, we can perhaps productively attend to lives that "haunt" the archives, clearly audible but dimly heard through multiple forms of absenting.

So long as white supremacy continues to shape the question of whose queer and trans lives and histories matter most, the ArQuives, like all efforts to document queer and trans histories, will continue to be both shaped by and resistant to this context.

When its holdings are presented not as *the* history of LGBTQ2+ life in Canada but as *a* form of historical record that can be read critically along and against the grain—while simultaneously celebrating the moments of solidarity across difference that Jennex and Eswaran's archival curation reveals—we can start to see why the painstaking labour of amassing such an archive remains as crucially important today as it was when the Canadian Gay Liberation Movement Archives was first conceived.

We dedicate our afterword to our mentor, colleague, friend, and queer confidant Dr. Don Goellnicht, whose loss we were mourning as we were finishing this piece.

Phanuel Antwi is assistant professor of English at the University of British Columbia where he writes, researches, and teaches critical Black studies, Black Atlantic and diaspora studies, gender and sexuality studies, and Canadian literature and culture.

Amber Dean is associate professor of Cultural Studies and Gender Studies at McMaster University. She is the author of *Remembering Vancouver's Disappeared Women: Settler Colonialism and the Difficulty of Inheritance* (University of Toronto Press, 2015).

ACKNOWLEDGEMENTS

This book has been a collective project from its beginning to end, and we would like to offer our deepest gratitude to the many people who made this work possible. Thank you to the Canada History Fund, the Pride and Remembrance Foundation, the S.M. Blair Family Foundation, and the Faculty of Arts at Ryerson University for their generous support.

Ed Jackson, Alan V. Miller, Donald McLeod, and Colin Deinhardt were integral to this project, stewarding us through the history of the ArQuives with great generosity. Thank you also to Rupert Raj, Robin Metcalfe, Lamar Van Dyke, Chris Fox, Tim McCaskell, Rachel Epstein, Elspeth Brown, and Amy Gottlieb for sharing their knowledge of queer life and political activism with us, and to Meredith Evans for all her support with research and editing as we rushed to meet our deadlines. Thanks, also, to Phanuel Antwi and Amber Dean—two thinkers we admire greatly—who wrote the afterword for this book.

Thanks to the ArQuives' Board of Directors for their trust, and to present and former staff members at the ArQuives whose help was invaluable to this project: Raegan Swanson, Jennifer Aja Fernandes, Carmen Tang, Lucie Handley-Girard, Tobaron Waxman, Adriana Ho, Jade Pichette, Caitlin Smith, Sajdeep Soomal, Zohar Freeman, Charly Wreggitt, Stefanie Martin, and Shamsa Abdullahi Mahmud.

Our deepest thanks to the team at Figure 1: Michelle Meade and Jessica Sullivan, whose ideas propelled this book forward, and to Lara Smith, Chris Labonté, Richard Nadeau, Mark Redmayne, and Michelle Young who each played a role in getting this done. Working together on this book has been transformative and we are grateful for their support in making it all possible. Stephanie Fysh, Alison Strobel, and Stephen Ullstrom provided copy editing, proofreading, and indexing, respectively, and we appreciate their attention and care.

I (Nisha) would like to thank Craig Jennex for the opportunity to work on this book about the queer histories of kinship to which I'm so attached. Many people saw me through this project, and my sincere gratitude goes to Kate Atkinson, Arti Mehta, Charlie Williams, Dex Thompson, Wanli Ou, Anita Castelino, and Nat Ko for sharing in the everyday excitement and struggles and for taking care of me throughout. Thank you to my family—Viju, Mukesh, and Hari Eswaran—for their steadfast faith in me and for their encouragement of my intellectual and emotional growth, and to my partner, Sita Balani, for trusting in—and helping me find—my place in the world of ideas. Thank you to my dissertation supervisor, Nadine Attewell, whose generous engagement with my work over the years has changed my thinking and writing for the better. My deepest gratitude goes to my friends and mentors Don Goellnicht and Brianna Hersey. Each passed away just before and during the writing of this book and remain integral to my conception of queer life and kinship. I miss them, and I thank them both.

I (Craig) would like to thank Nisha Eswaran for agreeing to participate in this massive project. Meredith Evans and Maria Murphy have supported this project from the start; their patience, friendship, and careful edits kept me going. Thanks also to Clorinde

Peters, Milé Komlen, Geoff Tobin, Joey Romkey, Melissa Burke, Liss Platt, Claudia Manley, Charity Marsh, Bev Vatamanuk, Allison Bent, Sarah McLaughlin, and Frank Bent-McLaughlin for incredible adventures that cleared my head during the writing of this book. I've been fortunate to enjoy unparalleled mentorship from individuals whose support continues to mean the world to me: Susan Fast, Amber Dean, Christina Baade, Jacqueline Warwick, and the late José Esteban Muñoz—thank you all. Halfway through this project I was welcomed into the Department of English at Ryerson University; I feel lucky to work among such intelligent and creative thinkers. Thanks to my family—Mom, Dad, Sara, John, and Cohen, as well as the broader Jennex, Fougere, Dalziel, Fraughton, Kuhn, and Furyk clans—for unwavering support and love. Even when complicated projects and tight deadlines turn me into a nightmare, Adam Kuhn is nothing short of a dream. Finally, the ArQuives has long been a site of intellectual inspiration and meaningful kinship; I feel truly fortunate to participate in the ongoing collective project of keeping these stories alive.

WORKS CITED

Anderson, Carolyn. "The Voices of Older Lesbian Women: An Oral History." PhD dissertation, University of Calgary, 2001.

Backhouse, Constance. *Colour-Coded: A Legal History of Racism in Canada, 1900–1950.* Toronto: Osgoode Society for Canadian Legal History; University of Toronto Press, 1999.

Bain, Beverly. "Fire, Passion, and Politics: The Creation of Blockorama as Black Queer Diasporic Space in the Toronto Pride Festivities." *We Still Demand: Redefining Resistance in Sex and Gender Struggles.* Edited by Patrizia Gentile, Gary Kinsman, and L. Pauline Rankin. Vancouver: UBC Press, 2017.

Bearchell, Chris. "Lesbian Pride March Is a First for Canada." *The Body Politic,* June 1981, 10.

Bébout, Rick. "1979." *Promiscuous Affections: A Life in the Bar, 1969–2000.* 1999; rev. 2003. At rbebout.com/bar/1979.htm

——. "Stashing the Evidence." *The Body Politic,* August 1979, 21–22.

——. "The Very Long & Contentious Career of 'Men Loving Boys Loving Men.'" *Text Crimes.* 2003. At rbebout.com/mlb/intro.htm

Brand, Dionne. *Map to the Door of No Return.* Toronto: Vintage Canada, 2001.

Britzman, Deborah P. *Lost Subjects, Contested Objects: Toward a Psychoanalytic Inquiry of Learning.* Albany: State University of New York Press, 1998.

Brown, Elspeth. "Canada's First Gay Student Activist Group." *Notches,* 5 February 2019. At notchesblog.com/2019/02/05/canadas-first-gay-student-activist-group/

Brown, Heather Ann. "History: The Toronto Dyke Scene."

Section 15.ca: Rebels without a Cause, 15 June 2004. At section15.ca/features/reviews/2004/06/15/toronto_dyke_history/

Catungal, John Paul. " 'We Had to Take Space, We Had to Create Space': Locating Queer of Colour Politics in 1980s Toronto." *Queering Urban Justice: Queer of Colour Formations in Toronto.* Edited by Jin Haritaworn, Ghaida Moussa, and Syrus Marcus Ware, with Río Rodríguez. Toronto: University of Toronto Press, 2018. 45–61.

Churchill, David S. "Demanding Possibilities: The Legacies and Potentials of Sex and Gender Activism," *Journal of Canadian Studies,* vol. 48, no. 1 (2014): 5–14.

Cowan, T.L. "Cabaret at grunt: Up Your Community." *(Queer) Intersections: Vancouver Performance in the 1990s.* 25 February 2012. At performance.gruntarchives.org/essay-cabaret-at-grunt.html

Cvetkovich, Ann. "The Queer Art of the Counterarchive." *Cruising the Archive: Queer Art and Culture in Los Angeles, 1945–1980.* Edited by David Evans Frantz and Mia Locks. Los Angeles: ONE National Lesbian and Gay Archives, 2011. 32–35.

Douglas, Debbie. "That Collective House on Dewson Street." *Any Other Way: How Toronto Got Queer.* Edited by John Lorinc et al. Toronto: Coach House Books, 2017. 176–77.

Dryden, OmiSoore H. " 'A Queer Too Far': Blackness, 'Gay Blood,' and Transgressive Possibilities." *Disrupting Queer Inclusion: Canadian Homonationalisms and the Politics of Belonging.* Edited by OmiSoore H. Dryden and Suzanne Lenon. Vancouver: UBC Press, 2015. 116–32.

Duder, Cameron. *Awfully Devoted Women: Lesbian Lives in Canada, 1900–65.* Vancouver: UBC Press, 2011.

Egan, Jim. *Challenging the Conspiracy of Silence: My Life as a Canadian Gay Activist.* Edited by Donald McLeod. Toronto: CLGA and Homewood Books, 1998.

Finley, Chris. "Decolonizing the Queer Native Body (and Recovering the Native Bull-Dyke): Bringing 'Sexy Back' and Out of Native Studies' Closet." *Queer Indigenous Studies: Critical Interventions in Theory, Politics, and Literature.* Edited by Qwo-Li Driskill, Chris Finley, Brian Joseph Gilley, and Scott Lauria Morgensen. Tucson: University of Arizona Press, 2011. 31–42.

Forbes, John. "Sara Ellen Dunlop and the Music Room: A Memory." *Any Other Way: How Toronto Got Queer.* Edited by John Lorinc et al. Toronto: Coach House Books, 2017. 127–29.

Foster, Marion, and Kent Murray. *A Not So Gay World: Homosexuality in Canada.* Toronto: McClelland and Stewart, 1972.

Fraser, James A., and Harold A. Averill. *Organizing an Archives: The Canadian Gay Archives Experience.* Toronto: The Canadian Gay Archives, 1983.

Gentile, Patrizia. " 'À bas la répression contre les homosexuels!': Resistance and Surveillance of Queers in Montreal, 1971–76." *We Still Demand: Redefining Resistance in Sex and Gender Struggles.* Edited by Patrizia Gentile, Gary Kinsman, and L. Pauline Rankin. Vancouver: UBC Press, 2017. 68–80.

Gottlieb, Amy. "Toronto's Unrecognized First Dyke March." *Any*

Other Way: How Toronto Got Queer.* Edited by John Lorinc et al. Toronto: Coach House Books, 2017. 330–32.

Haritaworn, Jin, interview with Richard Fung. "It Was a Heterotopia: Four Decades of Queer of Colour Art and Activism in Toronto." *Marvellous Grounds: Queer of Colour Formations in Toronto.* Edited by Jin Haritaworn, Ghaida Moussa, and Syrus Marcus Ware. Toronto: Between the Lines Press, 2018. 35–46.

Hooper, Tom. "Bathhouse Raids in Canada 1968–2004." Chart (March 2018). At anti-69.ca/wp-content/uploads/2019/01/Chart_Bathhouse_raids_in_Canada_1968-200-3.pdf

———. "'Enough Is Enough': The Right to Privacy Committee and Bathhouse Raids in Toronto, 1978–83." PhD dissertation, York University, 2016.

Hustak, Alan. "Celebrated Montreal Drag Queen Was First to Be Accepted without Moral Judgment." *Globe and Mail,* 9 July 2012; updated 1 May 2018. At theglobeandmail.com/news/national/celebrated-montreal-drag-queen-was-first-to-be-accepted-without-moral-judgment/article4401993/

Jackson, Ed, and Jarett Henderson. "Sex, Scandal, and Punishment in Early Toronto." *Any Other Way: How Toronto Got Queer.* Edited by John Lorinc et al. Toronto: Coach House Books, 2017. 86–89.

Jackson, Paul. *One of the Boys: Homosexuality in the Military during World War II.* Montreal and Kingston: McGill-Queen's University Press, 2004.

Jennex, Craig. "NO MORE SHIT! Complicated Collectivity, Past and Present." *GUTS: Canadian Feminist Magazine,* 20 January 2015. At gutsmagazine.ca/no-shit/

Jones, G.B., and Bruce LaBruce. "Don't Be Gay, or How I Learned to Stop Worrying and Fuck Punk Up the Ass." *Maximumrocknroll,* vol. 71 (1989): 52–53.

Khaki, El-Farouk. "Building the Unity Mosque." *Any Other Way: How*

Toronto Got Queer.* Edited by John Lorinc et al. Toronto: Coach House Books, 2017. 322–324.

Khan, Janaya, and LeRoi Newbold. "Black Lives Matter Toronto Teach-In." *Queering Urban Justice: Queer of Colour Formations in Toronto.* Edited by Jin Haritaworn, Ghaida Moussa, and Syrus Marcus Ware, with Río Rodríguez. Toronto: University of Toronto Press, 2018. 138–47.

Khosla, Punam. "Desh Pardesh: South Asian Culture in the Diaspora." *Rungh: A South Asian Quarterly of Culture, Comment, and Criticism,* vol 1., nos. 1/2, (1992): 5.

King, Moynan. "Playing Demented Women's Studies Professor Tour Guide, or Performing Monstrosity in Killjoy's Kastle." *Inside Killjoy's Kastle: Dykey Ghosts, Feminist Monsters, and Other Lesbian Hauntings.* Edited by Allyson Mitchell and Cait McKinney. Vancouver: UBC Press, 2019. 85–97.

Kinsman, Gary. *The Regulation of Desire: Homo and Hetero Sexualities.* Montreal: Black Rose Books, 1996.

Kinsman, Gary, and Patrizia Gentile, eds. *The Canadian War on Queers: National Security as Sexual Regulation.* Vancouver: UBC Press, 2010.

Knegt, Peter. "Canada Has Had Way More Than 69 Super Queeroes." *CBC Arts,* 27 June 2019. At cbc.ca/arts/canada-has-had-way-more-than-69-super-queeroes-here-are-a-few-we-missed-1.5179860

———. *Queer Rights.* Halifax: Fernwood Publishing, 2011.

Korinek, Valerie J. *Prairie Fairies: A History of Queer Communities and People in Western Canada, 1930–1985.* Toronto: University of Toronto Press, 2018.

Levy, Ariel. "Lesbian Nation." *The New Yorker,* 22 February 2009. At newyorker.com/magazine/2009/03/02/lesbian-nation

Li, Alan. "Power in Community: Queer Asian Activism from the 1980s to the 1990s." *Marvellous Grounds: Queer of Colour Formations in Toronto.* Edited by Jin Haritaworn,

Ghaida Moussa, and Syrus Marcus Ware. Toronto: Between the Lines Press, 2018. 47–60.

Liss, Sarah. *Army of Lovers: A Community History of Will Munro.* Toronto: Coach House Books, 2013.

Lord, Cassandra R., with Jamea Zuberi. "Blackness Yes! Blockorama: Making Black Queer Diasporic Space in Toronto Pride." *Any Other Way: How Toronto Got Queer.* Edited by John Lorinc et al. Toronto: Coach House Books, 2017. 342–45.

Lorde, Audre. *Sister Outsider: Essays and Speeches.* Freedom, CA: The Crossing Press, 1984.

Maracle, Aiyyana. "A Journey in Gender." *Torquere: Journal of the Canadian Lesbian and Gay Studies Association,* vol. 2 (2000): 36–57.

Matte, Nick. "Rupert Raj and the Rise of Transsexual Consumer Activism in the 1980s." *Trans Activism in Canada: A Reader.* Edited by Dan Irving and Rupert Raj. Toronto: Canadian Scholars' Press, 2014. 33–44.

McCaskell, Tim. *Queer Progress: From Homophobia to Homonationalism.* Toronto: Between the Lines Press, 2016.

McKay, Richard A. *Patient Zero and the Making of the AIDS Epidemic.* Chicago: University of Chicago Press, 2017.

McLeod, Albert. "Author Joseph Boyden and the Two-Spirit Human Rights Movement: Clarifying How the Two-Spirit Name Is Synonymous with Indigenous LGBTQ People." Press release. Two-Spirited People of Manitoba, 30 December 2016. At 2spirits.com

McLeod, Donald W. *A Brief History of GAY: Canada's First Gay Tabloid, 1964–1966.* Toronto: Homewood Books, 2003.

———. *Lesbian and Gay Liberation in Canada: A Selected Annotated Chronology, 1964–1975.* Toronto: ECW Press and Homewood Books, 1996.

Metcalfe, Robin. "Light in the Loafers: The Gaynor Photographs of Gaëtan Dugas and the Invention of Patient

Zero." *Image and Inscription: An Anthology of Contemporary Canadian Photography.* Edited by Robert Bean. Toronto: Gallery 44 and YYZ Books, 2005. 65–75.

———. "Queer Looking, Queer Acting, Seeks Same." *Out: Queer Looking, Queer Acting Revisited.* Edited by Robin Metcalfe. Halifax: Khyber Centre for the Arts, 2014.

Millward, Liz. *Making a Scene: Lesbians and Community across Canada, 1964–84.* Vancouver: UBC Press, 2015.

Moldenhauer, Jearld. "A Literary Breakthrough: Glad Day's Origins." *Any Other Way: How Toronto Got Queer.* Edited by John Lorinc et al. Toronto: Coach House Books, 2017. 158–60.

Muñoz, José Esteban. "Ephemera as Evidence: Introductory Notes to Queer Acts." *Women & Performance: a journal of feminist theory,* vol. 8, no. 2 (1996): 5–16.

Namaste, Viviane. " 'We Paved the Way for Whatever Tolerance They Have in Their Lives': An Interview with Michelle De Ville, 'The First Door Bitch in Montreal.' " *Trans Activism in Canada: A Reader.* Edited by Dan Irving and Rupert Raj. Toronto: Canadian Scholars' Press, 2014. 19–26.

Nash, Catherine. "Consuming Sexual Liberation: Gay Business, Politics, and Toronto's Barracks Bathhouse Raid." *Journal of Canadian Studies,* vol. 48, no. 1 (2014): 82–105.

Page, Morgan M. "The Forgotten Legacy of Trans Artist and Activist Mirha Soleil-Ross." *Dazed,* 12 February 2019. At dazeddigital.com/art-photography/article/43093/1/mirha-soleil-ross-morgan-m-page-chelsea-manning-trans-art

Rayside, David. *On the Fringe: Gays and Lesbians in Politics.* Ithaca, NY: Cornell University Press, 1998.

Rayside, David, and Evert Lindquist. "AIDS Activism and the State in Canada." *Studies in Political Economy: A Socialist Review,* vol. 39 (1992): 37–76. At doi.org/10.1080/19187033.1992.1 1675417

Rose, Rebecca. "Before the Parade." *The Coast* (Halifax), 21 July 2016. At thecoast.ca/halifax/before-the-parade/Content?oid=5523368

Ross, Becki. *The House That Jill Built: A Lesbian Nation in Formation.* Toronto: University of Toronto Press, 1995.

Russell, Victor, Karen Teeple, and Harold Averill. "James Andrew Fraser, 1946–1985." *Archivaria: The Journal of Canadian Archivists,* vol. 20 (1985): 245–46.

Silvera, Makeda. "From St. Helens Avenue to Dewson Street." *Any Other Way: How Toronto Got Queer.* Edited by John Lorinc et al. Toronto: Coach House Books, 2017. 178–80.

Simon, Roger I., Sharon Rosenberg, and Claudia Eppert, eds. *Between Hope and Despair: Pedagogy and the Remembrance of Historical Trauma.* Lanham, MD: Rowman and Littlefield, 2000.

Sismondo, Christine. "Halloween Balls: From Letros to the St. Charles." *Any Other Way: How Toronto Got Queer.* Edited by John Lorinc et al. Toronto: Coach House Books, 2017. 102–4.

Stoler, Ann Laura. *Along the Archival Grain: Epistemic Anxieties and Colonial Common Sense.* Princeton, NJ: Princeton University Press, 2008.

Taitt, Tanisha. *thirsty.* Study guide. Ottawa: National Arts Centre, no date. At nac-cna.ca/en/englishtheatre/studyguide/thirsty

Torres, Eric. "Queering the Pitch: On *J.D.s* and the Roots of Queercore." *Pitchfork,* 28 January 2015. At pitchfork.com/thepitch/650-queering-the-pitch-on-jds-and-the-roots-of-queercore/

Vacante, Jeffery. *National Manhood and the Creation of Modern Quebec.* Vancouver: UBC Press, 2017.

Veracini, Lorenzo. "Afterword: The Global Archive of Liminal Settlement." *Archiving Settler Colonialism: Culture, Space and Race.* Edited by Yu-ting Huang and Rebecca Weaver-Hightower. New York: Routledge, 2019. 269–75.

Wagner, Anton, dir. *John Herbert: Fortune and Men's Eyes* (film).

2001. At youtube.com/watch?v=_50kzdZA-OM

Walcott, Rinaldo. "Queer Returns: Human Rights, the Anglo-Caribbean, and Diaspora Politics." *Queer Returns: Essays on Multiculturalism, Diaspora, and Black Studies.* London, ON: Insomniac Press, 2016. 128–64.

Ware, Syrus Marcus. "All Power to All People? Black LGBTTI2QQ Activism, Remembrance, and Archiving in Toronto." *TSQ: Transgender Studies Quarterly,* vol. 4, no. 2 (2017): 170–80.

Warner, Tom. *Never Going Back: A History of Queer Activism in Canada.* Toronto: University of Toronto Press, 2002.

White, David, and Pat Sheppard. *Report on Police Raids on Gay Steambaths.* Toronto City Council, 1981.

Zaremba, Eve. "Shades of Lavender: Lesbian Sex and Sexuality." *Still Ain't Satisfied: Canadian Feminism Today.* Edited by Maureen FitzGerald, Connie Guberman, and Margie Wolfe. Toronto: The Women's Press, 1982. 85–92.

FURTHER READING ON QUEER
HISTORIES AND POLITICS IN CANADA

Airton, Lee. *Gender: Your Guide. A Gender-Friendly Primer on What to Know, What to Say, and What to Do in the New Gender Culture.* Avon, MA: Adams Media, 2018.

Callaghan, Tonya D. *Homophobia in the Hallways: Heterosexism and Transphobia in Canadian Catholic Schools.* Toronto: University of Toronto Press, 2018.

Corriveau, Patrice. *Judging Homosexuals: A History of Gay Persecution in Quebec and France.* Translated by Käthe Roth. Vancouver: UBC Press, 2012.

Coyote, Ivan. *Tomboy Survival Guide.* Vancouver: Arsenal Pulp Press, 2016.

Crichlow, Wesley. *Buller Men and Batty Bwoys: Hidden Men in Toronto and Halifax Black Communities.* Toronto: University of Toronto Press, 2003.

Dawn, Amber. *How Poetry Saved My Life: A Hustler's Memoir.* Vancouver: Arsenal Pulp Press, 2013.

Diaz, Robert, Marissa Largo, and Fritz Pino, eds. *Diasporic Intimacies: Queer Filipinos and Canadian Imaginaries.* Chicago: Northwestern University Press, 2017.

Driskill, Qwo-Li, Chris Finley, Brian Joseph Gilley, and Scott Lauria Morgensen, eds. *Queer Indigenous Studies: Critical Interventions in Theory, Politics, and Literature.* Tucson: University of Arizona Press, 2011.

Dryden, OmiSoore H., and Suzanne Lenon, eds. *Disrupting Queer Inclusion: Canadian Homonationalisms and the Politics of Belonging.* Vancouver: UBC Press, 2015.

Duder, Cameron. *Awfully Devoted Women: Lesbian Lives in Canada, 1900–65.* Vancouver: UBC Press, 2011.

Egan, Jim. *Challenging the Conspiracy of Silence: My Life as a Canadian Gay Activist.* Edited by Donald McLeod. Toronto: CLGA and Homewood Books, 1998.

Filax, Gloria. *Queer Youth in the Province of the "Severely Normal."* Vancouver: UBC Press, 2007.

FitzGerald, Maureen, and Scott Rayter, eds. *Queerly Canadian: An Introductory Reader in Sexuality Studies.* Toronto: Canadian Scholars' Press, 2012.

Gentile, Patrizia, Gary Kinsman, and L. Pauline Rankin, eds. *We Still Demand! Redefining Resistance in Sex and Gender Struggles.* Vancouver: UBC Press, 2017.

Goldie, Terry, ed. *In a Queer Country: Gay & Lesbian Studies in the Canadian Context.* Vancouver: Arsenal Pulp Press, 2001.

Grace, André P., with Kristopher Wells. *Growing into Resilience: Sexual and Gender Minority Youth in Canada.* Toronto: University of Toronto Press, 2015.

Haritaworn, Jin, Ghaida Moussa, and Syrus Marcus Ware, with Río Rodríguez, eds. *Queering Urban Justice: Queer of Colour Formations in Toronto.* Toronto: University of Toronto Press, 2018.

Irving, Dan, and Rupert Raj, eds. *Trans Activism in Canada: A Reader.* Toronto: Canadian Scholars' Press, 2014.

Jackson, Ed, and Stan Persky, eds. *Flaunting It! A Decade of Gay Journalism from* The Body Politic. Toronto: New Star Books and Pink Triangle Press, 1982.

Jackson, Paul. *One of the Boys: Homosexuality in the Military during World War II.* Montreal and Kingston:

McGill-Queen's University Press, 2004.

Janoff, Douglas. *Pink Blood: Homophobic Violence in Canada.* Toronto: University of Toronto Press, 2005.

Kinsman, Gary. *The Regulation of Desire: Homo and Hetero Sexualities.* Montreal: Black Rose Books, 1996.

Kinsman, Gary, and Patrizia Gentile, eds. *The Canadian War on Queers: National Security as Sexual Regulation.* Vancouver: UBC Press, 2010.

Knegt, Peter. *Queer Rights.* Halifax: Fernwood Publishing, 2011.

Korinek, Valerie J. *Prairie Fairies: A History of Queer Communities and People in Western Canada, 1930–1985.* Toronto: University of Toronto Press, 2018.

Lahey, Kathleen A. *Are We "Persons" Yet? Law and Sexuality in Canada.* Toronto: University of Toronto Press, 1999.

Liss, Sarah. *Army of Lovers: A Community History of Will Munro.* Toronto: Coach House Books, 2013.

Lorinc, John, Jane Farrow, Stephanie Chambers, Maureen FitzGerald, Tim McCaskell, Rebecka Sheffield, Tatum Taylor, Rahim Thawer, and Ed Jackson, eds. *Any Other Way: How Toronto Got Queer.* Toronto: Coach House Books, 2017.

MacDougall, Bruce. *Queer Judgments: Homosexuality, Expression, and the Courts in Canada.* Toronto: University of Toronto Press, 2000.

McCaskell, Tim. *Queer Progress: From Homophobia to Homonationalism.* Toronto: Between the Lines Press, 2016.

McKay, Richard A. *Patient Zero and the Making of the AIDS Epidemic.* Chicago: University of Chicago Press, 2017.

McLeod, Donald W. *A Brief History of* GAY: *Canada's First Gay Tabloid, 1964–1966*. Toronto: Homewood Books, 2003.

———. *Lesbian and Gay Liberation in Canada: A Selected Annotated Chronology, 1964–1975*. Toronto: ECW Press and Homewood Books, 1996.

———. *Lesbian and Gay Liberation in Canada: A Selected Annotated Chronology, 1976–1981*. Toronto: Homewood Books, 2017.

Metcalfe, Robin, ed. *Out: Queer Looking, Queer Acting Revisited*. Exhibition catalogue. Halifax: Khyber Centre for the Arts, 2014.

Millward, Liz. *Making a Scene: Lesbians and Community across Canada, 1964–84*. Vancouver: UBC Press, 2015.

Morgensen, Scott Lauria. *Spaces between Us: Queer Settler Colonialism and Indigenous Decolonization*. Minneapolis: University of Minnesota Press, 2011.

Raj, Rupert. *Dancing the Dialectic: True Tales of a Transgender Trailblazer*. 2nd ed. Victoria: TransGender Publishing, 2020.

Rayside, David. *On the Fringe: Gays and Lesbians in Politics*. Ithaca, NY: Cornell University Press, 1998.

———. *Queer Inclusions, Continental Divisions: Public Recognition of Sexual Diversity in Canada and the United States*. Toronto: University of Toronto Press, 2008.

Riordon, Michael. *Out Our Way: Gay and Lesbian Life in the Country*. Toronto: Between the Lines Press, 1996.

Rose, Rebecca. *Before the Parade: A History of Halifax's Gay, Lesbian, and Bisexual Communities, 1972–1984*. Halifax: Nimbus Publishing, 2020.

Ross, Becki. *The House That Jill Built: A Lesbian Nation in Formation*. Toronto: University of Toronto Press, 1995.

Rudakoff, Judith D. *TRANS(per)FORMING Nina Arsenault: An Unreasonable Body of Work*. Bristol, UK: Intellect, 2012.

Schuster, Marilyn, ed. *A Queer Love Story: The Letters of Jane Rule and Rick Bébout*. Vancouver: UBC Press, 2017.

Silversides, Ann. *AIDS Activist: Michael Lynch and the Politics of Community*. Toronto: Between the Lines Press, 2003.

Smith, Miriam. *Lesbian and Gay Rights in Canada: Social Movements and Equality-Seeking, 1971–1995*. Toronto: University of Toronto Press, 1999.

Spoon, Rae, and Ivan E. Coyote. *Gender Failure*. Vancouver: Arsenal Pulp Press, 2014.

Stone, Sharon Dale, ed. *Lesbians in Canada*. Toronto: Between the Lines Press, 1990.

Thom, Kai Cheng. *I Hope We Choose Love: A Trans Girl's Notes from the End of the World*. Vancouver: Arsenal Pulp Press, 2019.

Tremblay, Manon, ed. *Queer Mobilizations: Social Movement Activism and Canadian Public Policy*. Vancouver: UBC Press, 2016.

———, ed. *Queering Representation: LGBTQ People and Electoral Politics in Canada*. Vancouver: UBC Press, 2019.

Walcott, Rinaldo. *Queer Returns: Essays on Multiculturalism, Diaspora, and Black Studies*. Toronto: Insomniac Press, 2016.

Warner, Tom. *Never Going Back: A History of Queer Activism in Canada*. Toronto: University of Toronto Press, 2002.

ABOUT THE ARQUIVES

The ArQuives is Canada's LGBTQ2+ archive and is dedicated to celebrating, preserving, and collecting the stories and histories of LGBTQ2+ people in Canada. Staff members and a large volunteer collective maintain collections related to LGBTQ2+ life in Canada and beyond, including books, archival papers, artifacts, photographs, art, and more. Founded in 1973, The ArQuives has grown to become the largest independent LGBTQ2+ archive in the world. The ever-expanding collections held at The ArQuives are unique and serve to give voice to the lives, struggles, and accomplishments of LGBTQ2+ communities.

The ArQuives is a non-profit organization that needs assistance from the community in order to preserve, care for, and keep LGBTQ2+ stories alive. Please consider giving material or financial donations to The ArQuives. Your support will enable the continued digitization of the collection, the archiving of newly acquired collections, and greater outreach initiatives. For more information on how you can support The ArQuives, please visit www.arquives.ca.

ABOUT THE AUTHORS

Craig Jennex is an assistant professor of English at Ryerson University in Toronto, Ontario. He is editor, with Susan Fast, of *Popular Music and the Politics of Hope: Queer and Feminist Interventions* (Routledge, 2019). His work has been published in *TOPIA: Canadian Journal of Cultural Studies, Popular Music and Society, GUTS: Canadian Feminist Magazine,* and *The Spaces and Places of Canadian Popular Culture,* among others. He has been a volunteer at The ArQuives since 2012.

Nisha Eswaran is a writer and academic in Toronto, Ontario. Her work has appeared in *Postcolonial Text, South Asian Review, Kajal,* and *Jamhoor.* She is a PhD candidate in the Department of English and Cultural Studies at McMaster University in Hamilton, Ontario, where she researches friendship and anti-colonial history in South Asian literature.

INDEX

Barry, James, 16, *16*
basher, definition, 19
Bassnett, Sarah, 254
bathhouses: apology for Operation Soap, 235; police raids, 105, *105*, 152, 158, *159*, 166, 206, 233, 238; protests and organization against raids, 152, 156, 168, 180, *181*; Pussy Palace, 206, 233, 238, *238–39*
BC Gay and Lesbian Archives, 268
Bearchell, Chris: on Archives board of directors, 28; on Lesbian Pride March, 184; in National Portrait Collection, 266; No More Shit! protests and, 180; photographs, *25, 26, 100*; on Right to Privacy Committee, 152; in *Weekend Magazine*, *142*, 143
Bébout, Rick: on archiving queer history, 11, 23, 24; on The Barracks raid, 152; on James Fraser, 31; in National Portrait Collection, 266; and police raid on Archives and *The Body Politic*, *26*, 27
Belcourt, Billy-Ray: *This Wound Is a World*, 263
Benaway, Gwen: *Holy Wild*, 263, *263*
Bergman, S. Bear: *Gender Outlaws* (with Bornstein), 263
Bill C-16, 232
Bill C-23 (Modernization of Benefits and Obligations Act), 228
Bill C-38, 229
Bill C-150 (Criminal Law Amendment Act), 48–49, 99, 132
Bill C-279, 232
Bishop, Anne, 266
Bishop, Heather, 200, *200*
bitch, definition, 65
bitching, definition, 65
Black, Christopher E., 146
Blackbridge, Persimmon, 266
Black Coalition for AIDS Prevention, 173, 190, 192, *193*
Black Lives Matter, 222, 233, 252–53, *253*, 273
Blackness Yes!, 179, 190, 222, *222*
Black people: HIV status criminalization and, 234; political consciousness, 104; queer organizations, 177, 190, *191*, 222, *223*; Toronto Pride Parade and, 252–53, *253*
Black Women's Collective, 190
Blair, Elgin, *50*
Blizzard, Christina, 150

Blockorama, 179, 222, *223*
blood donation, 170–71, 188
The Blue Jay (Club Déjà Vu; Toronto), *186*
The Body Politic (periodical): on AIDS, 192; on CHAT community centre, 106; covers, *125*; editorial on Archives, *23*; establishment of Archives by, 22; *Flaunting It!* anthology, *124*; geographic tensions and, 13; incorporation as Pink Triangle Press, 25; members, *100*; "Men Loving Boys Loving Men" (Hannon), 26; offices, *23*; police raid and trial, 11, 26–27, *26–27*, 124; queer community formation and, 102, 124; separation of Archives from, 28, 33; on *Weekend Magazine* queer profile, 142–43
Boissonnault, Randy, 231
Bornstein, Kate: *Gender Outlaws* (with Bergman), 263
Boylesque, 264
Brand, Dionne, 273
Brindley, Kathleen, 107
British Columbia, 18, 172, 176, 228, 229, 246
Brodie, Shaun, 250
Brogaard, Eric, 228
Bronson, A.A., 173
Brossard, Nicole, 266, *267*
Brown, Elspeth, *36*, 90, 254
Brown, Heather Ann, 206
Brownlie, Robin, 34
Brunswick Four, 101, 131, *131*
Bryant, Anita, demonstrations against, 148, *148–49*
Buddies in Bad Times, 150, *150*, 249, 251
Bud's (Montreal), 156
buggery, definition, 19
bulldyke, definition, 19
burlesque, 264, *264–65*
Burrows, Betty, 72
Burt, John, 166
butch, definition, 19, 65
Butler, Alec, 266
buttons, 208, *208–9*
Byers, Heather, 131

C
cabaret, 264
Cabbagetown Softball League, *101*
Cabrera, Edimburgo, 36
Caldwell, Peter, 198
camping, definition, 65

campus-based organizations, 154, *154–55*
Canada: anti-homosexuality campaigns, 42–43, 46–47, 82, 235; decriminalization of homosexual acts, 48–49, 98, 120, 132, 158, 231–32; HIV/AIDS strategy, 172; human rights protection, 156, 176–77, 228, 232; immigration legislation, 14, 47, 100; Justin Trudeau's LGBTQ2+ support, 231–32; neoliberalization, 230; on pornography and prostitution, 168; rainbow refugees and, 236; same-sex marriage and, 12, 228–30, 231
Canadian Aboriginal AIDS Network, 173
Canadian AIDS memorial quilt, 214, *214*
Canadian AIDS Society (CAS), 172
Canadian AIDS Treatment Information Exchange (CATIE), 172
Canadian Blood Services, 170–71
Canadian Forces. *See* military; Second World War
The Canadian Gay Archives (CGA), 22, 24, 24–25. *See also* The ArQuives
Canadian Gay Liberation Movement Archives (CGLMA), 22, 270, 273. *See also* The ArQuives
Canadian HIV/AIDS Legal Network, 234
Canadian Human Rights Act, 146, 176–77
Canadian Lesbian and Gay Archives (CLGA), 34, *34*. *See also* The ArQuives
Canadian Women's Army Corps, *53*
Canadian Women's Movement Archives (CWMA), 14, 33, 268
Capital Rainbow Refuge, 236
Carleton University: AIDS Activist History Project, 268
Carousel Capers (periodical), *127*
Cassel, Jay, 33
CBC: CODCO, 179, 204, *204*; *Uncover: The Village* (podcast), 15, 233
CelebrAsian, 151, *151*
censorship, 92, 168–69, *169*, 216–17
Champagne, Robert, 33
Chan, Gerald, 151
Chenier, Elise, 42
chicken, definition, 19
chicken hawk, definition, 19
Cho, Tom: *Look Who's Morphing*, 263
Chrétien, Jean, 228, 229
Christianity, 84, 128, *129*, 229
Churchill, David S., 228

Cataloguing data are available from
Library and Archives Canada
ISBN 978-1-77327-100-2 (hbk.)

Design by Jessica Sullivan
Cover photographs by William Craddock
Front endsheet photograph by Ted Hebbes

Editing by Michelle Meade
Copy editing by Stephanie Fysh
Proofreading by Alison Strobel
Indexing by Stephen Ullstrom

Where a photography credit does not appear, the photographer is unknown.

Printed and bound in China by C&C Offset Printing Co., Ltd.
Distributed internationally by Publishers Group West

Figure 1 Publishing Inc.
Vancouver BC Canada
www.figure1publishing.com

The ArQuives: Canada's LGBTQ2+ Archives
Toronto ON Canada
www.arquives.ca

page 1 Protestors take part in the We Demand rally on Parliament Hill, Ottawa, August 28, 1971. Photograph by Jearld Moldenhauer.

page 2 Members of the Gay Alliance Toward Equality (GATE) take part in the We Demand rally, Vancouver, August 28, 1971. Contact sheet of photographs by Ron McLennan.

pages 20–21 Danny Cockerline—a tireless advocate for sex work, a member of *The Body Politic* collective, and an HIV+ activist who proudly identified as a "Safe Sex Slut"—conducts research in the Canadian Gay Archives at 24 Duncan Street, Toronto, 1983. Chris Bearchell once described Cockerline as "brilliant and reckless. Beautiful but insecure. Destined to provoke. Queer. But a queer queer; an outsider among outsiders." Cockerline committed suicide in 1995; he was thirty-five years old. In a note he left behind, Cockerline indicated that he did not want to put his loved ones through a difficult death and that he was increasingly worried that the Harris Government in Ontario would cut funding for medicines that he wouldn't be able to afford on his own. Photograph by Gerald Hannon.

pages 40–41 Phillip McLeod (*third from left*) and friends at Hanlan's Point, Toronto, c. mid-1950s.

pages 96–97 Activists stage a kiss-in at the corner of Yonge and Bloor streets to protest the earlier arrest of two men for kissing in the same place, Toronto. From left to right: David Foreman, Tim McCaskell, Ed Jackson, Merv Walker, David Gibson, and Michael Riordon, July 1976. Photograph by Gerald Hannon.

pages 164–65 Dykes on Bikes at Toronto Pride, 1984.

pages 226–27 Two-Spirited People of the First Nations at Toronto Pride, c. 1990s/2000s.

Funded by the Government of Canada | Canadá

💕 pride & remembrance run

S.M. BLAIR FAMILY FOUNDATION

 Faculty of Arts

THE PRODUCTION OF THIS BOOK WAS SUPPORTED BY A GRANT PROVIDED BY THE OFFICE OF THE DEAN OF ARTS, RYERSON UNIVERSITY.